algeria in others' languages

CORNELL FRENCH STUDIES SERIES

algeria in others' languages

Edited by
ANNE-EMMANUELLE
BERGER

CORNELL
UNIVERSITY
PRESS

*Ithaca
and
London*

Publication of this book was made possible, in part, by a
grant from Cornell French Studies, Cornell University

First published 2002 by Cornell University Press
First printing, Cornell Paperbacks, 2002

Printed in the United States of America

Library of Congress Cataloging-in-Publication Data

Algeria in others' languages/ edited by Anne-Emmanuelle Berger.
  p.cm.
  Includes bibliographical references and index.
  ISBN 0-8014-3919-1 (cloth : alk. paper)—ISBN 0-8014-8801-X (pbk. : alk. paper)
  1. Arabic language—Political aspects—Algeria. 2. Arabic
language—Social aspects—Algeria. 3. Multilingualism—Algeria. 4.
Languages in contact—Algeria. 5. French language—Influence on
Arabic. 6. Algeria—Languages. 7. Nationalism—Algeria. I. Berger,
Anne-Emmanuelle, 1958– .
  PJ6074 .A44 2002
  306.44'0965—dc21

2001005562

Cornell University Press strives to use environmentally
responsible suppliers and materials to the fullest extent
possible in the publishing of its books. Such materials
include vegetable-based, low-VOC inks and acid-
free papers that are recycled, totally chlorine-free, or
partly composed of nonwood fibers. For further
information, visit our website at
www.cornellpress.cornell.edu.

1 3 5 7 9 Cloth printing 10 8 6 4 2
1 3 5 7 9 Paperback printing 10 8 6 4 2

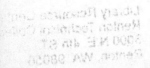

contents

preface

THE FOLLOWING collection of essays focuses primarily on the politics of language in postcolonial Algeria. Most of the essays were written between 1996 and 2000. Each contributor of the volume reflects in his or her own way on the specific cultural and historical status of both Arabic and French. The book as a whole can be read as an attempt to account for the tribulations and partial failure of the "politics of Arabization" in contemporary Algeria. Yet, this is no mere academic study. The vast majority of the contributors are Maghrebian or were born in the Maghreb (see my introduction). What unites them, beyond the heterogeneity of their approaches and positions, is the fact that they do not simply write as experts of a given field, be it the "field" of Algeria: they also write as individuals who are, or have been, immersed in the situation they describe.

As I write these lines, riots are taking place in Algeria, mostly in Algiers and in Kabylia; once again, the language issue resurfaces in violent ways, both as a real concern and as a metaphor for other concerns.

In the fall of 1996 I organized a conference on Algeria at Cornell University under the aegis of the newly founded interdisciplinary program of French Studies. The conference, entitled "Algeria in and out of French: Politics and Culture in Postcolonial Algeria" was the first of this scale, if not of its kind, to be organized in a U.S. academic setting.

My reasons for organizing such a conference were not primarily scholarly. I am not a specialist in Algeria, or even a specialist in Francophone literature. What compelled me was a mixture of what might be called ethico-political concerns and philosophical interest. At the time, the war against civilians, which has torn Algeria apart since the cancellation of the 1991 legislative election, was still raging. Intellectuals, journalists, artists, but also villagers and ordinary citizens were being put to death in cruel and spectacular ways. A hundred thousand people (some even say up to two-hundred thousand) have been killed since 1992. They were the hostages, if not the real targets, of the "war without a name," which pitted factions of the Algerian army in power against various Islamist armed groups. From 1993 on, many Algerians went into exile, most of them to France, despite France's deliberately restrictive visa policy, and some to the United States and Canada. I met a number of them in Paris, and was struck by the intricacy of their accounts of the situation and by their extraordinary resilience. Something important was happening in Algeria and, as a result, in and to France. I thought it deserved to be reported and reflected on, particularly since it was hardly making the news in the United States. Moreover, the U.S. academy could provide an opportunity for thoughtful exchange, precisely because it was neither Algeria nor France. This was also a time when Francophone studies were beginning to grow in traditional French literature departments, in the wake of the development of postcolonial studies. And it seemed to me that postcolonial scholars could help us (that is, both the public at large and the Algerians caught in the war) think more clearly about the situation.

The focus of the conference was deliberately broad and I invited a wide array of people. I wanted Algerian intellectuals or artists who had been part of Algeria's recent history to come and bear witness to what was happening. I wanted both experts in the field and nonspecialists, Algerian citizens and non-Algerians, to address the issues. I wanted people of different political persuasions and with different experiences of Algeria to talk to one another across their differences. All the people I invited, however, supported the cause of "democracy" in Algeria, that is, they were neither on the side of the regime in place, nor on that of the so-called Islamists. Yet, as those who are familiar with Algerian politics know, there are very strong divisions within the "democratic" camp, a situation that accounts at least in part for the failure of that camp to acquire political power. Some invited speakers could not come; others refused. The occasion was nonetheless momentous, thanks in part to the unexpectedly large audience of Algerians recently settled in the United States and Canada who attended. This book is a tribute to them.

Some may question the political significance of a conference organized under the aegis of the French Studies program. The conference might have had a different shape if it had been organized by Near Eastern Studies and had taken place in Arabic, for instance, instead of French and English. Yet it was my hope and my theoretical "wager" that the word "French" would not be taken simply as a symbol of neocolonialism. Indeed, one of the core assumptions of modern forms of nationalism that was repeatedly questioned during the conference in the light of Algeria's postcolonial makeup, was the ability of any language to speak for a nation and secure one's place within it. It was the persistence of the linguistic question and paradigm throughout the conference, a persistence that reflected the multilingual character of the event and the explicit or secret divisions of all utterances, that prompted me to edit the present collection of essays.

ANNE-EMMANUELLE BERGER

acknowledgments

I DEDICATE this book to those Algerians, exiled in France, who, from the moment I met them, left me shaken by their stories of horror. Seeing them survive terror with their humor intact and their gift for living unimpaired, I was moved to think again about Algeria. They added a dimension to the stories of my families and the memories of my childhood vacations spent in Algiers with my grandmother and great-grandmother. Hamida Ait El Hadj, theater director in exile, Nourredine Lamara, scenographer in exile, and the entire community of exiles, artists, intellectuals, hairdressers, journalists, schoolteachers, and so on, in France, in the United States, in Canada, and in Algeria itself are the real authors of this book—though not in English. Nancy Wood played an important role in the genesis of the project. Amy Staples and Carole Allamand lent a helping hand at its beginning stage. Through my conversations about Algeria with my father, Guy Berger, I gained precious insights: knowingly and unknowingly, he contributed to this book. Without Steven Kaplan's initiative, this book would not have seen the light of day. And I would also like to thank Michael Meeker, whose knowledge of the Middle East and whose kind interest in the endeavor encouraged me to pursue it. I am grateful to the contributors to the volume for the gift of their thoughts and friendship. Catherine Rice of the Cornell University Press gave gentle support and lucid suggestions. The anonymous readers also made many worthwhile suggestions and criticisms. Whitney Sanford translated the essays written in French; she and Tayeb Ould Aroussi helped in many other ways, and Peter Glidden made editing enjoyable. Finally, the book and I received an ultimate blessing: Rachid Koraïchi graciously authorized the reproduction of his artwork on the cover. In his displacements of the beautiful Arabic script, he shows us another dimension of the movement of language. I thank him heartily. To Jim Siegel, I owe the gift of English as my other-tongue, through which I can think and be anew.

algeria in others' languages

introduction

IN HIS FAMOUS lecture titled "What Is a Nation?" Ernest Renan reminded his audience that "language invites people to unite, but it does not force them to do so" (Renan 1990, 16). The remark was intended to contest the philosophical and political premises underpinning the then-popular view of nations as ethnolinguistic entities. A language, according to Renan, may foster union and, we might add, it may do so by dictating its rules; but it cannot (or ought not to) enforce the rule of the land or be the basis of political legitimacy. Nevertheless, as we know, modern nation-states and colonial enterprises have functioned in precisely that way: in contrast to old dynastic states and empires, they have made language a primary tool and coercive agent of national or colonial cohesion, whatever the grounds—ethnic or political—of their claim. The role of French in the discourse of the revolutionary proponents of modern France is well known; the process of "nationalizing" the French language initiated by the Revolution is all the more interesting in that it stemmed from a purely political—as opposed to ethnic—rationale. The role Arabic has played and continues to play in shaping Arabophone nations has been equally decisive, if not more so. Much has already been said about the multiple effects of the use for political purposes of a language considered sacred, including the fact that modern Western notions of the boundaries between the sociopolitical and the religious cannot help our understanding in this matter. What, then, of national, postcolonial Algeria today?

The language question is one of the most intricate, conflictual, and enduring aspects of Algeria's postcolonial politics. "Arabization," as it was termed, was a stated goal of independent Algeria from its inception. It was advocated in the Tripoli program devised by the Front de Libération Nationale (FLN) in 1962, a few months after independence was formally achieved. It was reasserted as a necessary and fundamental feature of the newly independent Algeria in the constitution of 1963. It was officially supported by both Ahmed Ben Bella, who headed the new state until 1965, and by Houari Boumediene, who deposed him and ruled until his death in 1978. It was also pursued by President Chadli Benjedid until his demise in 1991.[1] "Total Arabization" was once again declared by President Liamine Zeroual in the mid-1990s and was supposed to have been definitively implemented as of 5 July 1998. On 25 June of the same year, a few days before "total Arabization" was to take effect at all levels of public life, Matoub Lounès, a famous Kabyle singer and a fierce proponent of Berberism, was murdered under mysterious circumstances.[2] Once again, the process stalled. After the election of Abdelazziz Bouteflika in 1999, government statements of language policy seem to have softened, but it is still unclear where Algeria is heading and what role language is to play.

But what exactly does the "Arabization" of postcolonial Algeria mean, and what has it entailed? The newly independent leaders of the revolution sought to "Arabize" Algeria and to make "Arabic" the only national language because they perceived Algeria as no longer, or not yet, an Arabic-speaking country, much less an Arab country. Indeed, French colonial policies had denied Arabic any official or educational existence. By the time Algeria became independent, the language of its administration and judicial system was French, as was that of its school system, where only an extremely restricted number of indigenous Algerians were educated. "Arabization," then, was a matter of cultural decolonization and social equity, since those educated in French had access to positions barred to the majority of the population, which remained illiterate.

Yet the matter was complicated by the fact that, contrary to what the term "Arabization" seems to suggest, the vast majority of the indigenous population actually did speak—but not write—a type of Arabic. This Arabic, however, deemed "dialectal Arabic," was denied any legitimacy and therefore any ability to become the—or a—national language. In spite of the nationalist rhetoric describing Arabization as a recovery of Algeria's "true personality," the process entailed the teaching and generalized use of an Arabic foreign to the speakers of dialectal Arabic (the majority of the Algerian population), who therefore were not considered "Arabophones." The question was then: Which Arabic should the Algerians be taught in order for them to become proper Arabophone speakers and hence legitimate citizens of the new Algerian nation? This very ambiguity seems to have impinged on the nationalist movement from the start. Whatever the diversity of its origins, the nationalist movement really took shape as such in the 1930s, in a dual—cultural and political—movement: on the one hand, the Ulema movement, led by Sheikh Ben Badis, a learned Arabic scholar and fluent French speaker from a prominent Constantine family, advocated (and started to implement) a return to the study of Koranic and classical Arabic, as a way to retrieve Algeria's cultural roots. The famous saying by Ben Badis ("Islam is our religion, Arabic is our language, Algeria is our country") summed up the claims of this cultural nationalism. The Arabic to which the Ulema movement referred was indeed both Koranic and standard or classical Arabic. On the other hand, the less educated and populist-leaning Messali Hadj, who cofounded the first nationalist party (the Etoile Nord-Africaine, or North-African Star) in the late 1920s, when he was working in France as an "immigré," and who later headed the PPA (Parti du Peuple Algérien), which led the fight for independence until the creation of the FLN, took a linguistic stance that remains open to interpretation. In August 1937, echoing the words of Ben Badis, the PPA made the following statement in French, "Muslim Algeria is a people with its mother tongue, its religion, its glorious past, its thinkers, its heroes, and its Islamic traditions. In spite of colonization, we remain extremely attached to this past."[3]

What is this Arabic "mother tongue" to which Messali-Hadj and his fellow nationalists refer? Very likely, dialectal Arabic.

It is this founding ambiguity of the politics of Arabization, along with the difficulty of effectively achieving linguistic decolonization, that explains in part the present conflicts over language in Algeria. This situation has produced endless and fascinating "performative paradoxes." Arabization was often advocated in French, in the Francophone media, for instance, which to this day outnumber their Arabophone counterparts.[4] One of the proponents and theorists of Arabization, Taleb Ibrahimi, who was minister of national education under Boumediene and who recently ran for the presidency under the banner of a moderate Islamic party, made countless pro-Arabization speeches in French. A "true bilingual," educated in both French and "standard" Arabic, Ibrahimi has continued to use French in his public statements. Even the Front Islamique du Salut (FIS), which, since the 1980s, has led the battle against what it identified as an internal *hizb franza* (party of France) chooses to identify itself to the world and to its fellow citizens by a French acronym. Kateb Yacine, a founding figure of Francophone postcolonial literature, wrote in French against French, but, in the 1970s, he also mounted a defense in French of dialectal Arabic, for which he was attacked in Arabophone newspapers and in Francophone media that supported Arabization.[5] French was also used as a privileged medium to voice the Berberophone claim inside and outside Algeria. Berber languages are still the native language of about 20 percent of the Algerian population and they too have been threatened by the prospect of a "total Arabization" of the country. Add to that the fact that the Berberophone and Francophone issues have tended to be conflated, in part because of the failure of modern North African nations, and Algeria in particular, to come to terms with their founding ethnocultural duality, and in part as a result of the exploitation by the French colonial powers of this duality. Even though, over the centuries, the Berber and Arab tribes became largely mixed throughout the country (with the exception of the region of Kabylia, which remained Berber), the French always insisted on the once Latin (hence "European") culture of the Berbers, as opposed to that of the Bedouin tribes. In their struggle against Arabic hegemony, the native speakers of Berber languages have in turn played this card.

As of the early 1980s, with what could be termed the culturalization of Algerian politics, language politics began to take center stage. It was no longer merely a matter of contradictory and often brutal government policies. The stance individuals took on language became a defining feature of the newly emerging political landscape, characterized by the growing influence of what was to become the FIS and by the growing mobilization of Berber "culturalists."[6] In his groundbreaking book on the politics of Arabization in the Maghreb (*Arabisation et politique linguistique au Maghreb*), which covers the period from independence to the aftermath of Boumediene's death in 1980, the French scholar Gilbert Grandguillaume ends his description of the Algerian linguistic predicament with a report on two events that occurred in 1980: the first was a strike by Arabophone students demanding that Arabization be decisively and effectively implemented at all levels of social, economic, and cultural life; the second was a series of demonstrations, strikes, and riots in the region of Kabylia, following the cancellation by government authorities of a lecture on Kabyle poetry to be given by Mouloud Mammeri, a famous Kabyle Francophone writer. The Kabyle riots gave rise to the creation of a "Berber Cultural Movement" (Mouvement pour la Culture Berbère), still active in spite of internal feuds.[7] These events marked the beginning of a new era in Algerian politics. What they showed was that language issues had begun to both mobilize and polarize the society at large. The public debate surrounding language might in fact be coterminous with the formation of an Algerian postcolonial civil society.

One might expect that the emphasis on language and the issue of cultural diversity would bring about a revival or resurgence of ethnicist discourses and identity claims, as indeed the Berber movement seems to indicate. Let us be cautious, however, when applying the categories of "ethnicity" and "ethnic identity." To begin with, and by definition, the overarching Islamic framework that informs cultural identity is not based on ethnicity, whether conceived in racial terms, in linguistic terms, or in both. Bernard Lewis provides a useful overview of the general thinking about ethnic and tribal differences in an Arabo-Islamic context. In particular, he stresses the principled distrust of Islam toward any factionalism or regional particularism that might threaten the unity of the community of believers, a stance that is precisely reflected in the successful imposition of Arabic as the dominant language across so many different regions and populations of the Muslim world (Lewis 1998, 84–85). More specifically, we need to take a careful look at the history of Algeria's colonization and its ensuing nationalist movements. In 1863, the French officially put an end to the tribal system inherited from nomadic times, refusing thereafter to recognize the traditional organization of the Algerian population into Arabo-Berber or Berber tribes and subtribal clans. What the colonizers substituted for the tribal divisions was a typically French grid, which contributed to the "topographization" of old tribal distinctions. The new administrative and hence political organization of Algeria followed geographical and regional lines and fostered a new type of internal boundaries. Thus Kabylia as a new entity supplanted former tribal denominations and elicited new forms of identification without really erasing the former ones. Present-day Kabylia is a product of the superimposition of the old tribal system, the Islamic encompassing grid, and the French geopolitical reapportionment. Such a conflation affects the nature of Kabyle "Berberism." The Algerian historian Mohammed Harbi (1992, 74–84) gives an interesting analysis of the "Berberist crisis" of 1949, which divided the nationalist movement and led to the expulsion from the PPA of the early proponents of a culturally pluralist Algeria. He insists quite accurately that, even though they were considered "factionalists" and expelled as such, the Berberists were primarily nationalists who had no regional or particularist agenda. At the time, they did not even put forward the issue of the status of Tamazight, the Berber name given to the language spoken by Kabyles, but they clearly resisted the dominant Arabist ideology, comparing the political conflation of nationalism and Arabism to Pan-Germanist ideology.[8] After independence, the same "Berberist" leaders and their heirs founded the only two secular parties to contest the rule of the FLN in the name of democratic pluralism: the FFS (Front des Forces Socialistes) and later, when a multiparty system was officially allowed in 1988, the RCD (Rassemblement pour la culture et la démocratie). Although both parties are notably Kabyle, their platforms are indeed national. According to Harbi, the ethnicization of "Berberism" is an effect of political repression, with one notable and interesting exception: it is in France among the Kabyle immigrants that an ethnocultural view of the issue really took hold (Harbi 1992, 77): the Kabyles invented themselves as such from the outside, some would say from the side of the former colonizer. But, then again, the last upheaval against French rule in the nineteenth century was launched in 1871 by one of the most powerful tribes of Kabylia.

Ultimately, Berberism is the product of the state's authoritarian politics of language on the one hand, and, on the other, of a longstanding difference internal to the nationalist movement regarding the nature and foundations of the Algerian political contract. The complicated and convoluted character of Harbi's description of the Berber issue results from the superimposition of various imported hermeneutic models and reflects the failure of any one of them taken alone to account for "Algeria." The prominence of the Kabyles on the national scene has indeed awakened neotribal rivalries. Other Berber groups, such as the Arabophone Chaouis, deny the Kabyles any right to speak for all of *Berberie*. The fact is, as Hafid Gafaïti reminds us in his essay in this volume, that Kabyles have held important political positions throughout the FLN's rule. But they did not hold these positions as Kabyles and certainly did not advance the "Berberist" cause. Here again, their prominence in certain sectors of the government, and the prominence of the Chaouis in others, stem from an old politics of influence based on clan rather than from new regional and cultural affiliations.

The creation by the Algerian national educational system of an effectively (if oddly) "Arabized" but underemployed class of citizens, who came of age in the early 1980s, led to a radicalization of the linguistic issues. I mentioned earlier the strikes of the Arabophone university students in 1980. This was the onset of a movement the FIS would enlist and compound soon thereafter. Mixing—accurately at a certain level—cultural and socioeconomic considerations, the FIS launched an attack in the name of Arabo-Islamic values against both the corruption of the FLN regime and what it called the "party of France," in an attempt to appropriate the still meaningful anticolonial nationalist rhetoric. The anti-Francophone and, for that matter, anti-Berberophone rhetoric of the FIS took a grim turn when its armed branches (the Armée Islamique du Salut, or AIS, and the Groupes Islamiques Armés, or GIA)[9] began targeting and killing women, government employees (especially from the police and the army), and so-called Francophones (primarily intellectuals, journalists, and artists), after the elections that saw the victory of their party were voided.

As a result, a number of Algerian intellectuals and scholars began to take up the issue that had been forced on them by both the "Islamists" and the regime in power, which continued to make contradictory proclamations on the language question. These intellectuals did so both from within Algeria and from France. Some of them had been living and working in France for a long time, such as the writer Assia Djebar and the historian Mohammed Harbi. A number of them (those who managed to escape death and to overcome France's reluctance to issue visas) went into exile beginning in 1992.

The bloody events brought about a definitive change in the critical landscape regarding language issues. Although the politics of language in the Maghreb had elicited specific scholarly interest soon after Tunisia and Algeria became independent, the main linguistic focus until then had been on education, with scholarship, primarily in French, and a number of writings by Algerian sociologists and pedagogues (see Mazouni 1969; Colonna 1975; Haddab 1979). Special mention should be made, however, of Mostefa Lacheraf, perhaps the first modern Algerian "intellectual" (in the French sense of the word). Lacheraf, who was educated in France and was briefly minister of national education at the end of the Boumediene years, pursued a sustained reflection on the prospects of both bilingualism and Arabization in Algeria within the framework of a larger political and anthropological study of Algerian modern society. For a number of Algerian Francophone writers as well, the linguistic question had been a long-standing concern, for obvious reasons, but, as of the late 1980s or early 1990s, it became an even more insistent theme.[10] Contrary to what had generally been the case before the 1990s, then, Algerian scholars, historians, intellectuals, and artists actually took the lead in reframing the linguistic issue and bringing it to the fore.[11] The debates took place primarily in the written media, both Algerian and French.[12] They elicited immediate interest and a prompt response on the part of French scholars in the field, numerous French intellectuals with a long-standing or renewed interest in Algeria, and American and Anglophone scholars, who opened the field of postcolonial studies and were the first to launch a Francophone field of study. Some have found the passionate interest the French media took in the issues suspicious. Was it not an occasion to advance the neocolonial cause of *Francophonie*? Whatever the case, in this new context, the complex weaving together of the linguistic and the political in Algeria gave rise to a variety of strong responses, inextricably political and analytical. Hence the often polemical nature of the critical discourse addressing the issue.

In a special issue of *Les Temps Modernes* devoted to the Algerian "brothers' war" *(la guerre des frères)* in 1995, Harbi's conclusion to an article on violence, nationalism, and Islamism is typical:

> Il est une autre tragédie qui déborde la scène politique et qui
> est comme un clivage interne, une fissure dans l'identité. C'est
> la distance qui sépare et oppose berbérophones, francophones et
> arabophones. Et ce clivage autodestructeur aboutit à la mort de
> ceux qui rêvent de la suture, à savoir les intellectuels.(Harbi
> 1995, 33)

> There is yet another tragedy, which extends beyond the political scene, and which is like an internal cleavage, a split in
> identity. I mean the distance that separates and sets Berberophones, Francophones, and Arabophones against each other.
> This self-destructive cleavage leads to the death of those who
> dream of stitching the cut together, namely the intellectuals.
> (my translation)

Here, the linguistic question is designated as the most severe problem of Algeria in its present and troubled state. A most painful and destructive issue, it "extends beyond the political scene," to use

Harbi's own words, while at the same time framing it. Indeed, each time a pronouncement is made on a public issue in Algeria, it is also a statement about language, since the language(s) in which it is made convey(s) something, possibly contradictory, about the speaker's position. In echoing the divisive discourse commonly used in Algeria, and in France, to identify the opposing factions—the "Francophones" are identified and sometimes self-identified as the "democrats," the "Arabophones" as supporters of political Islamism, and the Berberophones as separatists (though the latter claim they are the true native "Algerians")—Harbi risks reproducing the simplified cleavages and classifications he himself warns against, and which indeed have brought death to those who contest them—the intellectuals, but not only them. In fact, the so-called Francophones are not simply Francophones: they all speak dialectal Arabic or Berber, sometimes both. The Berberophones often speak French and usually dialectal Arabic, although it is true that some, the less educated and those less exposed to the successive invasions and constructions of "Algeria," continue to speak only a Berber language. Conversely, some pro-Berbers are barely able to speak any Berber. As for the Arabophones who were educated in standard Arabic, they often still know some French and speak dialectal Arabic, which has until now remained the language of the home and of the street.

Linguistic practices thus greatly complicate the lines of political opposition or complicity that are said to define the Algerian landscape today. Rather than corresponding to neat geo-ethnic borders, they point to numerous internal political and cultural splits. Taken seriously, Algerian di- or polyglossia is a good vantage point from which to examine a number of issues defining the postcolonial predicament: issues of cultural and national identity or autonomy; issues of political domination, but also of "power," a much more complex and opaque notion when it comes to defining the power(s) of language(s), as Benedict Anderson's study (1990) of the politics of language in Indonesia beautifully shows.[13] More generally, the case of Algeria raises issues of belonging: Who does a language "belong" to? Can it actually "belong to," or make the subject who speaks it belong (but to what exactly)? Dealing with these questions with the specific example of Algeria in mind might help us rearticulate (if not displace) the colonial and neocolonial closure and its founding antinomies.

In keeping with the spirit of the conference on postcolonialism held at Cornell University in 1996, and with what I believe best exemplifies the present phase of the language question in Algeria, this volume brings people and views not ordinarily heard in the United States, alongside more recognized voices, to the attention of U.S. readers. The great majority of contributors are not only scholars but are also from the areas concerned: some, such as Réda Bensmaia, Hafid Gafaïti, and Djamila Mochrane-Saadi are Algerians settled in France or in the United States. Réda Bensmaia established himself early as a scholar in the United States. Hafid Gafaïti was the young dean of the university of Siddi-Bel Abbès before he moved, first briefly to France and then to the United States in 1993, in the wake of the events of the 1990s. Around the same time, Djamila Saadi-Mokrane was forced out of Algeria, where she was teaching at the University of Algiers; she now lives in Lille, France. Others, such as Hélène Cixous and Lucette Valensi, are French of Jewish-Maghrebian descent (from Algeria and Tunisia, respectively). Omar Carlier is an Algerian of French descent recently forced to move back to France from Algeria; born Jean-Paul Carlier, he did his military service in Algeria in the late 1960s, shortly after the end of the war, fell in love with Algeria and an Algerian woman, married her, converted to Islam, and settled in Oran, where he taught until 1993. Abdelkebir Khatibi is a Moroccan living and working primarily in Morocco, in French. A number of the contributors were, to varying degrees, involved or caught up in the events and cultural struggles that forced the linguistic issue to the fore. Although they may not conform to current scholarly styles in the United States, their personal and historical engagement with the issues at stake is part of what makes their contributions interesting. Even Lucette Valensi, a well-known historian of early colonial Maghreb from the Ottoman period, ventured out of her field of expertise into contemporary Algerian literature out of a kind of "personal interest" in the Algerian predicament.

By featuring firsthand accounts of the politics of language in postcolonial Algeria, along with more "distanced" appraisals or studies of these politics, the present collection ultimately seeks to present both the case and the study of the case. It is my hope, then, that it will elicit a two-tier reading: most of the essays, including the more literary ones, have an obvious analytical and critical dimension and can therefore be classified as "secondary sources" for the study of the politics of language in a postcolonial context. But a number of them, whether written by Algerian or French nationals, also provide primary material for thinking about these issues. They should therefore be read not only as critical assessments but as partial illustrations of what they analyze.

There are, of course, exemplary sites for the study of the politics of language: one is the field of literature, since literature can never be far away when language is at stake. Another is the field of political discourse and policy-making. In a way, however, the foremost site is "popular" discourse, heterogeneous as it is. These fields call for several types of analysis or treatment: historical (political and cultural history), anthropological, philosophical, and literary. I believe that these approaches are well represented in this volume.

The story of Algeria's languages, which is recounted several times in this book, can be told in different ways, each giving rise to different arguments. In spite of its heterogeneity of fields and perspectives, however, the volume presents strikingly convergent motifs, including the exploration of the specific connection between violence and linguistic issues in a postcolonial context. That connection is more or less directly investigated, albeit from different vantage points, by Omar Carlier in "Civil War, Private Violence," by Ranjana Khanna in "The Experience of Evidence: Language, the Law, and the Mockery of Justice," and by Lucette Valensi in "The Scheherazade Syndrome: Literature and Politics in Postcolonial Algeria." Violence can also be said to haunt Khatibi's ongoing reflection on the peculiar diglossic condition of Maghrebian speakers, confronted as they are with a "double idiomatic discontinuity between, on the one hand, classical Arabic and what is called dialectal Arabic, and on the other hand, between Tamazight (Berber) and the Arabic language in all its diglossia." (Khatibi). Khatibi both celebrates and laments the internal splits produced by Maghrebian diglossia, a situation that predated French colonization, but that was aggravated, intensified, and, at the same time, displaced by it. In this sense, and although Khatibi lovingly coined the term *bilangue* (*bi*language), he shows "diglossia" to be much more than merely the recourse to two and only two identifiable languages. Although Khatibi's meditation is directed at the Maghreb as a whole, Algeria can be said to provide the most extreme example of the splits and binds he describes and makes use of in his own writings. The acts of speaking and writing about the violence of language politics may be infused with the very violence they address. Indeed, when Algerians talk about this issue, they often resort to a strikingly emotional rhetoric: In his short piece (1995), Harbi speaks of a "tragedy" that induces an "identity split," which in turn leads to the infliction of death. In her essay, tellingly entitled "The Algerian Linguicide," the sociolinguist Djamila Saadi describes Algerian language politics as a politics of death. Her use of the words "mutilation" and "castration" to depict the wounds inflicted on the linguistic body of Algeria suggests that she views the linguistic history of Algeria as the history of a war repeatedly waged against a kind of archaic phallic mother. Hafid Gafaïti, who, in "Monotheism of the Other," purports to deconstruct the political uses of the opposition between Arabic and French, ends up mounting a forceful, albeit conflicted, defense of Algeria's national language. These two compelling essays not only comment on Algeria's linguistic "cleavages" but actually document them, from divergent if not opposing perspectives.

All the essays are quite expectedly concerned with the lasting but changing legacy of French. Interestingly, however, a significant number of them either interweave the issue of "French" with gender issues or show in various respects how the complicated language play in Algeria becomes gendered in specific and insistent ways.

At the end of his essay on the causes of violence in postcolonial Algeria ("Civil war, Private violence"), Carlier remarks, for instance, on the "gender change" undergone by "Algeria" between dialectal Arabic and standard Arabic. In dialectal Arabic, Algeria is called "L'Algérie," from the French transcription of _El Djeza'ir,_ and is gendered feminine, whereas it becomes (again?) masculine in "proper" standard Arabic.[14] Is it significant that, in dialectal Arabic (that is, an Arabic that carries with it the scar of historical memory, the French inscription of Arabic), Algeria becomes feminized, or conversely, that it is or becomes masculine in proper standard Arabic?

In her far-reaching essay on the relationship between language, justice, and the law in colonial France and postcolonial Algeria ("The Experience of Evidence: Language, the Law, and the Mockery of Justice"), Ranjana Khanna ponders the complex use of French by some Algerian women in the mock trial they staged against Islamic "terrorists": during the trial, the terrorist men are made to speak standard Arabic, while the "terrorized" women, both victims and accusers, speak French. Here, French is revived as the language of the law, which it indeed was under French rule,[15] but it is also invoked in another way, as the language of the possibility of justice and, more specifically in this case, of justice for women.

In his close and inspired reading of _Amour bilingue_ (_Love in two Languages_), Réda Bensmaia shows how _writing_ (in) French, rather than simply speaking it, opens the possibility,—for Khatibi, and, beyond him, for any Maghrebian whose "being and language always consist in at least two languages, two cultural scenes, and two bodies"—of affirming French, albeit an "other(ed)" French, rather than submitting to it. Writing would allow Khatibi to invent a French that would be neither an appropriation of the colonial language nor the betrayal or an evasive original language. Following Khatibi's lead, Bensmaia ultimately articulates the connection between the "language change" that occurs within "bilingual French" and the "sex change" the narrator of *Amour bilingue* claims to have experienced at some point. Bensmaia defines the Maghrebian writer of "bilingual French" as an androgyne, who would be "the other of the two sexes" (and of the two languages) rather than the combination or neutralization of the two.

Continuing the gender play between languages and the language play between genders in Algeria, a number of these essays, including "The Impossible Wedding," ultimately raise the question of the status and meaning of what is called a "mother tongue," an expression that suggests a link between the primordial relation to language and the relation to the mother. Bensmaia opens his essay with a passage from Kafka's diary regarding the role played by the German language in which he was raised in preventing him from fully loving his (Jewish, Central European) mother. This passage brings to the fore the complicated relation to the mother introduced by diglossia.

Interestingly, Algerian nationals often refer to France as a "stepmother figure," (une marâtre) rather than as a father figure. Now, it is well known that the stepmother is the abhorred figure in any child's (and adult's) family romance, precisely because she dares to take the place of the irreplaceable: the mother. A number of essays, however, explore the possibility that, by a strange turn of history, French has turned not only into the language of the "stepmother" but into that of a good stepmother, an oxymoron if ever there was one.[16] In her dense and informative study of Algerian postcolonial literature, written in her characteristically direct style, Lucette Valensi highlights the peculiarities of Francophone Algerian literature with respect to the status of French and Arabic, which she contrasts with the neighboring Maghrebian Francophone literatures of Morocco and Tunisia. In doing so, she comes close to asserting that, against conventional—and correct—political thinking, French (that is, French in/as writing)[17] has recently become almost a (albeit contested) mother tongue for Algerian intellectuals. Both she and Carlier recall the familiar (and familial) nickname—"stepmother"—given to France. As for Ranjana Khanna, she writes: "French paradoxically becomes the language of protest even as it carries with it the ghosts of the past. Perhaps it is the case that the uncanniness of the language—its paradoxical status as the language of the Other and simultaneously as an elusive mother language that gave opportunities—has paradoxically become the only viable alternative, however haunted it may be by its own colonial specters" (36).

The mythical force of a notion such as "mother tongue" may well stem from the fact that language itself is experienced as motherly and mothering, as if the irreplaceable uniqueness of the idiom through which the subject is "brought to identity," recalled—or, as it were, "replaced"—the irreplaceable uniqueness of the mother. Indeed, the locution *langue maternelle* in French, perhaps even more than its English equivalent, is an ambiguous expression, since it can mean either the language of the mother, or language itself as mother.

For Hélène Cixous, the mother tongue is really a (mothering) "tongue." But, contrary to what the mother tongue conventionally connotes, the mother tongue in "The Names of Oran" does not tie a particular idiom and the subject who speaks it to the original place of its communal utterance. The mother tongue that enchants its speaker in Algeria (and which she characterizes as an "Arabying Franco-German charabia"[18]) is nothing other than language itself, before it is really known and understood to be knowing (hence its "desirable foreignness"), before it becomes partitioned into mutually exclusive idioms, before it becomes attached to places and shapes identities, before it serves to stabilize and characterize the relation between those places and those identities. To speak the mother tongue, then, is really to speak in tongue(s). Hélène Cixous describes the pleasures and possibilities opened by "illiteracy," by the fact of not knowing how to spell the words heard, indeed, by misspelling them (intentionally or unintentionally), because they evoke and mingle several idioms at once. The mother tongue, this one at least, is in this sense the origin (and aim) of literature; for what is true literature, if not an improper way of writing, and of writing the improper?

In *Monolingualism of the Other* (1998a), Jacques Derrida writes:

There are situations, experiences, and subjects who are, precisely, in a situation (but what does *situating* mean in this

case?) to testify exemplarily to them. This exemplarity . . .
would be the exemplarity—remarkable and remarking—that allows one to read in a more dazzling, intense, or even traumatic
manner the truth of a universal necessity. The structure appears in the experience of the injury *(blessure)*, the offense,
vengeance and the lesion. In the experience of terror. (26)

"Structure"—any structure, but more specifically, the structure of
language and language as structure—would appear and only appear in
the experience of the *blessure* (wound, injury) that remarks it and
makes it legible. For the wound, which both incises and inscribes the
body (a given body of language and the body of the speaking subject),
marks the mark as such, and calls attention to it. In the same thrust,
the wound "situates" both the mark and the bearer of the mark. The
double scarring of dialectal Arabic and French in Algeria, the mutual,
albeit unequal historical cross-inscription of languages, the symbolic
and literal wounding of Algerian speakers, split as they are by each
utterance, may indeed reveal something about the experience of language, or, more precisely, of language as it is embodied in a particular
idiom, in the cutting singularity of the utterance. For, as Derrida repeats several times, "there is no metalanguage, and . . . a language
shall always be called upon to speak about *the* language—because the
latter does not exist" (1998a, 69).[19] The split hurts; the wounds inflicted, the injuries suffered can bring death, as Algeria and Algerians
remind us. But they may also give life; a dangerous life. Indeed, the
forays made by one language into another in a truly di- or polyglossic
context,[20] though they threaten the integrity and closure of the linguistic body and the subject who inhabits it, force that body and that
subject to remain open to the other, hence, to the possibility of love
as well as conflict and death.

Derrida, however, contends provocatively that he is a true Maghrebian, perhaps even the only true Maghrebian or the most Maghrebian
of all Maghrebians, not because he speaks all or even some of the languages of the Maghreb, but precisely because he speaks only one language and this language is French. He speaks only one language and
this language is not his own; this language that claims him cannot be
claimed as a mother tongue. From the point of view of history and
culture, the language that his mother passed down to him is neither
her language nor his. His is the language of the Other, worse, of the
other side, *l'autre côté de la mer(e)* (the other side of the sea/mother).

And yet it is the only one. It is as if, for someone who was born in Algeria, and an Algerian Jew at that, French monolingualism, far from signifying the assertion and consolidation of a homogeneous identity, introduced the experience of an infinite and originary division—and rejection—of the origin, as if it re-marked, in the guise of a hyphen across the sea, the originary separation from the mother. The monolingual speaker, provided he was born and lived in or through "Algeria," would thus be the most radically alienated, the most threatened by the absolute hegemony of one language. French in Algeria, from Algeria, for one who speaks only that language, would subject the speaker to the experience of an unstoppable othering in the guise and place of self-gathering; it would make the speaker forever "other than"—other than French and nothing else. But, in this sense, would it not expose (and thus enlarge) the wound that its homogeneous uniqueness is supposed to suture or mask? That is why, even while introducing the speaker to the dimension of the promise, as all languages do, as language in general does, French would also bring about the reign of terror: "I finally know how not to have to distinguish any longer between promise and terror" (73). Such are the last words of *Monolingualism of the Other*.

There is, then, always a "twist" to the "a priori universal truth of an essential alienation in language—which is always of the other—and by the same token, in all culture" (58). "This necessity," Derrida continues, "is revealed one more time, still one more first time, in an incomparable setting. A setting called historical and singular, one might say idiomatic, which determines and phenomenalizes it by referring it back to iself" (58, translation modified).

This book explores some of the "twists" and paradoxes produced by the idiomatic situation of Algeria.

PART I
ALGERIA IN
OTHER(S')
LANGUAGES

the monotheism of the other

Language and De/Construction of National Identity in Postcolonial Algeria

HAFID GAFAÏTI

Salut, petit frère. Salut en bâtardise!

—JEAN-PAUL SARTRE

ON 5 JULY 1998, following the recommendation of the (undemo-cratically elected) National Assembly, the Algerian government uni-laterally declared that Arabic is the only official language of the coun-try. The passage of this law calling for the generalized use of Modern Standard Arabic[1] and the prohibition of the use of French, Berber, or Algerian Arabic in official documents, commercial venues, and the media—and the reactions that followed—confirm the fact that the linguistic situation in Algeria is explosive.[2] Its official implementa-tion had been postponed many times because of recurrent opposition to the governmental policy, primarily on the part of the Kabyle cul-turalists[3] speaking for the Kabyle community, which constitutes about one-sixth of the total Algerian population. The date chosen, 5 July 1998, coincided, some say not by chance, with the murder of Ma-toub Lounès, the famous Kabyle singer and radical opponent not only to the central government but also to Arabic language and Arab-Mus-lim culture and civilization per se. For this reason, beyond the appar-ently straightforward ideological positions of the supporters and op-ponents of Arabization, we need to explore what is at stake beyond and beneath the question of language. To do so, we must study the evolution of linguistic practices in Algeria and situate the debate within the colonial and postcolonial contexts.

In this essay, I will try to show how, at various times, colonial and postcolonial political forces have attempted to reconstruct the national identity of North African countries in general and Algeria in particular on the basis of cultural representations and ideological constructions closely linked to nationalist, ethnolinguistic discourses. I will also attempt to illustrate how the issue of language is at the center of the current cultural and political debate in a situation that, until recently, some have described as a civil war.

In the process, I do not pretend to give the "right" answer to an intricate problem that presents one of the most important challenges to the young and already tragically wounded Algerian nation. My only ambition is to invite the reader to look in a new way at a situation whose description and assessment are in great part dominated by emotional reactions, ethnic and linguistic identities, ideological and political biases, and reductive misrepresentations. In other words, my main objective is to deconstruct the dominant discourses on the linguistic and, necessarily, cultural and political issues in Algeria produced in the social and political sphere by, on the one hand, the official regime and its allies and, on the other, the regime's opponents. In short, I do not have solutions. What I offer is an invitation to consider the different visions of Algerian cultures and identities and to look at this extremely sensitive issue from a more comprehensive point of view.

Beyond Manichaeism

Until recently, there has been a tendency among political observers, journalists, and critics to analyze and explain the current Algerian crisis over the problem of language in relatively simplistic terms. Indeed, the sociopolitical situation has been understood for the most part in Manichaean terms, with all or most of the blame placed on so-called Muslim fundamentalists and their Arabophone allies, primarily linked to the FLN and its regime.[4] Many scholars and media in Algeria and in the Western world, particularly France, have unreasonably and unilaterally presented the Francophones as representatives of democratic and progressive ideals, while their Arabophone opponents have been described as obscure barbarians linked to international Muslim fundamentalist terrorism. In a recent article (Gafaïti 1997), I myself fell into this simplistic perspective at times, even though I made every effort to avoid it.

This tendency is probably linked to the fact that, originally, it seemed we were confronted with a classic situation in which political adversaries in Algeria were divided between Arabophones and Francophones, conservatives and progressives, and totalitarians and democrats. In light of the evolution of the situation in the last two or three years, however, it appears that the issues are much more complicated. Therefore, whatever side one may naturally, ideologically, and politically favor, and whatever the cost, intellectual integrity demands a reassessment of the Algerian conflict from a less partisan perspective.

It is increasingly apparent that information is closely monitored by the regime, that both national and international media are subject to various forms of censorship and other manipulative tactics. Furthermore, it is now clear that forces other than those linked to the Muslim fundamentalist movement have been involved in violence and repression in Algeria. However, a mechanical analysis of the crisis based on an opposition between Arabophones and Francophones is usually more a repetition of clichés and a reflection of biases than an expression of reality, given that Algerians share many ideological characteristics independent of their ethnolinguistic origin or political allegiance and unrelated to the kind of education they received. Indeed, although many issues divide them, it is also true that many factors unite them and contribute to a widely shared cultural and national consensus. It should be noted, for example, that the most important nationalist leaders who brought about the liberation of the country from French colonialism were Francophone. Although current falsifications of the history of the Algerian revolution do not reflect it, it is well established that many so-called Arabophones and the Muslim religious leaders (the Ulema in particular) did not question French colonial rule and were ready to accept it as long as it promised protection to Islam. Similarly, it was only in 1956, that is, two years after the general insurrection, that the Algerian Communist Party actively joined the armed resistance that led to independence. These facts provide a glimpse of the tendency, by all parties, inside and outside the regime, inside and outside the country, to oversimplify the situation and misrepresent the linguistic policy and other sensitive questions—such as the role the bourgeoisie, the National Popular Army (which currently controls political life), the various regions, and women played in the national liberation war and, after independence, in the making of modern Algeria.

The Terms of the Debate

Since independence, the debate on language has centered on the confrontation between Francophones and Arabophones, and therefore, on the opposition between Arabic and French. Thus, the controversy has often been characterized as—or reduced to—the opposition between two languages, two entities, two ideological perspectives, in short, two different and antagonistic cultures or visions of the world. According to the "Arabophones," French is: the language of the enemy; the language of colonialism; the expression of Western culture; and the negation of Algerian national identity. Arabic is: the language of the Algerian nation; the recuperation of Algerian identity; the expression of the Algerian soul (the language of the Koran and Islam); and the crucible of the Arab-Muslim community to which Algeria belongs.

To this classification, another has always been added, both by Arabophones and Francophones, the opposition between Berberophones and non-Berberophones. This has often been presented as an opposition between the Arabs and the Berbers. It is generally associated with the affirmation that, in Algeria, power rests in the hands of the "Arabs," who impose their political and cultural domination on the Berber minority. On this basis, some have construed what is often negatively called a "Berberist" discourse, which consists of the following: Arabic is: the language of Arab colonialism imposed on North Africa in the seventh century; an archaic language which, because of its underdevelopment and sclerosis, is not capable of adapting to the needs of the modern world; the vehicle of Islam and Pan-Arab ideology, which are alien and inauthentic traditions imposed on Algeria from the outside. Berber (Tamazight) and Algerian Arabic dialect are: authentic because they are ancestral; the real media of popular communication. French is: the language of modernity, science, and technology; the expression of rationality and the opening to the Western democratic model.

It is crucial to note that this construction has been based in great part on the appropriation of the term "Berber" by one of the ethnic groups at the center of the controversy, the Kabyles. Indeed, although most Algerians, including the so-called Arabs, are in fact also Berber, the Kabyles, concentrated in the northeastern part of the country and constituting a community of 5 million out of Algeria's 30 million residents, have tended to limit the meaning of "Berber" to themselves in order to oppose the "other" (non-Kabyle) Algerians, scornfully designated as "Arabs." Historically, this tendency has stemmed from two equally biased and oppositional discourses of exclusion. On the one hand, in an act of self-hatred and denial, the so-called Arabized Algerians refuse to acknowledge the essential, foundational, and paramount importance of Berberitude in the country and attempt to repress the expression of a Berber, or Tamazight, specificity as a fundamental element of their identity. On the other hand, by appropriating the term "Berber" and excluding the "Arabs" from their representation of themselves, the Kabyles, who are only one of the five important ethnic Berber groups that make up the Algerian people as a whole, in fact repress the ethnic diversity of the Berbers not only in Algeria but also in North Africa and elsewhere, including sub-Saharan Africa and Spain, for example. In so doing, they simultaneously reject the unquestionable and equally important Arabness of their own identity, culture, and nation. Unfortunately, the claim of purity by both parties is a reflection of their equally dogmatic and dangerous ethnic discourse of exclusion, based on a fundamentally racist view of each other.

Rewriting the Nation

Traditionally, Algerians relied on the oral transmission of culture. During the nineteenth and twentieth centuries, their culture was systematically eradicated by the French *mission civilisatrice*, which in fact closed the existing Arabic and Berber schools and offered very limited access to education in French. In 1938, the French government went so far as to classify Arabic as a foreign language and forbade its use in schools and in administrative and official documents. As a result, at the time of independence, more than 80 percent of Algeria's population was illiterate. During French colonial rule, after 132 years of French colonization, only 6 percent of girls had been schooled. By contrast, after only twenty-five years under an Algerian government, 67 percent of the girls benefit from education. And yet, the anti-Algerian discourse in so-called developed, democratic, and secular France, often perpetuated by the Kabyles regarding their so-called Arab compatriots, has consistently and exclusively emphasized the poor record of the Algerian government in matters of women's rights. After independence, the Algerian government

launched an extensive campaign against illiteracy; and it was precisely during the first decade of independence, through the educational programs of the nationalist government—not through the so-
called civilizing mission—that the generalized use of French began to
develop (see Achour 1985 and Djeghloul 1986).

Many factors explain this apparent paradox. First, because of
French colonial policy, most teachers and administrators were educated in French only. Second, Algerians had to rebuild a country rav-
aged by war and the systematic destruction of its economic and cultural foundations; therefore, they had to set priorities. Third, like
most newly independent countries, Algeria still depended in great
part on the former metropolis, which used any means possible—economic, political, or ideological—to perpetuate its domination.
Clearly, the use of the French language by Algerians played a crucial
role. Within a short period of time, however, at both the ideological
and the practical level, nationalist sentiment prompted political leaders to promote the use of Arabic in place of French. In Algeria, despite
what naive or manipulative politicians, too quickly erasing the rav-
ages of history, would have us believe, French was not only the language of modernity, the instrument of science, and the vehicle of
"universal and democratic ideals," but also and above all the language of colonialism, segregation, ignorance (for the majority), religious intolerance, mass destruction, and the eradication of Algerian
identities and their linguistic expressions, whether Arabic or Berber.

The result of this complicated and often contradictory dynamic is
that, according to a simplistic view that currently holds sway, the educated elite can be divided into two main groups: the Arabophones,
usually described as affiliated with the Arab-Muslim conservative
tradition, and the Francophones, generally characterized as favoring
a Western conception of society and thought. In fact, after the liberation of the country, the dividing line between Francophones
and Arabophones was initially economic, though some ideological
and cultural distinctions followed. To apprehend the present crisis
and the controversy over linguistic policies in other than stereotypi-
cal terms or along lines that are not strictly ideological, we need to
emphasize the decisiveness of the economic factor. As Rachida
Yacine notes in "The Impact of the French Colonial Heritage on Policies in Independent North Africa" (1993):

> At independence, the French language has emerged as a mod-
> ernising vector and as an instrument of social and political mo-

bility. It was used by Maghrebi intellectuals, and by those who attended the French schools. Once again, this language was not accessible to all. The linguistic situation generated the birth of two groups called "Arabophones" and "Francophone" which were to complicate the Maghrebi social climate. The Maghrebi desire for rapid modernisation has increased dependence on France and the West. Consequently, the utilisation of the French language has been reinforced and French was considered as an instrument of development and modernisation. The important use of this language restricted the development of Arabic in the Maghreb. The linguistic problem became even more crucial with the existence of a colloquial spoken form and a more refined written form of Arabic, plus the borrowing of French words. (225)

Indeed, ideologically, both Arabophones and Francophones shared the same nationalist feeling and opposed the attempts of France to control the country after its independence. They shared the objective of building a modern Algerian nation. Furthermore, apart from some rare exceptions, the majority of the leaders were in fact educated primarily in French, and the policy of Arabization that followed in later years was in large part originally conceived and often carried out by *Francophone* leaders, administrators, and civil servants.

To Arabize or Not to Arabize?

In the course of the twentieth century, Algeria has become a trilingual country, at least.[5] Since the mid-1960s, however, the state has attempted to repress the use of both local Arabic and Berber dialects and French. Nevertheless, in the realm of culture and the arts, all these languages have, in recent decades, undergone a revival. Certain aspects of formal education, research, and the dissemination of knowledge are still carried out in French, and a significant part of the industrial and economic sectors, namely the strategically important oil industry, as well as various state institutions and administrations, and an important number of press publications still use French extensively.[6]

More recently, the regime has attempted to impose Arabic as the sole official language, which, it claims, is the only language that can express the authentic identity and culture of the people. The political discourse that justifies this move constructs a unified national identity in reaction to the systematic attempts on the part of the French to dismantle the foundations of the country and to cut it off from its roots. In *Islamist Challenge in Algeria: A Political History* (1997), Michael Willis writes:

> The *Révolution Culturelle*, with its essentially nationalistic aim of establishing a distinct cultural identity for Algerians in place of the overwhelmingly French one that 130 years of colonial rule had imprinted on the country, primarily influenced the growth of the Islamist movement, through its core objective of securing the linguistic "Arabisation" of Algeria. Algeria's programme of Arabisation had actually begun as early as 1964 with Ben Bella's Arabisation of primary education and introduction of compulsory religious instruction. It was under President Boumediene, however, that Arabisation became a real priority for the Algerian government. (51)

Teachers, writers, artists, and intellectuals have been called upon to express the Arabness of the nation. The ultimate expression of this nationalist sentiment has been the abandonment of the language of the colonizer. For example, as a consequence of this mandate, Malek Haddad, himself a famous Francophone novelist, who, in 1968, became the country's minister of culture, decided to stop writing, simply because he had not mastered Arabic. He asked the other writers at the time to reject French and, in doing so, complete the process of national independence through cultural liberation. The decision, made from a different political perspective, that of Kateb Yacine, the most important Algerian writer and one of the greatest twentieth-century novelists, to stop writing in French in 1970 and use only Algerian vernacular languages proceeded from a similar rationale.

Although the popular rejection of French was part of a political and aesthetic debate in the 1960s, when it was appropriated by the state in the 1970s, it evolved into something very different and far more repressive. Under the "socialist" regime, Algerians were asked to complete the task initiated by the war of liberation, to generate a nationalist and anti-imperialist discourse and to create a socialist society. They were called upon to comply with the official ideology of the FLN and to abandon French and use only Arabic as the language of science, administration, and official communication. Rachida Yacine (1993) describes the evolution of this policy in North Africa:

The Maghrebi claim for Arab-Islamic characteristics, with the
emphasis on a national language, has been used either as a political issue, as was the case in Algeria and Morocco, or as a
means of political legitimacy as in Tunisia. As soon as independence occurred, these nations selected Arabic language as an
official national language. Their preferences were found in official documents and speeches. For Algeria, this choice appears
in the Tripoli programme of 1962 which underlines the process
of Arabisation. In this programme which states the main political options of the Algerian nation, it is declared that the Algerian culture will be national and that its role will include that of
the restoration of Arabic language (at first) to reflect the values
of the nation and its dignity, and to make the language itself effective as a language of civilization. Articles of the Algerian
Constitution of 1963 focused on Arabic as a national language.

The National Constitution of 1963 described Arabic as an element of national identity. Again, article 273 of the Second
Constitution of 1976 stipulated that Islam is the religion of the
state, Arabic its national language, and that the government
will work to generalise the use of the national language at the
official level. (227–28)

In the postcolonial era, the use of Arabic became such an ideologically charged issue that, as Mostefa Lacheraf, an important revolutionary and distinguished intellectual, has pointed out, the Arabic
language became the "hostage of nationalism" (1964, 323).

Beginning in the late 1960s, the forced "Arabization" of education
in schools and universities, carried out with the assistance of teachers from the Middle East, quickly cut off the Berberophone and
Francophone Algerians from their fellow citizens. Thus, language use
continued to be an important element of social stratification and political struggles. In the late 1970s and 1980s, the "Islamization" that
followed the policy of systematic and authoritarian "Arabization"
further separated even progressive or secular Arabophones from other
Algerians. These developments have contributed substantially to the
violence of recent times. Analyzing this situation, Rachida Yacine
again explains:

At independence, the national governments of Algeria, Morocco and Tunisia sought to encourage the use of Arabic as a
means of asserting national identity. However, it was limited

in use and development. The claim for Arabic as a national language, and the expansion of the French language to all activities of life in the Maghreb, generated contradictions and often provoked conflicts. It is commonly assumed that the linguistic situation has been dramatic in the first decade of independence, and considering the political tensions of the transition there were no national debates on the linguistic issues. In that period, the French language had become an instrument of social promotion, progress and power. It established conflicting social and political relationships in the Maghreb; at first it was an obstacle to national development and modernisation, then later a contradiction to the official claims for authenticity and national identity. (1993, 225–26)

The desire to exercise total control over linguistic expression and production led the Party and the government to create an Academy of Arabic Language. The aim of this body was to regulate linguistic expression not only in schools and universities, but also in the media and at every level of social communication (on signs, in official documents, on inscriptions, and so on). The ironic side to this development is that it was promoted, implemented, and supervised by Mouloud Kassim, the *Kabyle* minister who later created the first Islamic Studies Institutes in Algeria![7] As these examples clearly demonstrate, there is no transparent connection between one's ethnic identity and one's political position on language policy.

The Linguistic "Purification"

According to the official ideology of the FLN regime, Algeria is a strictly Arab-Muslim nation. In this respect, it has always tried to rewrite the history of the country. This rewriting has entailed what most Algerians see as the fully legitimate necessity of eradicating French colonial discourse, ideological structures, and imperialist constructions aimed at destroying the collective memory of Algerians. Unfortunately, it has also entailed an attempt to erase ethnic and linguistic differences and other expressions of a multicultural community. In this sense, it has also been fighting and repressing the reality of Algeria, and of North Africa in general, which involves a complex interplay of peoples who, for more than a millennium, have lived together and produced this country's uniquely rich culture.

Since independence, successive governments have attempted to deny the cultural specificity of important ethnic minorities, such as the Kabyles, but also of various groups that have for centuries contributed to the richness of Algerian culture, such as the Jews and Algerians of European—primarily French—origin. Since most foreigners and Algerians of European and Jewish descent left the country immediately after 1962, the repression has concentrated on Berber, and in particular, Kabyle, cultural specificity. Recently, both the government and its Muslim fundamentalist opponents have revealed their homogenizing inclinations. Indeed, fundamentalist groups forced most foreigners to leave the country, either through threats of violence or actual murders. The government, for its part, has increasingly undermined the possibility of an inclusive society and instead has attempted to produce a monolithic, conformist, and intolerant society based on a fictional purity and artificial unity.

The FLN regime's unilateral imposition of Modern Standard Arabic as the country's sole official language and its repression of Tamazight and Algerian Arabic, the vernacular languages of the country, and of French, a language used by a large part of the Algerian elite, is an act of linguistic "purification" that marginalizes significant segments of Algerian society. This operation can be understood only from within a historical perspective that takes into account the genesis of the current linguistic and cultural crisis. The attempt to construct the myth of a modern nation-state in Algeria is based on at least three fundamental elements: an independent Algerian nation, Arabic as the national language, and Islam as the religion of the country. These factors are linked to other cultural, ideological, and political orientations, most importantly: opposition to the economic and cultural domination of France in particular and the West in general, along with an association, at the political level, with the "Third World" and, at an ideological level, with the Arab-Muslim world. After the liberation of the country from French rule, and with this set of orientations in mind, the Algerian government began to promote the exclusive use of Arabic. In this respect, the two immediate targets were the French language and the vernacular dialects of Algeria.

Whereas the justification for the fight against a generalized use of French was clearly ideological and political and based primarily on nationalistic rhetoric, the attack on Algerian Arabic and Berber was linked to the veneration of Arabic as a superior and even sacred language.

In *Translating the Message* (1989), Lamin Sanneh explains one aspect of the status of Arabic:

> Muslims ascribe to Arabic the status of a revealed language, for it is the medium in which the Qur'an, the sacred Scripture of Islam, was revealed. In several passages the Qur'an bears testimony to its own Arabic uniqueness, what the authorities call its *i'jaz*, or "inimitable eloquence" (see Qur'an 10:38–39; 11:1–2; 16:104–5; 28:49; 39:24, 29; 41:41–42; 43:1–3). The author of the Qur'an, which is God, thus came to be associated with its speech, so that the very sounds of the language are believed to originate in heaven. . . . Consequently, Muslims have instituted the sacred Arabic for the canonical devotions. Given the lay character of Islam, these canonical devotions have brought the sacred Arabic to the level of the ordinary believer, although normally it is only religious specialists who understand the language in any satisfactory fashion. . . .
>
> The active participation of lay Muslims in the ritual acts of worship *(salat)*, fasting *(sawm)*, and, less frequently, the pilgrimage *(hajj)* to Mecca means that Arabic phrases, however imperfectly understood, remain on the lips of the believers wherever and whoever they happen to be. In thinly or unevenly Islamized areas, the natural imperfections arising from the obligation to employ the sacred Arabic provide the motivation for reforming local practice, rather than yielding to indigenous forms.
>
> An intriguing situation arises in which the prestigious and revered status of Arabic acts to disfranchise the vernacular. Mother-tongue speakers find themselves in the anomalous position of conceding that their languages are "profane" or "mundane" *('ajami')* for the decisive acts of the religious code, a concession that bears little relationship to one's fluency in Arabic. In fact, both the expert Arabs and the illiterate convert share a common veneration for the sacred language, with the knowledge of the expert being the standard toward which the convert aspires or, at any rate, the rule to which he or she concedes prescriptive authority. (212)

It is important to note, however, that for proponents of Arabization, the supposedly sacred origins of the Arabic language provide only part of the ideological justification. The other important part is economic and political. Furthermore, Koranic or so-called classical Arabic is not the language of Arabization.

Economic and Political Factors

Throughout the colonial period, and even after the end of the colonial occupation, French remained not only the language of administration and industrialization but also the instrument of economic and social advancement. Consequently, the postindependence government promoted the continued use of French in education. This pro-French policy created a two-tiered society, a kind of bicephalous economy based on two different standards, and resulted in incalculable social, cultural, and ideological contradictions. Michael Willis (1997) explains:

> Arabisation aimed to make modern literary Arabic the national language of Algeria through the important state controlled channels of education and the state administration. Arabisation proceeded quite rapidly through the education system but it advanced at a far slower pace through Algeria's large state administration. The net result of this was that the education system was turning out far more Arabic-speaking students or "Arabisants" than could be absorbed by the administrative sector, which in many places was largely still Francophone. There were also few jobs for Arabic only speakers in the state sector and the large corporations. The corporations, in particular, preferred students fluent in French or other European languages to deal with their mainly Western clients and suppliers. (51)

Because Francophonie has been linked in the popular mind to the government's elitist, oppressive, and illegitimate rule, the Francophone elite has tried to extend its own life by advocating a false populism based on Arabization. Thus, Arabic has come to embody a dual claim: on the one hand, the recuperation of Arab-Muslim identity in the context of Pan-Arab nationalism (Carré 1993), and, later, the Gulf War (Fregosi 1994, 36), which coincided with the rise of the FIS;[8] and, on the other, the basis for a new inclusion of a postindependence generation educated entirely in Arabic—and, for this very reason, unemployed, marginalized, and despised. Willis (1997) further explains:

> The implications of this problem for the government and for the potential revival of Islamist agitation and sentiment were severalfold. Two particular groups suffered from the lack of employment opportunities for Arabic-educated students. A high proportion of Arabisants came from poor, originally rural, families which migrated in large numbers to Algeria's large towns and cities over the past few decades. Not only, then, did this increasingly frustrated group become a significant source of agitation in urban areas, but moreover, in coming from the rural hinterland they retained much of the religious conservatism of those areas (which had largely been left untouched by the modernist ideas of post-independence governments) and thus were more likely to be sympathetic to Islamic activism and ideas. The fact that it tended to be poorer, more rural Algerians that became Arabisants, whilst the wealthy, more urban groups stayed largely Francophone (through choice), also meant that the social and economic cleavages between the two groups widened as the language preferences of both met with differing success in the job market, thus enhancing already present social tensions. . . . A significant proportion of "Arabised" students, particularly from wealthier and better-educated backgrounds, chose to study Arabic and Islamic law and literature at university rather than follow more Francophone-based courses in science and technology. This, however, did not do much more to improve their job opportunities over the poor Arabisant school-leavers. (51–52)

In view of the evolution of the situation after the cancellation of the 1991 legislative election, the insurrection that followed, the wave of terrorism, violence, and repression, and the various economic and political readjustments carried out by the regime, it appears that Arabization reflects the continuity of the FLN's nationalist and Arab-Muslim ideology, which a majority of Algerians share. (This point needs to be stressed, even in the face of opposition from the Kabyles and the French.) Arabization also stands as a sign of the FLN's solidarity with political allies from the moderate Islamic movement. Indeed, after the 1995 presidential elections, the Algerian regime continued to deny the FIS's right to exist, even as it included members from other Islamic parties.

In light of these events, the politics of Arabization can be seen to serve many functions. It fosters an ideological continuity with the FLN's anticolonial discourse, a discourse that emerged during the period of colonial dependence and has endured since independence from French rule. Although the opponents of Arabization may not like to admit it, this continuity is essential. Furthermore, because Francophones have dominated political life and civil society in the period since independence, and because they have controlled a disproportionate share of Algerian wealth, Arabization makes it possible to redistribute wealth in a more equitable manner: social well-being, in other words, will no longer be determined solely by the ease with which one adjusts to or manipulates colonial norms.[9] Finally, and most critically, the politics of Arabization sends a message to Islamic fundamentalists: by co-opting the fundamentalists' potential allies, Arabization has a moderating effect on a politically volatile situation. In *Islamist Challenge in Algeria: A Political History* (1997), Willis writes again:

> It was therefore almost inevitable that both frustrated groups would find themselves identifying with opposition to the government which identified itself with Islamic values, since not only were both groups far more aware, through their education, of Arabo-Muslim ideas and concepts, but both believed that it was the persistence of secular and French influence that was responsible for their frustration. A return to the sort of Islamic, Arabised order advocated by most Islamist critics of the government would clearly be in their interests. Indeed, Jean-Claude Vatin indicates that calls for greater Islamisation of Algeria, which clearly grew amongst Arabisants in the 1970s, were linked to calls for Arabisation "as a mere device for gaining access to those jobs more or less monopolised by their French-speaking co-religionists." (52)

It is also important to realize, however, that the Algerian government's current strategy may be based on dangerous miscalculations. First, it may be naive for the regime to imagine that, by depriving the fundamentalists of potential recruits, it has secured reliable allies for itself. Second, in view of the catastrophic situation of the country's economy, it is not certain that the new "Arabized" generation will ever benefit from these reforms. The combination of corruption in all institutions and at every level of government and the radical changes imposed by the International Monetary Fund may undermine the potentially ameliorative effects of Arabization. Third, both the form of this policy of Arabization and the pace at which it is carried out seem to repeat—to an exaggerated degree—the failed attempts of previous governments to allow only the use of Arabic in a country that is effectively trilingual. Indeed, given the degree of "globalization," the prohibition against other languages may well be regarded as a gesture that limits rather than expands the possibilities open to *all* Algerians. In other words, the cultural and political claims of Arabization may be irrelevant if they limit Algerians' access to a wider (economic and cultural) world.

From One Monotheism to Another?

Although the program of Arabization has extensive popular support, especially among those who seek to recover the part of their culture that was violently suppressed by the French, it is also clear that numerous mistakes in policy and method have generated resentment within Algeria and alarm in the international community (which, it should be remarked, expressed no opposition to the French suppression of Arabic). There is no doubt that the Arabization of Algerian schools and universities has been carried out in an irrational manner: rather than being realized gradually, allowing time for everyone to adjust, Arabization was abruptly imposed. The explanation for these irrational policies lies in the extent to which politics rather than pedagogy and reason determined the pace and range of Arabization. In this respect, it is undeniable that the Algerian regime shares much of the responsibility for the turmoil associated with Arabization. Nevertheless, although we cannot excuse the ineptitude and bad faith of the regime, it is equally important to stress that its policy was not based, as is so often asserted, on a blindly nationalist ideology; on the contrary, the regime also faces enormous political and economic pressures.

It is striking that in recent publications (primarily from France, let us note), it is principally Arabophones and teachers from the Middle

East who are blamed for Arabization and for the increasingly poor quality of education, whether in French or in Arabic. There is no doubt that teachers from the Middle East nurtured an already considerable Islamist movement in Algeria. However, the failures of Algerian-French cooperation—and the disastrous consequences for the educational system in Algeria—are also quite stunning and must be included in discussions of why the apparent radicalism of Arabization has such extensive support. Although most critics of Arabization ignore the conditions that precipitated the move toward Arabization, we need to consider them.

First, the initial wave of Arabization was linked to the affirmation of Algerian nationalism within the framework of Third World and Pan-Arab unity. Second, it was related to the economic situation of Algeria in the 1970s, and more specifically, to the disagreement between the Algerians and the French regarding the price of oil and gas, which are the basis of economic development in Algeria. Indeed, following President Houari Boumediene's unilateral decision, on 24 February 1972, to nationalize the oil industry, French president Valéry Giscard d'Estaing ordered the return, within forty-eight hours, of twenty-eight thousand French engineers and technicians, most of whom were managing the companies and supervising the extraction of oil and gas, the most critical of Algerian resources and the source of 98 percent of the country's currency for foreign exchange. This gesture, which was intended to destroy the Algerian economy, was also accompanied by the French government's blocking of bilateral cooperation in the education sector. It was on this occasion that Giscard d'Estaing made his infamous statement: "They [the OPEC countries] have oil, but we have ideas." This was also the context in which he proclaimed that the oil of Algerians was "red." Even though Giscard d'Estaing was clearly criticizing what he perceived to be communism, the Algerian president responded: "Yes, our oil is red because of the blood of our martyrs." It was in this same context (in 1974, to be precise) that France suddenly began to restrict North African and especially Algerian immigration to France, a practice that has evolved into the increasingly racist and fascist politics of anti-immigration in France today. By the mid-1970s, Algerian-French relations had dangerously deteriorated: each government pressured the other with all the means available to it: economic, propagandistic, and even military (in the case of the anticolonial war in the western Sahara).

It was under these circumstances that Algeria began to initiate a multidimensional policy to diversify its economic, cultural, political, and international relations. Faced with attempts by France to sabotage Algerian independence, the Algerian government turned to Soviet bloc countries, which quickly furnished engineers, technicians, and teachers in the natural sciences, and to the countries of the Middle East, whose assistance consisted principally of providing teachers in the humanities. It was also at that time that Algeria increased its military cooperation with the Soviet bloc, developed new ties with the United States and Japan, particularly in the oil industry, and began to send thousands of students to study in countries other than France.

Between 1981 and 1986, I myself was director of the Foreign Languages Institute and vice president of the University of Sidi-Bel-Abbès, Algeria. I was in charge of this academic institution's external relations and cultural exchanges and, in that capacity, I initiated more than a dozen exchanges with universities in Western Europe, Eastern Europe, and the Middle East. What my colleagues and I observed is that the teachers sent to Algeria from France were usually no better than the Russian, Romanian, Polish, East German, Belgian, Swiss, Egyptian, or Syrian teachers, and that they were rarely of the high caliber of the Palestinians. It is essential to recall that, in the mid-1970s, when the move toward Arabization was taking place, the French government rarely provided us with the qualified and experienced faculty we so urgently needed; instead, the French sent Volontaires du Service National Actif (VSNA), that is, inexperienced individuals who, most of the time, had absolutely no teaching experience and also lacked the emotional and intellectual qualities that would have allowed them to adjust to the conditions of Algerian students and schools.[10] It should be stressed that the VSNA are French youth who can avoid doing military service in France by becoming teachers (obviously at salaries far lower than those of regular teachers belonging to the French Fonction Publique, or civil service) in "Third World" countries, principally in the former colonies of France. After the 1981 Algerian-French Conférence des Recteurs et Présidents d'Universités (Summit of National Administrators and University Presidents) that took place in Constantine, where Algerians expressed their disillusionment and disappointment with the mediocrity of French instructors, there were many occasions when we sent incompetent teachers back to France, or refused to receive them in the first place. It became increasingly clear that unqualified teachers were continually being sent not inadvertently, but because of the systematic and calculated refusal on the part of the French Ministry of Education to provide us with the kind of skilled and high-quality teachers we were willing—and indeed, very desperate—to hire.

Thus, as far as foreign teachers are concerned, the quality of teaching in Algeria declined not only because of Arabization, which was carried out by young Algerian teachers who were also minimally trained and who relied, therefore, on supposedly mediocre teachers from the Middle East, even though this racist claim has been made by Algerians themselves. It also declined because of the increasingly poor quality of the French teachers who gradually replaced the older and better-trained generation of teachers from France. What resulted from the conjunction of these factors is that, in the 1970s, Algerian education—in French as well as Arabic—declined precipitously. The problems that confront us today, in other words, do not simply stem from Arabization—Arabization in itself is not a diabolic phenomenon. Our problems stem from the fact that the quality of both Arabophone and Francophone education suffered from an insidious combination of bad administrative and political decisions on the one hand and global conditions on the other.

Ethnic Discourse and the Colonial Subconscious

One of the strategies of those who oppose Arabization is to present it as the instrument of ethnic oppression—the oppression of Berbers by Arabs. But this argument is based on some unspoken—and disingenuous—assumptions. First, to present Arabization as a tool of Arabs' domination of the Berbers is to neglect the fact that the Berber population is not a homogeneous group. In fact, in Algeria at least five different groups make up the population known collectively as "Berber." The opposition to Arabization comes principally from the radical ethnic activists of one of these five groups, the Kabyle, who, far from recognizing the heterogeneity of the Berber community, present it as monolithic; and on this basis they simplistically argue that Arabs have dominated Berbers in the past and intend to do so more completely in the future. Second, this argument is misleading in the extreme because political, economic, and military power has traditionally rested with the Chaouis, another of the five Berber groups. Unlike the Kabyles, the Chaouis have to a great extent embraced the Arabic language and Arab-Muslim culture. Third, the Kabyle Francophone elite themselves have, for at least a century or more, benefited from a disproportionate share of political and economic power. The advantages of the Kabyle Francophone elite in the political and economic arenas derive unmistakably from French colonial policy based on the "Kabyle Myth" that Kabyles are ethnically linked to Europeans rather than Africans or Middle Easterners (see Lorcin 1995, esp. 252–53). Favored by the colonial government, the Kabyle elite quickly mastered the French language, which became the basis for their social and political promotion during the colonial period and after independence.[11] Generally speaking, power has been distributed in the following way: the Chaouis have commanded the army—which explains why, so far, all but one Algerian president, most key governmental advisers, and most generals and senior officers have been Chaouis; and Kabyles have largely monopolized industry, state administrative positions, and the Francophone media. This is so true that the capital, Algiers—the country's economic, political, and administrative center—is to a large extent a Kabyle city. In reality, the so-called Arabs—that is, the strictly non-Berber Algerians concentrated primarily in the western regions of the country— are those who have thus far benefited the least from the share of economic development and political power. This can be explained by the regime's clanish, ethnic, and regional structures and policies for which the traditional Kabyle leaders and economic, ideological, and political groups are equally responsible.

The extremism that Kabyle culturalists—and not Berbers in general—attribute to the proponents of Arabization has its counterpart in the extremism of the Kabyle ethnic activists themselves. It is true that the FLN-military regime has developed policies that repress Berber culture (and the Tamazight language in particular). But let us recall that the regime itself is principally Berber (Chaoui and Kabyle), not "Arab." Kabyle culturalists have wisely presented themselves as Francophiles, democrats, and modernists, and, knowing that the anti-Algerian, anti-Arab, and anti-Muslim bias is still pathologically strong in the West in general and in France in particular,[12] they often succeed in masking the fact that their own attitudes and ideological positions are marked by an equally exclusive, tribalist, and racist discourse against the so-called Arab-Muslims (a group that also includes Berbers of Chaoui and Mozabite descent).

The extremism of the Kabyle culturalists sheds light on one of the

more virulent strains of tribalism. Like many other Algerians, they
may be persecuted by the regime, but, though it is true that they
themselves may be victims of tribalist hatred, they are also some of
its most visible disseminators. For example, they systematically deny
the Arab-Muslim dimension of Algeria; they systematically reject the
fact that Arabic is spoken by at least 80 percent of their country's
population. They also demonstrate an astonishing ignorance of the
fact that French has also been the language of the negation and alienation of Algerian identity. It is staggering that, more than thirty years
after the independence of their country, they boast that they know
only Kabyle and French and have no knowledge of the language spoken by the other 25 million Algerians, for whom they, as so-called
democrats and modernists, claim to speak.

Those who oppose Arabization often do so by oversimplifying the
linguistic situation in Algeria. They overlook the distinction between the vernacular languages of Algeria and what is—inappropri-
ately—called classical Arabic. In his otherwise useful book, *The
Agony of Algeria* (1997), for example, Martin Stone repeats this
cliché:

> The language spoken in the home and on the streets, despite
> the meddling of the politicians and the imams, is a rich and
> unique mix of Classical and Maghrebi Arabic, various local
> Berber dialects and "roumiya." This hybrid is a relatively re-
> cent development: before the French occupation, all inhabi-
> tants of the coastal littoral (though not all Kabyles) would have
> been proficient in Maghrebi Arabic as well as Classical Arabic.
> Maghrebi Arabic itself is spoken across North Africa, and de-
> veloped in the late Middle Ages from Classical Arabic with a
> few borrowings from Spanish, Berber dialects and Turkish. As
> with all spoken languages, it is constantly changing but has a
> special ability to seize French words and mutate them into ac-
> ceptably Algerian-sounding forms.
>
> In contrast, the language of broadcasting and official
> speeches is stilted and reflects the speaker's political or socio-
> economic status. Government ministers often lapse into
> French in the middle of a speech, frequently replying to ques-
> tions put to them in French. Moreover, many Algerians have
> enormous difficulty understanding the Classical Arabic used in
> television news broadcasts, and prefer to watch the French

satellite channels beamed from across the Mediterranean. In
the political and social crises of the 1990s satellite dishes became a frequent target for Islamic extremists in heavily Is-
lamist-influenced areas such as Blida and parts of Algiers.
(22–23)

In fact, apart from some courses in literature—dealing, in fact,
with *pre*-Islamic poetry and culture—or religious studies, the Arabic
taught at school is not classical or Koranic Arabic. In recognition of
the *Nahda,* a nineteenth-century *secularist* movement that sought to
revive Arab culture by modernizing it, Algerians are instructed in
modernized Arabic. This is the version of Arabic that is designated by
universities in the United States and Europe as Modern Standard Arabic. The distinction between classical and modern Arabic is similar
to the difference between ancient and modern Greek or ancient and
modern Hebrew. Against all evidence, the fact that Arabic is a *living*
language is systematically and willfully ignored because of the ignorance, bad faith, and ideologically driven misrepresentation of the opponents of Arabic.

I will not fetishize Arab-Muslim civilization as one of the most
important of humankind, though it certainly is that. Let us simply
recall that Arabic, in addition to being the language of the Koran, is
also the language of literature and poetry, of mathematics and astronomy, of geography and history, of philosophy and medicine, the
language of anticolonial resistance and popular revolutions. Given
that, in many countries, the exact sciences are still taught in the language of Ibn Rushd (or Averroës), Ibn Sina (or Avicenna), Al
Khawarizmi, and Al Hallaj;[13] given that Naguib Mahfouz was
awarded the Nobel Prize for Literature and that Adonis and Mah-
moud Darwish are two of the greatest poets of the twentieth century,
who enjoy international acclaim both as poets and as progressive
thinkers, and who have been widely translated into other languages;
and given that software programs provide a seamless transition between Arabic and the language of computers, the characterization of
Arabic as an obscurantist, antimodernist language is quite simply
racist!

The tribalist instincts of the Kabyle culturalists reflect a position
that is no different from that of the Arabophone reactionary writer
Tahar Ouettar, who declared on the French-German television chan-

nel *Arte* that the death of the poet Tahar Djaout, who was ethnically Kabyle (I personally would identify him simply as an Algerian and as a friend who is deeply missed) was a loss for his family but certainly not for his country. This kind of tribalism undermines the hope for a genuine multiculturalism. The Kabyles' struggle for recognition of their identity, language, and culture should not blind us to the fact that the ideological discourse that their movement defends is both a legitimate claim to Berberitude, one of the fundamental dimensions of Algerian identity, *and* a dangerous discourse of ethnic exclusion structurally identical to that of the enemies—the regime or the Muslim fundamentalists—they claim to fight.

This unidimensionalism further feeds an already volatile situation and reduces the likelihood that Algerians will engage in a conversation based on tolerance and mutual recognition rather than hypocrisy and political calculation, as was the case at the Saint Eugedio conclave.[14] The Algerian historian Mohammed Harbi, a dissident of long standing, has perspicaciously traced the genesis of the current controversy over language and cultural difference in Algeria. In "Violence, nationalisme, Islamisme" (1995), he writes:

> At the linguistic level, the Ulema [Muslim theologians] have been the initiators of a Jacobin strategy. As a language of science, Arabic, the language of the Koran, the language of revelation, did not, in the seventh century, displace vernacular Berber language but Latin. As a monotheistic religion, Islam overcame a Christianity whose influence had not defeated the paganism that thrived in the interior of the country. Monotheism was a coastal phenomenon. The dissemination of the Arabic language was carried out by the conquering army, the Ulema, and the Arab or Berber merchants. It accompanied the establishment of state institutions and Islamization but was not accompanied by a total Arabization of the Berber worlds. I use the plural in saying "Berber worlds" because the idea of unifying heterogeneous spaces without taking into account time and social processes has become an Algerian national mania. For example, the Kabyle culturalists challenge the Jacobinism of the Arab-Muslims in the name of a strategy that is equally Jacobin. (26, my translation)

The claim that Algerians do not understand what is improperly called "classical" Arabic, which has been characterized by the opponents of Arabization as the official language of the regime, the language of a medieval elite, the language of obscurantist Arabism and Islam, distant from the authentic languages of the people, is simply ludicrous. Although this may be the case for illiterate people or for Francophone Algerians who were educated almost exclusively in French—the generation of Algerians who are now in their forties—it is certainly not the case for the majority of the postindependence generation, for whom Arabic has been the language of instruction.

In other words, it is not the opposition between Modern Standard Arabic on the one hand and Berber and Algerian Arabic on the other that should be stressed, but the opposition between Arabic and French. Unlike Modern Standard Arabic or French, neither Berber nor Algerian Arabic has yet developed into a language of science and technology or administration. Thus the unspoken part of the argument against Arabization is that the official language of Algeria should be French!

The assumption that Arabic is a backward and archaic language, that it is unable to operate in the modern world, that it cannot serve as the instrument of science and technology, and that it is incapable of communicating progressive values such as democracy and modernity cannot be rationally defended, particularly when one considers the international stature of Arab-Muslim culture and the Arabic language. Ideologically, however, this assumption powerfully echoes French colonial discourse after the 1830 conquest of Algeria and the neocolonial discourse that has developed since independence in 1962—within the French right and extreme right, as one would expect, but, to a great extent, within the French left[15] as well. After all, the left was the proponent of a savage war against Algeria and currently enforces racist anti-immigration laws that do not displease the fascist National Front. Indeed, it was in these same terms that colonial ideologists described Arabic. Furthermore, this attitude toward the indigenous language was an assumption applied not only in North Africa but also in other French colonies.[16]

A comparable kind of Jacobinism explains why the Arabophone elite hold Berber and Algerian Arabic in contempt and why the Kabyle culturalists and members of the Francophone intelligentsia express scorn for so-called literary or classical Arabic and deny an important dimension of the country's identity and culture. It is important to note, however, that these views are not shared by the more representative, consistent, and politically lucid Rassemblement pour la Culture et la Démocratie (RCD). Originally a Kabyle party for the most part, the RCD is thus far the only significant Algerian organization that has been trying to move beyond the ideological imprisonment of ethnicism. It is also the only significant political organization that clearly positions itself as a party that is both secular and national in the complete sense of those terms. In this respect, the RCD's position on the linguistic issue is remarkable. As Ramdan Redjala and Smaïl Aouli (1995) eloquently comment in their essay, "La Kabylie face à la dérive intégriste, "On the basis of a systematic pedagogical endeavor, the militants of the RCD have been able to articulate the principles of the Algerian personality: Berberitude, Islam, and Arabness, without renouncing the colonial legacy. This certainly means that cultural recognition is not a Kabyle issue only." (208, my translation)

In short, the linguistic issue in Algeria is dominated by multiple and mutually exclusive discourses and positions. This discourse of exclusion is often reproduced by Francophone Algerian[17] and French media and, at times, unfortunately, by intellectuals. I would like to insist that these intellectuals are often sincere and full of goodwill: nevertheless, because of their personal ideological inclinations or political sympathies, they have a limited appreciation of the Algerian global situation. This tragic situation is certainly not unrelated to the current crisis and the violence that is tearing the country apart. Linguistic forms of monotheism and cultural dogma correspond to sociopolitical and ideological forms. In this case, it is no exaggeration to say that Algerians are to a large extent the victims of their own perpetuation of what one might call the colonial subconscious.[18]

[2]

the algerian linguicide

DJAMILA SAADI-MOKRANE

SINCE COLONIZATION and the emergence of a national movement, then Algeria's independence in 1962, conflict has dominated the cultural and linguistic features through which people display their sense of belonging to a community. Some lay claim to the colonial legacy as an asset that opens a universal dialogue; others recognize only Arabic and Islamic currents; and still others seek to preserve the Berber characteristics of the primordial, pre-Islamic Algerian self. The issue of language arose with such violence that, in the space of half a century, the death of three different languages was predicted: of Arabic during colonization, and of Berber, and French after independence. "Linguicide" stands as a strategy elaborated to subjugate and reshape the identity of the country and its inhabitants by separating them from their points of reference.

For the French colonizer, it was necessary to cut to the quick the Arabic and Islamic roots of a conquered land in order to crush its core values, which offered a refuge and thus a source of resistance. Algerian leaders needed to muzzle other languages to impose the hegemony of the Arabic language on the entire nation. In fact, the existence of the pre-Islamic Berber language serves as a reminder of historical periods that many would prefer to see forgotten, a reminder that Algeria was not a blank slate before Islamization, and that the Arabization of the country was the consequence of an Arab conquest. The persistence of the use of French supposedly reveals Algerians' alienated affinity for the West and its secular values. This affinity is summed up in the label *hizb franza*, literally, "the side of France," which is used to designate a traitor to the country.

This chapter was translated by Whitney Sanford.

Imagined Strategies of Glottocide

The first death was predicted by the Orientalist William Marçais and the colonial society of his time. He envisioned the "natural death" of Arabic, given the growing importance of French in daily communication (Souriau 1975). French would become indispensable in oral exchanges between communities, since the majority of colonizers did not speak Arabic. The "natives," excluded from colonial education but required to use French in their encounters with the colonial administration or with employers, would eventually forget how to speak Arabic, retaining only its written form! This is precisely the definition of a dead language, as Latin is today. The Latin model held a prominent place in the colonial consciousness because literary written Arabic was confined to Koranic schools and medersas (that is, Islamic secondary schools), which only a tiny minority of students could attend, and also because the colonial school system relegated literary Arabic to the status of a foreign language. The common people, having access neither to the colonial school nor to the medersa, knew only oral Arabic. It was assumed they would forget it, since they would often be using French. Literary written Arabic would be maintained by the few scholars of the period. This occurrence was made possible by the fact that most speakers did not understand literary Arabic. A parallel was even drawn between this situation and that of early speakers of Romance languages, since most Romance speakers did not understand the more erudite Latin.

We can attribute the second death sentence to a leader of the only political party of the postindependence period, the FLN. He too foresaw the "natural death" of a language—Berber. With the rise of Arabic education after independence, the Kabyle child would eventually be unable to understand his own mother. Arabic would gradually supplant Berber, a purely oral language, confining it to rudimentary intrafamilial exchanges. However, the proverb "no one is a prophet in his own land" sums up the situation, because this "leader" was far from suspecting that Berber resistance would overcome the imperium of the sacred Arabic language, and would be on its way to overthrowing its hegemonic postindependence status.

The third prediction was the death of French, which was expected to disappear entirely from Algerian society. In primary schools, French was supposed to be gradually replaced by another foreign language, English. The institutional use of French in public administration was forbidden by a 1990 law, called the "generalization of the Arabic language," which foresaw the total Arabization of public administration by 1992, and of the university by 1997. The application decree, pushed back several times, took effect on 5 July 1998, the anniversary of independence. It had a strong effect on public opinion, expressed principally in the French language press, which feared the worst for its future and its freedom of expression. But, according to recent information, nothing has greatly changed in the use of language in Algeria.

Let us also remember that the death of dialectal Arabic by means of public schooling was also planned. Introductions in first- and second-year textbooks explain that the assignment of students who learn the rules of written language in class is to correct members of their families. Many teachers make this censoring role explicit to their students. As a result of being corrected by their children, parents would lose their "bad" linguistic habits—that is, their native language—and would conform to the code of a written language that is, for the most part, foreign to them. Thus the school knowingly makes the student an agent of linguicide. There is hardly a household with school-age children that has not experienced this sort of correction in the use of the mother tongue, and anecdotes centering on this role assigned to the child abound. School is thus founded on teaching a foreign language to children, who are duty bound to spread it to their family circle.

The media took over this offensive: a radio program called "Arabic on the Radio" was broadcast during prime time. The program relied on a simple Manichaean principle, which everyone remembers: "Say this. Don't say that." It thus corrected all dialectal usages in favor of literary Arabic. The attempt to destroy native languages went so far that incomprehension often reigned in institutional, political, and administrative relations; as a result, the people never understood their leaders very well. It was not until President Mohammed Boudiaf was called upon to lead the country in February 1992, after the electoral process, which was about to result in the election of the FIS, was halted, that the leader and the people spoke the same language. It was the first time that a leader had addressed the people in dialectal Arabic and had been understood. Boudiaf, unlike his predecessors, had mastered dialectal Arabic, which allowed him to speak to the nation in a language accessible to the majority.

Neither the cultural, sociological, or political programs on television and radio nor the news shows were perfectly understood by most people. Listeners were obliged to guess and interpret, which often led to interminable discussions of what each thought he or she had understood. At the same time, we could hear and scoff at numerous business leaders who, when invited to comment in the media, stuttered and stammered in literary Arabic, a language they barely knew but were required to use publicly. Sounding foolish, they would repeat the appropriate word whispered to them by their hosts, thus consenting to linguistic mutilation. The masquerade was pushed so far that we witnessed a president of the Republic, giving his first televised speech, deciphering a written text, which he delivered with some difficulty.

In some ways, the planned deaths of popular linguistic practices are reminiscent of the psychic hell that George Orwell described. The Arabic, French, and Berber languages are all connected to the country's history, but in different ways. They exist as a collision of words, and endure all the fractures that destabilize society. Fantasized deaths and aborted oral drives, trace macabre patterns of linguistic suffering; a will to omnipotence endeavors to penetrate the intimacy of the ineffable human being and to remake the ontological character of the people of Algeria. To use a brutal metaphor, the leaders of Algeria would like to linguistically castrate the people, and, to do this, have used the resources of the state to recreate a lost image of the Orient. In this context, it is clear that no linguistic usage can be neutral, nor can it be a simple tool for communication. Every language is a source of frustration. Literary Arabic is still misunderstood by the majority; dialectal Arabic and Berber cannot express things in writing since they are exclusively oral languages; French, often poorly spoken, is considered the language of colonial alienation. In spite of all these deficiencies, the imposition of one language as a national language, in this case Arabic, has not led to the establishment of a national cultural and linguistic unity. Nevertheless, this is the objective of Arabization, as stated in a founding text of the Algerian revolution, the Tripoli program, which declares that Algerian culture must be Arabized to fight against "the cultural cosmopolitanism and pervasive Westernization which has contributed to teaching many Algerians to disdain their national language and values." It is clear that this text assigns an aim to literary Arabic that is not linguistic but political—the unity of a liberated nation.

Warring Languages

Let me recall the basic assumption of sociolinguistics: most societies, for the sake of mutual comprehension among their members, try to find a common language. The common language develops, usually in a multilingual context, at the expense of other languages, or even in direct conflict with them. Generally, in societies where several languages coexist, one of them eventually emerges as the common language, as a result either of legal measures or of cultural or economic supremacy. This is precisely the situation in Algeria, where oral native languages (Berber and dialectal Arabic) and written languages (literary Arabic and French), are all in use and in conflict, and all have a historical basis that accounts for their emergence. But although literary Arabic is the only officially recognized national language, French and the various native tongues continue to grow and develop, within a context we will now attempt to clarify.

Berber, the oldest language in Algeria, is attested in Lybic inscriptions dating from the Neolithic period. It is the native language of one-fifth of the population. An alphabet using the *tifinagh* script is still in use today among the Tuareg; elsewhere, exchanges in Berber are exclusively oral. The word "Berber" apparently comes from the Latin word *barbarus,* which designated "uncultured," foreign peoples outside Roman civilization (Boukous 1989). The word "Kabyle," on the other hand, means "the tribes," and comes from Arabic. Today the term "Tamazight," which refers to a number of regional variations of Berber throughout the country, is preferred. In the north, speakers of Chenoui, Chouaia, and Kabyle are the most numerous. In the Sahara, three other dialects predominate: Mozabite, Zenete, and Tamachek. Tamachek is the only linguistic form that uses the *tifinagh* written script. Many Berber-speaking areas have yet to be completely inventoried by specialists, who estimate the Berberophone population of Algeria at about 20 percent (Youssi 1991). However, no linguistic study has corroborated this estimate, since the public use of Berber remains taboo.

This taboo originated in what historians have named "the Berberist crisis" (Gallissot 1995). Within the national movement, a conflict over the definition of the Algerian nation erupted in 1945–49, a conflict whose consequences are far from ended. Following the doctrine of the Ulema (religious scholars), Arabo-Islamism intends to impose Islamic authority on society via Arabization and moral reform. The word "Arabization" should be understood as a translation of *ta'arroub*, that is, to "become Arab": in other words, the aim is not only for Algerians to become Arabic speakers, but to become "Arabs" by adopting their language, their customs, and their culture. This suggests that one social group consents, even seeks, to integrate into another, which is defined in terms of the civilization to which it is connected. In the Maghreb, the Islamic aspect of Arab civilization is practically the only one perceived in religious, social, and cultural arenas (Souriau 1975). Islamism has imposed its views on all the country's founding texts, thereby pushing Francophone, Berberist, and Marxist intellectuals into clandestine opposition. These groups instead ascribe to a national Arabo-Berber popular culture without reference to Islam. In 1963, just after independence, war broke out in Kabylia; it ended in 1965 with a crackdown on the use of a different language and claims to a separate identity. Thereafter, the Berber language was violently repressed. Students caught with copies of the forbidden "*tifinagh* alphabet" were thrown into prison, because the regime saw use of the alphabet as a symbol of Kabyle separatism.

At the same time, the Berber Academy founded in Paris solidified the movement's claims and coordinated a significant level of cultural activity in Algeria, which each year is repressed by the police acting on the authority of the current regime. The "Berber spring" erupted in Tizi-Ouzou in 1980 (Chaker 1986), after a conference on ancient Kabyle poetry, which was to be chaired by the great Berber novelist Mouloud Mammeri, was banned. People joked that "Berber is a language we can sing, but not speak"; indeed, Kabyle songs had already disseminated the community's identity claims. Today, Tamazight classes are allowed at Tizi-Ouzou University, where the language is the subject of much postgraduate research. The Berber movement is trying to emerge from the ivory tower; after a strike was launched in schools and universities of Kabylia, the teaching of Berber in primary schools was authorized for the 1995–96 academic year. All this suggests the possibility that Berber will become the second national language, once it is taught in all the country's schools. As for the public, opinions about language vary greatly, and we may wonder whether Tamazight education will be limited to Berberophone regions or expanded to include the entire school system (*Rapport de prise en charge du dossier amazigh* 1998).

The absence of a written tradition in Tamazight leaves many issues unresolved, however. For example, the use of the ancient *tifi-nagh* alphabet may have the drawback of further isolating Berber culture, since this writing system is very little used. For transcriptions, the Latin or Arabic alphabets, depending on which audience is targeted, have most often been used until now. But, for general use, this practice clashes with linguistic sentiments, that is, the Berbers' self-representation of their own language, or, as linguists say, "the intuition of the speaking subject that allows him to judge grammaticality and to appreciate different registers in the language" (Arrivé, Gadet, and Galmiche 1986). Writing Tamazight with Latin characters might constitute a move toward universalism for Berberophones, insofar as the language's readability would make it accessible to the greatest possible number. Arabophones, however, perceive such a move as a rejection of national identity and even as an indication of Francophilia. Yet the use of the Arabic alphabet is felt by some Berberophones to diminish the importance of their language, by reducing it to a subcategory of Arabic. For now, the first schoolbook has been composed using a collection of texts transcribed into all three alphabets and translated into five Berber dialects. Furthermore, the existence of regional variants not yet inventoried requires a careful reflection on how to codify linguistic norms in order to synthesize them for teaching purposes. Discussions on this topic are ongoing.

The situation of classical Arabic presents very different characteristics. Arabic was introduced to the Maghreb as the language for Koranic study in medersas with the first wave of Islamization in the urban centers in the seventh century. It spread further in the eleventh century with the Hilal invasions of the countryside and the Sahara.

Classical Arabic is the sacred language of the Koran. It is a language of civilization that was used in the translations of texts from the Greco-Roman tradition transmitted to Europe in the Middle Ages, and was also used in the works of numerous scholars of the Muslim world in the fields of medicine, mathematics, astronomy, and grammar. Today it is primarily a liturgical language.

Literary Arabic (or modern Arabic) is taught in school systems throughout the Arab world. It is important to distinguish between classical Arabic, linked to the Koran and to Islamic territorial conquests, and literary or modern Arabic, a written form of Arabic more readily associated with the modern media. Literary or modern Arabic was developed in the nineteenth century at the instigation of the modernizing elites of the Middle East, known as *Nahda*, the Revival

(Arkoun 1984). Among writers and intellectuals open to Western culture, and in particular to English, a consensus emerged regarding the simplification of classical Arabic, both at the level of syntax, which was relieved of affected or uncommon turns of phrase, and at the lexical level, which integrated neologisms to designate discoveries of the modern world. This is the basis of the linguistic community called "the Arab world," and the same norms are in use in modern literature, administration, political life, the press, and the school system. Modern or literary Arabic is also the basis for Arabization in Algeria; but because it comes from the Middle East, many Algerians have difficulty understanding it. Some university scholars even say that the form of Arabic taught in primary school in Algeria "is really a methodological artifact that corresponds neither to the spontaneous oral usage of the language represented by different vernaculars in use throughout the Arab world, nor to actual production of standard Arabic in formal situations which require its use" (Taleb-Ibrahimi 1993). This means that students are taught an "artificial" language with no connection to the ordinary speech of Algerians or to that of educated speakers in the Arab world.

Dialectal Arabic, the native language of most speakers, is divided into numerous regional variants. A recent and original hypothesis maintains that Maghribi is a natural language descended from Punic, the language of Carthage, which evolved under the influence of Arabic after the Arab conquest of North Africa (Elimam 1997). Dialectal Arabic consists of a primarily oral form that has given rise to popular poetry, tales, legends, songs, and, to a lesser extent, plays for stage and screen, which, until recent years, conformed to the standards of literary Arabic. Since the country's independence in 1962, only amateur theater has used dialect, and the script was never written down. This is the case for Kateb Yacine's plays *Mohamed prends ta valise* (Mohamed, take your suitcase) and *La guerre de deux mille ans* (The two-thousand-year war). Until 1988 films were almost entirely in literary Arabic, with the exception of the famous television series "Hassan Terro." Since the colonial period, data collected from the oral tradition have given rise to numerous studies and translations, most of them in French. Berber and dialectal Arabic are ordinarily used by native speakers of those languages, and are also used to voice protest by a "turbulent" popular culture, still harshly suppressed by the police.

Arabic has been subject to the vicissitudes of the colonial experi-

ence. In 1938 it was declared a foreign language by a law that was re-
scinded only in 1961, just prior to independence, by Charles de Gaulle.
In 1962, the newly sovereign country was Arabized through a massive
education program. Then, in 1968, a decree designated Arabic as the
language to be used in all civil service positions. In 1988, the "French
Mission in Algeria" schools were barred to Algerians and to children of
mixed couples (usually Franco-Algerian), but remained opened to all
other foreigners. The French lycée (high school) of Algiers was moved
to another neighborhood, and the highly selective school formerly
called the Lycée Descartes took in students from the *nomenclatura*
class (the *tchitchi*—children of the wealthy—as opposed to the *bohi*—
rejects). The deceived public did not know that a specific program had
been established there, giving higher priority to the teaching of French
than in other Algerian high schools. Many of the students in this
school went on to pursue their university studies abroad.

The 1990 law, which generalized the exclusive use of Arabic in institutions and public service, was accompanied by sanctions as severe as imprisonment for violating the law. As a result, the linguistic
war against French also excluded Berber, thereby provoking an unprecedented protest movement. After popular demonstrations, the
law was temporarily suspended; nevertheless, Arabic hegemony remained secure in legal and religious administrations and in the
school system. More recently, the murder of the popular Kabyle
singer Matoub Lounès, which took place during the implementation
of this law (July 1998), sparked many demonstrations throughout
Kabylia, rendering this issue all the more problematic. But Arabization is not Algerianization—far from it. The debate over the content
of Arabization is motivated by an anxiety about education in Arabic.
There are serious ideological and cultural issues at stake in the teaching of any language. In the case of Arabic, the sacredness of the language means it is often conflated with Islam. This is not purely a
problem of form, since today Arabization continues the work of ac-
culturation once provided by French. In its choice of outdated texts
and pedagogical methods, and in the importance given to the teaching of the Koran from primary school to high school, the education
program in Arabic has cut itself off from its Algerian roots.

The French language asserted itself in Algeria amid the tumult of
colonization. At the time of independence, the country inherited a
French-speaking elite who continued to use French as the language of

economic, scientific, and technical power. It is still taught as a foreign language from the fourth year of elementary school through the last year of high school. In high school, it is used in the medical sciences, the exact sciences, and in technology studies; some fields of specialization give parallel courses in Arabic, but these have low enrollments. In the social sciences, French is also used in graduate study. In all disciplines, it provides access to the literature, which is in French for the most part. To measure the distance traveled since independence, let us recall that, for an estimated population of 10 million in 1962, "there were 770,000 Algerians enrolled in primary school, 11,200 in middle school, and 14,000 in high school. As for university enrollments, they counted 7,000 students, the majority of whom were European" (André Adam, quoted in Sraïeb 1975). By 1980, when the population had almost tripled, the proportion of students educated in French was estimated at 51 percent, and it is anticipated that it will have reached 74 percent by the year 2000 (Santucci 1986). To these estimates let us add the 800,000 Algerian emigrés who live in France, and who contribute to the influence of French via familial and economic relations with their native country. Let us mention as well the popularity of satellite antennae, which allow people to pick up French television channels, which are much watched throughout the country. Book publishers and the press distribute many French titles. Given the circulation of the French language, some might say that Algeria is the second-largest Francophone country, after France itself. We find ourselves confronted with a disconcerting paradox, since the school system, which has been the principal vector of Arabization, is at the same time the agent of Gallicization because of the number of students enrolled in school; although the society has officially been in the process of Arabization since independence, French has, through a variety of mechanisms, expanded even more widely than during colonization. Today, a monolingual Arabic speaker educated in the Algerian school system has to learn French to have access to jobs. Knowledge is transmitted in French, the language in which more than 60 percent of university students are educated, while Arabic is confined to ancient texts, ideology, and religion.

The situation outlined above explains the conflicts that link the linguistic question to cultural, religious, and identity claims, which involve antagonistic social projects (Saadi-Mokrane 1985).

Mal-vie *and* mal-langue

The lead curtain of linguistic repression has fallen on all cultural domains, since everything that escapes "Islamic nationalism" is assumed to be incompatible with it, and thus to undermine it at its foundation. Repression is preferred to the lively ferment of creation. The old colonial fissures that split the country have been revived with even more bitterness. So we've been left to ourselves, then? Therefore we reinvent troubles that weaken and sterilize creativity. For a long time, reading committees cut off free speech with the proverbial carving knife. Scripts, commentaries, movie and documentary dialogues in French or in native languages? Banned! Popular theater? Outlawed! Or confined to the margins of amateur theater. Raï music, Berber music, protest songs that unsettle sexual taboos and ideology? Prohibited! Literary works put through the censorship mill? Banned! Berber and dialectal Arabic classes in high schools and universities? Canceled!

The "cultural civil war" has been waged without respite during the thirty years of independence. In this "voyage to the end of the night," we discover we are guilty as well, because we contribute to the reproduction of a manufactured split between Arabophones and Francophones—a split in which we hardly recognize ourselves, a split that reduces the impact of critical thought and open reflection on social issues. But we are also cut up into slices of culture, a fragmentation that we endure, like horrific aftereffects of a colonial illness that would best be eradicated so that we can recover the original purity of the nation.

There is also the denial of otherness—"one religion, Islam, one language, Arabic, one nation, Algeria." The unitary credo of the Ulema (the Algerian Islamic movement under French Occupation) has deep roots in the history of this country; in its name, an entire people continues to be muzzled and made foreign to itself. An observer of Algerian society summed it up: "This territory which produced Apuleius, Saint Augustine, Ibn Khaldun, Emir Abdelkader, Albert Camus, Kateb Yacine, Jules Roy and so many other original talents has ended up resembling a cultural desert." How did things come to this?

Research conducted recently on Algerian youth, who represent two-thirds of the population, suggests the heavy toll exacted by the failure of the schools. To begin with, the whole education system is in crisis. It seems that Islamic fundamentalism has entered Algerian schools through foreign service workers. A widespread account has it that, because the French government refused to send teachers for the new school year at independence, Algerian authorities addressed their request to Egypt, which dispatched its "Muslim Brothers" to be rid of them. This prevalent notion would need to be verified, but it is common to hear people accuse the schools of helping to propagate Islamist ideas. In quantitative terms, after nine years of compulsory schooling, middle schools reject more than 800,000 sixteen-year-olds who are failing or having language trouble—a situation everyone facetiously calls "bilingual illiteracy." This oxymoron expresses in humorous terms the difficulties in expressing themselves encountered by an entire generation taught in Algerian schools, hence supposedly bilingual. Indeed, monolingualism is rare in Algeria, since it is characteristic of people who have never been to school and have no contacts outside the milieu into which they were born. The most common pairs of languages that people know are Berber and dialectal or literary Arabic, Berber and French, French and dialectal or literary Arabic, and dialectal Arabic and literary Arabic. It is, of course, the gaps in literary Arabic and in French that lead to talk of "illiteracy," insofar as these are written languages taught in school. Rules of proper usage are often transgressed, leading to a linguistic mixing of all the various languages in use, and this situation is amplified by the effects of a counterculture at work at all levels of society. Each speaker, mocking himself in language play, tries to transgress the rules and to show linguistic creativity or audacity through code-switching, mixing, interference, and so on.

The high schools reject almost 1,200,000 teenagers, who cannot go on to higher education. Unemployment grips 840,000 of them, the majority from the most disadvantaged classes (Munier 1991). At the university, the vacuum caused by the brain drain has taken on vast proportions in recent years with the emergence of terrorism, for which universities have paid a heavy price. Because of the education it provides, school is a decisive battleground for the forces that are tearing one another apart. While some factions believed they could lead schools to strike for the establishment of an Islamic regime, others deplore the thousands of schools destroyed, the teachers murdered, often in front of their students, and the hundreds of young students killed in front of their classmates. Should we give credence to the idea that the general decline in students' education level and the massive failures that have driven a large number of young people to idleness in the streets are responsible for the current situation?

It is true that at least 21 percent of young people suffer in a "cultural vacuum," and their only leisure activity is going to mosque. Research conducted in the high schools of Oran points to even higher numbers (Bengharbit-Remaoun 1993). It is also not uncommon to hear now and then, even from teachers, that fanaticism is a product of a school system that has cut students off from all their cultural and historical roots. Native languages have been devalued, popular culture denied, the Algerian personality humiliated, the roots of the ancient Maghreb forgotten. The only positive image standing against all this self-negation is that, however theoretical, of the good Muslim, and it is the duty of all to identify with this image in order to change a badly flawed world.

The identity crisis caused by the school system has been perpetuated by the state-owned media. Their pompous language, relying on formal rhetorical techniques, does not echo people's daily preoccupations and feelings. Since 1988, market-oriented economic policies have substantially changed the press, but it remains gagged by restrictive rules that heavily penalize attacks leveled at Islam and state security. Thus a politicolinguistic "dissensus" undermines the credibility of institutional discourses. The myth of a more lenient "elsewhere"—Canada, the United States, or Australia—becomes a refuge, feeding an unfulfilled desire for departure, success, even salvation. These places are imaginary, populated by every sort of illusion and enhanced by exotic tales. Economic, cultural, sexual, and emotional deprivation plunges an entire generation into a profound sense of suffering an unjust fate, forcefully expressed by the word *hogra*, that is, the injustice and contempt in which the overwhelming mass of "rejects" are held.

The state of Algerian literature brings out this malaise all the more acutely. Native languages are noticeably absent. Because they are oral for the most part, they nourish literature through stories and legends, proverbs, and an inexhaustible multilingual play, but never gain full access to it. As if arduously crafted from the raw materials of an oral language, literature in French has often developed a halting idiom, as in Rachid Mimouni's "splintered French." Born in the 1950s, this literature became the witness of its time, acting as a spokesperson for an illiterate society that could not understand it by denouncing colonialism. At independence, the themes of protest that sustained this literature often obliged its authors to flee the censors and to seek recognition in France. Thus major works remain unknown or circulate clandestinely, which cuts them off even more from their natural audience. Such is the case for the novels of Rachid Boudjedra. Jean Déjeux has compiled a list of 510 works of fiction published between 1945 and 1984. With the climate of terror that reigns in the country today, a literature of exile has come into being in France through an unprecedented wave of publications—essays, chronicles, plays, poetry. It is a literature born of exceptional circumstances, whose real value remains to be appraised.

The first literary works in Arabic appeared in the 1970s. From 1967 to 1985, only about thirty novels and short stories were published (Bois 1986). Very few authors are known to the general public; among them we should mention two novelists, Tahar Ouettar and Abdelhamid Benhedouga, whose works are even praised abroad. They draw their inspiration from the national literary tradition and from popular protest; they have a pronounced sociological bent. Today some Arabic writers publish their work in France (and in French); this is the case of Waciny Larej's *La gardienne des ombres* (1996) of *Calamus* (1997), written and translated by Merzak Bagtache, and of Abdelhamid Benhedouga's *Je rêve d'un monde . . .* (1997). But the difficulties of publication and distribution in Algeria also deprive these authors of a readership corresponding to their aspirations.

Berber literature is primarily oral and comprises stories, poetry, and songs for the most part. The Algerian press has made much of a few written works recently published, in particular theatrical plays, but these remain unknown to the general public.

It is as if the passage from oral to written language has been struck by the curse of Babel. Multilingualism takes place in a context of multiculturalism, one of the inalienable sources of creativity in any society. And yet, guilt-ridden Algerians wonder about the legitimacy of such a legacy. They ask themselves: Is it a feature of a thriving society or of an alienated one? Should they continue to use all their languages? Might they lose themselves, or rather, find themselves, in so doing? The fear of the unknown undermines their convictions, because the only reality most have experienced is what I call *mal-langue* (ill-language), the offspring of *mal-vie* (ill-life). This is the unfinished story of an orphaned people, repeatedly severed from (their) culture.

In a historical situation of ferment that is far from revealing all its secrets, it is wise to postpone any conclusion. In Algeria as in the rest of the world, we are witnessing a "crisis of languages," which is "a permanent aspect of social crisis, and perhaps a way of masking languages' essentially political nature" (Rey 1985, Sanford's translation).

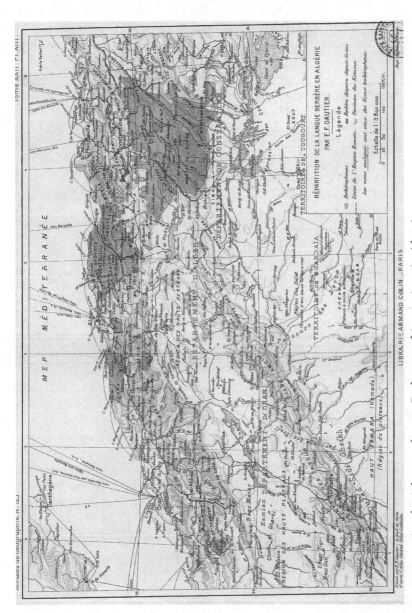

FIGURE 1. A colonial map of 1913: Berber-speaking regions in Algeria

[3]

the impossible wedding

Nationalism, Languages, and the Mother Tongue in Postcolonial Algeria

ANNE-EMMANUELLE BERGER

> The language one does not know how
> to write has a magic authority.
> It is she ["language"] who spoke to me,
> and at her words I traveled.
>
> —HÉLÈNE CIXOUS, "The Names of Oran"

I WANT TO START BY looking at a picture. It is a picture of a photograph or series of photographs imagined by Benedict Anderson in his famous book on the origins of nationalism: *Imagined Communities*. The imagined photographs are the ultimate figure for the happy ending of both the book and nationalism. The figure appears in the last paragraph of what used to be the last chapter in the first edition of the book: thus, in a way, it is Anderson's last word on the topic. The chapter, entitled "Patriotism and Racism," is devoted to the exploration of the nature of *amor patriae,* the love for one's country or homeland. Against the grain of the current liberal cosmopolitan distrust of nationalism, Anderson seeks to remind us "that nations inspire love, and often profoundly self-sacrificing love" (Anderson 1992, 141), and that nationalism gives rise to a wealth of cultural productions, which he reads, in a Freudian manner, as a work of "love." Let me quote what was the last paragraph of *Imagined Communities:*

> It may appear paradoxical that the objects of all these [patriotic] attachments are "imagined"—anonymous, faceless fellow-

Tagalogs, exterminated tribes. . . . But amor patriae does not
differ in this respect from the other affections, in which there
is always an element of fond imagining. (This is why looking at
the photos-album of strangers' weddings is like studying the
archeologist's groundplan of the Hanging Gardens of Babylon.)
What the eye is to the lover—that particular, ordinary eye he or
she is born with—language—whatever language history has
made his or her mother-tongue—is to the patriot. Through that
language, encountered at mother's knee and parted with only
at the grave, pasts are restored, fellowships are imagined and
future dreamed. (154)

Let me try to unravel the various threads of the complex simile
woven by Anderson: to love one's country and to embrace one's fellow countrymen in this love is like looking at a wedding picture. It is
not, of course, the picture of a stranger's wedding, whose contemplation elicits no particular feeling since it is as indifferent to the viewer
as, let us say—to provide an alternative to Anderson's Babylonian
comparison—the map of the parking lot at Cornell University; the
photograph would have to be, then, the picture of the beholder's own
wedding. The mother tongue, adds Anderson, is to the lover of the
homeland what the lover's eye is to the contemplation of his own
wedding pictures: in both cases, a certain channel of representation
(the gaze—a language) allows the "lovers" to see and fancy the object
of their love. Without the "eye" or lens of the mother tongue, there
would be no amorous vision, no "fond imagining" of the subject's
"wedding" with the nation. The analogy between language and the
gaze points to the specular power of language, understood not merely
as a tool for communication but as a means of identification. What
are the implications of Anderson's comparison for an understanding
of the link between language and *amor patriae*?
   In keeping with Anderson's forceful argument regarding the role of
print capitalism in the development of modern nationalism and the
birth of nation-states, the photograph is itself a kind of print, a product of the industrial and capitalistic age of mechanical reproduction.
As a picture, it prompts or facilitates the processes of specularity and
recognition that are at play in the formation of what is called
identity, be it personal or national. It is well known that any image of
oneself, and, to begin with, one's image in the mirror, elicits pleasure
and provokes a cathexis of love on the part of the beholder. It is im-

portant, then, as the first line of Anderson's paragraph suggests, to give a face to the faceless, in this case, to one's unknown fellow human beings. Indeed, without a "face"—imagined or represented—an object might not be "loved." As an industrial picture that is infinitely reproducible and can therefore be made available to the community at large, the photograph is also one of the tools in the formation of an archive shared by its viewers. The image in the mirror vanishes with the beholder, but a photograph remains, like writing, even after the death of the subject, thus manifesting the intimate connection between representation and memory.[1] And, as we know, there can be no concept of a nation without something like a collective memory, be it mythical, fictitious, or palimpsestic, as it always is. But the photograph might not work as both a tool and a metaphor for *amor patriae* if it were not a wedding picture. As such, it features the paradigmatic union of the self with the other: it is a "self-portrait with other." The union symbolized by the wedding is not any kind of union. It is not only the erotic union between a man and a woman who, as such, stand for the paradigmatic other; it is also the figure for and agent of community formation through the contract of an exogamic alliance. To get married means to step outside the endogamic circle of the biological (or quasi-biological) family and into the contractual circle of the community at large. Some might say that to get married is to distance oneself from the mother and from one's own childishness. Indeed, in the eyes of his mother, or as he sees himself seen by her, the subject remains a "child" and therefore fails to identify himself as a citizen.

Yet the mother, or rather her substitute and symbol, the mother tongue, is overwhelmingly present in Anderson's last glowing picture of nationalism's power of union, a union that, like all weddings, is an attempt to turn the union with the other into a reunion with oneself, past, present, and future. Let me recall the last lines of the paragraph: "What the eye is to the lover . . . language—whatever language history has made his or her mother-tongue—is to the patriot. Through that language, encountered at mother's knee and parted with only at the grave, pasts are restored, fellowships are imagined and future dreamed" (154).

Hence Anderson ultimately turns or returns to the mother's knee after the world tour of what he calls "print languages." It is not that the mother tongue, defined as the language spoken by one's mother and transmitted in that capacity to her children, is endowed with any more naturalness or historical anteriority than any language whatsoever. As Anderson says, a language is made into a mother tongue as a result of a historical process and, we might add, in the case of the formation of modern nation-states, as a result of a deliberate political process. In his overview of the rise of nationalism, Anderson encounters and describes a variety of situations of this kind. In some cases, Central Europe, for example, the vernacular language became the national language; in others, South America, for example it was the colonial language, Spanish or Portuguese, that successfully became the mother tongue of the majority of the inhabitants. In still other cases, in Russia, for example, it was the dynastic language that became the national mother tongue. It all depended on which language assumed the form and acquired the status of a "print language."

Nevertheless, the reassertion of "the primordialness of languages"[2] in the experience of any subject and in the formation of a national consciousness does beg the question of the status of the mother tongue. The real question raised by modern nationalism, then, is whether a national language can be successfully converted into a "mother tongue," or conversely, whether a mother tongue can assume the status of a national language. Again, the decision to promote a language to the status of national language, whether there is one national language or several, is taken by the state, and it has been a fundamental concern and feature of nation-states since their inception. The choice of a national language is an extraordinary, almost demiurgic act; the nationalization of the French language (and the suppression of the regional languages) undertaken by the French Revolution was indeed conceived by the revolutionaries as an anti-Babelian endeavor, seeking to undo the linguistic confusion God imposed at the Tower of Babel, and therefore to overthrow and replace God's (dis)order with the order of the nation (see Grégoire 1975). But how does one successfully convert a political decision into a social reality? And how do the familial and the national translate into each other?

Indeed, Anderson's last sentence seems to suggest that, for a loving and nostalgic gaze at the wedding picture to function as an allegory for the happy nationalist's awareness of his or her national belonging and historical existence, the "national language" in which national consciousness comes into being must be learned at one's mother's knee. In other words, the successful assimilation of the familial into the national and of the national into the familiar occurs when the mother tongue and the national language coincide as a result of historical and political processes.[3] The fantasized wedding would then

represent the union of two speakers of the same national mother
tongue.

Interestingly, a certain notion of "wedding," taken both literally
and figuratively, is also at the core of Ernest Renan's seminal meditation on the notion of "nation" at the turn of the nineteenth century.
Reflecting on the birth of modern Western nations, Renan describes
the decisive proto-national hold of a certain feudal group over a given
area in terms of what he calls "a marriage contracted with the soil"
(Renan 1990, 12). More precisely, Renan attributes the success of
proto-national formations in Western Europe, and more particularly
in France, to the fact that the Franquish conquerors quickly forgot
their own language and adopted instead the (Romance) language(s) of
the people they conquered. According to Renan, they did that by
forming sexual and hence familial bonds, if not bonds of love, with
the women of the land:

> The grandsons of Clovis, Alaric, Gundebald, Alboin, and
> Roland were already speaking the Roman tongue. This fact was
> itself the consequence of another important feature, namely
> the fact that the Franks, Burgundians, Goths, Lombards, and
> Normans had very few women of their own race with them.
> For several generations, the chiefs only married German
> women, but their concubines were Latin, as were the wet
> nurses of their children; the tribe as a whole married Latin
> women, which meant that, from the time the Franks and the
> Goths established themselves on Roman territory, the *lingua
> francica* and the *lingua gothica* did not last too long. (10)

Renan does not say (or care) if the bonds formed with the native
women were coerced or voluntary. But his account of the successful
hold of the French language ultimately reads as an allegory of the
sway of the mother tongue over the destinies of modern nations. For
the language of the concubines and wet nurses adopted by the conquerors and their children is literally a mothers' tongue. At the same
time, its appeal cannot serve to found any claim to ethnic purity.
Quite the contrary, the circumstances of its development—a generalized exogamic mating—radically undermine the fiction of a homoge-
nous origin. Linked as it is to the development of heterosexual relations across ethnic differences, the promotion of the mother tongue
fosters the formation and thriving of proto-national ties beyond tribal
and ethnic divides. It is indeed Renan's political and philosophical

aim in this essay to mount a forceful argument against any ethno-racial view of the foundations of nations. While Renan stresses the initial violence of the colonial (and sexual) encounter and, beyond, of all national foundations, his emphasis on the seminal role of the mother tongue in this instance allows him to assert with equal force the functionality of a certain "wedding" in the formation of modern nations.

To go back to Anderson's argument, the hold of the mother tongue whose amorous power prompts the wedding with the fellow speaker, turns the act of stepping outside the family, which the wedding both performs and symbolizes, into a return home—but to another home, the home with the other: the "*home*land." (Anderson rightly stresses the familial character of this expression, used to connote one's affective relation to one's country.) Thus, in a manner reminiscent of Rousseau's argument in *Essay on the Origin of Languages* concerning the origin and "popularity" of "popular languages"—that is, protonational languages, as opposed to domestic or vernacular idioms—Anderson describes a double movement: a move away from the familial circle of the mother into the national sphere, achieved through the symbolic wedding of the subject with his fellow nationals; and a move back, if not to the mother's knee, at least to a point at which the subject-become-citizen can enjoy, through the lens of the mother tongue, the lingering memory of the time when he/she was a child at the feet of his/her mother. Like a child, but as a man, or perhaps a woman, he/she can then dream of the future.

Now, along with this Oedipian or even pre-Oedipian fable if one were to consider it from the point of view of the development of the girl, Anderson outlines another scenario, without clearly articulating the connection, or the difference, between these two models or stages of national consciousness. The subject-become-national is ready to be killed and to kill others for his homeland, he reminds us at the beginning of the chapter, thus emphasizing, albeit unwittingly, a certain gendered character of the national subject. Indeed, if this double sacrifice is proof of the passionate nature of his love for the homeland, it is also the manifestation of the national subject's access to full manhood; is not the ability, even the will, to sacrifice one's life in war, the ultimate assertion of a certain type of virility? At any rate, it points to a moment and a space—that of war—when the national community is assimilated, at least traditionally, with the community of men, thus casting a very different picture from that of the wedding I have just commented on.

As we follow Anderson's argument, a question arises: what happens when a national language fails to become a mother tongue, and vice versa, and when, as a result, the speakers of a given "nation" live in a state of permanent diglossia?

Keeping these questions in mind, let me now turn to the linguistic picture offered by Algeria today.

Several languages are currently used to various degrees and at various levels of proficiency in postcolonial Algeria.

The most ancient populations to have settled in the Maghreb are those tribes the Romans called "Berber" (barbarous). After being partially Romanized and Christianized, they were, to a greater degree, Islamized and Arabized starting with the Arab conquest in the seventh century. According to Bernard Lewis (1998), "the total and final obliteration of the [pre-Islamic] civilizations [in North Africa] and their replacement by Arab Islam must rank as one of the most successful cultural revolutions in human history" (53).[4] Yet the Berbers have continued to speak their own language to a certain extent over the centuries and under different colonial rules. In Algeria, the Berbers of Kabylia, an Arabic name designating the "tribal people," still speak Tamazight, the indigenous name for their language, which belongs to the Hamidic, as opposed to the Semitic, family of languages. Tamazight is the language of the "Amazigh," a term that means "free men," a generic name often used by protonations to celebrate their awareness of themselves as an autonomous entity. To this day, about 20 percent of the population of Algeria still use Tamazight, either as their principal language, or as the language spoken at home, hence, indeed, their first language. This population is concentrated in Kabylia, a mountainous region whose isolation explains in part the incomplete penetration of Arabic. Tamazight remains an essentially oral language, even though various written transcriptions were attempted, first in an old Lybic alphabet called *tifinagh*, still in use by the Tuareg, and now in either Arabic or Roman script. The competition between these transcriptions has political and ideological implications: the Arabic script is a way of tying Tamazight to Arabic culture; the Western Roman script ties the language to a genealogical line stretching from the Roman empire to the French conquest.

Arabic is, then, the primary language of 80 percent of the Algerian population. But to simply say that 80 percent of Algerians—if not more, since a number of Kabyles, those who live in the cities for instance, also speak Arabic—are Arabophone is to cover over a gap that is at the core of Algeria's linguistic predicament. In fact, the language spoken daily at home and in the streets is a dialectal form of Arabic, quite different from the official national language, to the point that those Algerians who were born before independence, and who therefore did not attend the newly Arabized schools, do not understand it. The national language, a form of standard or "median" Arabic developed from the nineteenth century on by reformers throughout the Arab world in an attempt to modernize Koranic Arabic, is designated in various ways by Algerians (and Maghrebians in general): they call it "literary Arabic," "classical Arabic," or "oriental Arabic." These terms all imply a distance, whether cultural or geographical, from the familiar language. It is another Arabic, if not the Arabic of the Other.

Now it may well be true that a certain degree of internal diglossia characterizes most Arabic-speaking countries due to the particular status of Arabic as the sacred language of the Koran, untranslatable and invariable as such. The modernization of Arabic and the attempt to make various Arab peoples and nations communicate with one another in this language probably widened the gap, or at least increased the awareness of a gap between two Arabics: Koranic Arabic, the language of the community of believers (*Umma*), which is used "vertically" as it were, to communicate with God, and standard Arabic, which is used "horizontally," to promote another kind of communal affiliation along ethnocultural and national lines (Pan-Arabism). The symbolic "verticality" of Koranic Arabic is probably reinforced by the fact that knowledge of it also reveals and at the same time creates a hierarchical split, both social and symbolic, between those who are well versed in the language and those who are not, those who can read Koranic Arabic, and those who cannot.

In the Maghreb, as the Francophone Moroccan writer Abdelkhebir Khatibi reminds us, diglossia in this sense predates French colonization:

> In the Maghreb, actual bilingualism or multilingualism is not
> born of the colonial situation, it preexists it. . . . Well before
> French and Spanish colonization of the Maghreb, there was a
> double idiomatic discontinuity. ("Diglossia")

Yet there is no doubt that both French colonization and the resulting Algerian nationalist movement(s) that informed the politics of

decolonization do account for the incredibly conflictual and distress-
ing linguistic predicament of postcolonial Algeria.

Perhaps the most striking feature of Algeria's present linguistic
landscape is the embattled and debased situation of the country's
"mother tongues," not only Tamazight, whose regional importance
can be seen to threaten national unity, but also dialectal Arabic itself.

The suppression of the vernaculars may be both an old story and a
structural feature of linguistic policies throughout the Arabic-speaking world, as Lewis (1998) once again suggests.[5] The contempt and
suspicion in which the Algerian form of dialectal Arabic has been
held by the political leadership since the inception of the independent state in 1962 nonetheless deserves to be analyzed on its own
terms.

Algeria's official linguistic policies have had both pragmatic and
symbolic effects, which I would like to address. But first, let me recall
briefly the main features of the linguistic policies pursued by the
French colonial powers and then by the newly independent Algerian
state, which have led to the present situation. French colonial policies
were complicated quite early on by the ongoing political dispute and
the disagreement about goals between the metropolitan leadership
and the French settlers, who regarded themselves as Algerians—they
were the first to do so—and who, at the end of the nineteenth century,
for instance, wanted nothing to do with France's reassertion of Enlightenment principles in matters of education. In any case, the situation was roughly as follows: the medersas and other Koranic schools
that existed in Algeria, and everywhere else in the Islamic world, were
closed down or put under French supervision, until their revival in the
1930s at the instigation of the Ulema or reformers' movement, led by
Ben Badis. The bilingual education system, which was tried for a time
with the establishment of bicephalous Franco-Arabic primary schools,
was dropped in favor of an all-French education system. A form of cultural and protopolitical resistance developed in response to these policies: the indigenous population often refused to send their children to
French primary schools even when education became compulsory
(this movement underwent a reversal after World War II), and mas-
sively refused, until the end of the colonial era, to educate their
daughters (see Ruedy 1996, 347–48; and Turin 1971). The dynamic
was somewhat reversed at the secondary and upper levels of education, with the French rulers barring indigenous Algerians from higher
education through a drastic system of quotas. The colonial administration was more successful in alphabetizing the indigenous popula-

tion of Kabylia, due in part to the former's attachment to what historians have called the *mythe Kabyle*, which stipulated a greater cultural proximity between Berbers and Europeans, and distinguished the Kabyles (that is, Berbers) from the Arabs. Arabic, that is, written, classical Arabic, which was now rarely taught, was reintroduced as an elective in French schools just before independence. As a result, when independence came, a vast proportion of the population was illiterate[6] and therefore only spoke dialectal Arabic or Tamazight, in addition to the minimal French necessary to perform work for the French rulers. A small proportion of the indigenous population had been educated in French schools, including many leaders of the nationalist movement.[7] Knowledge of Koranic Arabic, which in any case was the exclusive privilege of the male literate population, had dropped. A significant proportion of Kabyles spoke fluent French along with Tamazight, as a result of the Arab/Berber divide to which I alluded, and also because Kabyles accounted for the bulk of Algerians who went to France as construction workers. The number of Algerian immigrants, who continued to go back and forth between France and their native villages— a movement that began with the need to replace French workers who had gone to war during World War I—peaked between 1950 and the end of the 1970s, notwithstanding Algeria's victorious fight for its independence. To this day, French teachers in Algeria are often recruited from among Kabyles.

It is in this context that, following Ben Badis's early formulation of the basis of Algeria's cultural nationalism,—"Islam is our religion, Arabic is our language, Algeria is our country"—the victorious nationalists decreed standard Arabic, which most of them hardly knew and had not studied, as the only national language.

In this sense, the politics of Arabization conducted by the state since independence has aimed not only at replacing French as the language of the state and of established forms of public expression (literature and the media), but at replacing Algerian Arabic and effacing Tamazight. What is called "total Arabization" has been the official goal since independence. It was included as such in the constitution along with a statement that makes Islam part of the definition of Algerian citizenship. The politics of Arabization really took off under the presidency of Houari Boumediene (1965–78), who himself was educated in Egypt. Indeed, even today, the term "Arabophone" designates primarily those people who have been educated in the Middle East, rather than in French-speaking institutions. The best way to achieve this kind of Arabization was obviously through schooling.

Many teachers were brought in from Egypt and the Middle East to help convert Algerian citizens into "real Arabophones." Standard Arabic became the language of schooling up to the university level, where French still holds sway in some sectors. (Officially, the university was to be entirely Arabized as of December 1980.) In 1985, an end was put to bilingual education at all levels, while President Chadli officially barred Algerian nationals from attending all-French schools; yet the elite and the powerful, most often educated in French, continued to send their children to these schools.[8]

The purpose of mass schooling in Arabic was twofold: first, the new state wanted to give Algerians access to literacy, that is, allow Algerians to overcome the gap, so great that it is experienced as a form of diglossia, between spoken and written Arabic. It may be that the greater proximity of the written word to the sacred Koranic text will always prevent the hierarchical division between spoken and written Arabic from disappearing—at least until the next cultural revolution. Thus, even a secular writer such as Khatibi repeatedly stresses the split that affects and structures the practice of language: "Writing is not speaking; such would be the internal bilingualism of every language." Yet, whatever the case, writing is fundamentally implicated in the conception and establishment of modern states, as modern political thinkers from Jean-Jacques Rousseau to Anderson have pointed out. The modern state is coterminous with the order of representation, and there can be no representation without some form of "writing": from writing down the "social contract" (or constitution) to posting the letter of the law for all citizens, from forming "imagined" communities through printed media to establishing political representation and registering "voices," transformed into votes, modern nations represent themselves "in writing." More specifically, however, the purpose of Arabization, as the official instructions from the Ministry of Education make clear, was to use the properly Arabized child as a weapon for correcting the language of the family.[9]

Despite the coercive and punitive measures taken or announced by the state, the most recent of them dating back to July 1998, total Arabization has yet to be achieved. Although it is true that a new generation of "Arabophones" is emerging, the state policies have elicited a strong reaction in Tamazight-speaking areas and prompted the organization of a Berber cultural movement demanding official recognition of its language. Francophone newspapers and literary texts, born of the Western tradition of readership and relying on a well-established publishing and distribution network with ties to metropolitan France, are thriving. French is believed to have paradoxically increased its hold as a result of the progress in literacy and its status as Algeria's primary "second language" of education.[10] Broadcasting French television in Algerian homes is also said to contribute to the preservation of French. Ironically then but quite understandably, the democratization of French really started after independence, when knowing the language was no longer tied to the enforcement of social stratification through quotas, and did not have to mean subjection to colonial rule. Yet we ought to be careful to distinguish various kinds of Francophones: The younger generation that wasn't raised in bilingual schools knows and uses French as a foreign language, or possibly as a limited lingua franca; in contrast, the Francophones of the first generations following independence, still numerous, were raised as true bilinguals. To counter the endurance of French, the state has now decided to replace French with English at school, a move approved by the supporters of Islamism.[11]

Why, then, the choice of standard Arabic at independence as the only national language?

In addition to keeping in mind the status of writing in nation-states (and standard Arabic is supposed to be both written and spoken), we need to remember that Algeria became independent in the context of what appeared to be a triumphant, albeit secular, wave of Pan-Arabism, exemplified by Gamal Abdel Nasser's rule over the nation he renamed the "United Arab Republic." Moreover, most historians of colonial and postcolonial Algeria now agree that the first "imagined" community to unite colonized Algerians was indeed the community of believers, the Umma, before any modern idea of the nation took shape.[12] In this sense, Algerians concurred with the French, who identified them as "Muslims," or "Arabs," precisely inasmuch as Arabic is an essential component of Islamic identity. For this reason, the countries of the "Arabic world" functioned as a kind of ego ideal for the nascent Algeria, one that could reinforce Algeria's new identity claim against a very forceful and long-standing national "ego," that of France. In addition, Algeria as such was to some extent an invention of the French: the ethnonational denomination "Algerian" was first used by the French settlers, before it was reclaimed by young indigenous nationalists (see Ageron 1979 and Prochaska 1990). The first "Algerian" cultural and literary movement, which called itself Algérianiste, came from settlers of European descent. But all this does not quite explain the fate of dialectal

Arabic, which "postnationalists" now present as the true Algerian language.

In a recent essay, Gilbert Grandguillaume, arguably the best specialist on the linguistic question in Algeria, and certainly very even-handed,[13] draws an interesting parallel between what has happened to native women and what has happened to the native language in independent Algeria. Recalling the active role played by women during the war of liberation and the bold steps they took, unveiled, into the public sphere (a process famously described by Frantz Fanon in his 1959 article "L'Algérie se dévoile"), Grandguillaume reminds us of the multiple ways in which independent Algeria strove to send the women back "home" and confine them to the domestic sphere. The so-called family code that was finally promulgated in 1984 was apparently in the works of the regime as early as 1963. This code is a "nationalized" version of the Shari'a (code of Islamic law), with specific legal and political restrictions applied to women. The code clearly prevents Algerian women from achieving the status of full "national" subjects. Women were also encouraged to once more put on the veil, an encouragement that became a campaign of terror with the growing sociopolitical impact of the FIS (or Islamic Salvation Front). But what does this have to do with languages? This is precisely the question Grandguillaume asks himself. And he answers tentatively, "in both cases, it is as if something intimate was showing that had to be hidden, as if true Algerianness scared people off" (Grandguillaume 1998, 74, my translation).

In my opinion, Grandguillaume's parallel, which is prompted by his panoramic view of Algeria's social policies, is far from arbitrary. Dialectal Arabic would be, then, the equivalent of unveiled women, who, like the language they speak inside and outside the home with their fellow Algerians, are a symbol or metonymy for "true Algerianness." "True Algerianness," like any essentializing concept, is a suspect notion; it cannot, however, be understood as the revival of an original or traditional form, since Algeria is a modern invention. When women are degraded, then, the native language is degraded. When they are sent back to the home, it is also dialectal Arabic, the everyday spoken language, that is in a sense "veiled." Linguistic and social policies concur, one might say, in their attempt to veil "the intimate," perceived as a source of shame. One could also say that "intimacy" does not actually exist prior to veiling; it is the veiling that turns the veiled object or subject into something "intimate," that is,

haram.[14] But what does this make standard (promoted to "national")
Arabic? It makes it into the veil that hides the shameful spoken language; as a result, dialectal Arabic is literally turned into a mother
tongue, spoken between mothers and preschool children, or between
adults in their capacity as former children, precisely because of the
close and forced association of this language with the women barred,
if not from the public space, then at least from the national sphere—
unless they appear veiled. Now, the reimposition of the veil on Algerian women—like "Arabization," only a partial success—was no mere
return to the past. The veil that women are asked to wear these days
is not the traditional white haik; it is a new kind of veil, common to
all Islamic countries: the *hidjab*. I would suggest that standard Arabic is indeed a symbolic equivalent of the hidjab.

In an earlier essay entitled "The Newly Veiled Woman: Irigaray,
Specularity and the Islamic Veil," I argued that the promotion of the
hidjab in Islamic countries or communities is part of a politics of "re-
active phallicization" against the perceived "feminization" of the
"Orient" by the Western colonial imaginary. The young women who
decide to wear the hidjab in Algeria, Egypt, or even France, are described and describe themselves as endowed not only with a new legitimacy, but also with a new authority. It is as if wearing the hidjab
made them more assertive as well as more self-controlled. The fact
that they choose to take the veil also emphasizes their sense of autonomy, making them, in this regard, "modern" women. In fact, in
something of a reversal of the meaning of the old prescription of the
veil, the hidjab is not so much designed to hide women's "shame"
(*aourat*)—or, in contemporary Western parlance, their castration—as
to assert their identity as Muslims. Indeed, the word *hidjab* in the
Koran does not designate the veils women are supposed to wear,[15] but
rather the curtain that separates and protects the devout Muslim
from the nonbeliever.[16] In this sense, the separation the hidjab establishes is not only that between genders: it operates like the defining
border separating and protecting the community of believers from
the outside world. It is because modern Muslim women are thus
made into the guardians of the symbolic border of the Islamic world
that the newly veiled women acquire a sense of power. The hidjab
does not so much make them invisible as grant them a new visibility,
whose aim is to catch the attention of the Western world. The politics of the hidjab make sense within the specular structure that or-
ganizes the contemporary relation between the Islamic world and the

West, in that the forging of (new) identities depends on the Other's recognition, be it a negative recognition: it is as if dependence on Western recognition had replaced the old colonial ties. In short, the newly veiled women are not so much hiding as showing off, and showing off to the imagined West. It is this type of identity building, combining the desire to appropriate authority for oneself with a defiant display, that I call "phallic." The hidjab in this sense functions more like a flag—an ostentatious sign of a communal or national sense of belonging—than like a feminine garment.

It seems to me that standard Arabic functions in similar ways for its Algerian proponents. As the national language, it is both the linguistic flag brandished and the holy curtain imposed by the nationalist leadership to secure the national community's symbolic borders, while signaling its legitimate place within the Arabo-Islamic world. Moreover, standard Arabic is not only aimed at protecting the national speaking community from French, which Algerian dialectal Arabic, full of terms borrowed from the French, fails to do; the adoption of standard Arabic is also an attempt to shield and sever the speaking subjects of Algeria from the infantilizing effect of a dialect construed as weak, impure, and improper. I have been told by Algerian Arabic speakers that the word most commonly used to designate a dialect in Algeria is the Arabic word transcribed as *lêeja*, which is related both to the notion of accent and to that of infantile speech or stammering. If that is true, then the dialect is indeed perceived as keeping its speakers in a state of infancy, which involves a proximity to and dependency on the mother. The notion of accent also stresses the organic link of the dialect to speech and the voice, as opposed to writing. The Algerian form of Arabic may well be a dialect according to a scientific taxonomy, in that it is derived chronologically and linguistically from peninsular Arabic,[17] although one suspects that the classification of idioms into "dialects" and full-fledged "languages" is as much a matter of politics as of science.[18] In any case, it is different from a regional language such as Tamazight, the language of "free men." Tamazight's relation to standard Arabic may be more similar to the relation between Javanese and Indonesian Malay, as described by Anderson (1990).

The phallicization of the national language and hence of its speakers is not specific to Algeria. The nationalization of the French language undertaken by the French revolutionaries at the end of the eighteenth century, in their attempt to make France a modern nation-state leading to the liberation of men, was also thought by its proponents to require a measure of linguistic virilization.[19] National French was presented as having to fight a double internal evil, not unlike standard Arabic in Algeria: on the one hand, it was to be a democratic language distinct from the deemed "effeminacy" of the French ruling class, an effeminacy interpreted by Rousseau and other democrats of the time as a sign of the perversion of male aristocrats, who, along with France as a whole, yielded to the power of aristocratic women. On the other hand, it was supposed to "annihilate" the dialects called *patois*—a derogatory term suggesting roughness and awkwardness in speech—to achieve both unity and respectability. Dialects, like the idioms of the peasants and the lower classes in general, were indeed considered an unwanted mark of subjugation. The famous reports on the "universalization of the French Language" and on the fate of regional "idioms" that Baptiste-Henri Grégoire, known as Abbé Grégoire, and Bertrand Barère read to the "Convention" (that is, the people's legislative assembly) in 1794, brought together all these themes: virility, modernity, the fight to eliminate accents, the insistence on the institution of writing, and the role of print in the dissemination of new state laws. And indeed, the Napoleonic Code, which crowned the new legal system put forward by the Revolution, was characterized by the symbolic confinement of women to the domestic sphere. Perhaps this thematic convergence suggests something about what we might call the infantile stage (or is it a permanent state?) of nationalism in general.

The emancipation of Algerians through the acquisition of a new language deemed "national" thus implied not only that they shake off a "foreign" authority but also that they turn against and away from the indigenous powerlessness of the mother, by violently renouncing the mother tongue. Young women were encouraged to participate in the effort at national Arabic literacy, on the condition, we might say, that they adopt the new veiling order, symbolized by the hidjab and standard Arabic. Carlier corroborates this view in his insightful formulation of the connection between "Arabization" and the changes in family roles and relations.

The debasement of dialectal Arabic has reinforced the diglossic condition of Algerians along both gender and generational lines. The illiterate mothers born before independence cannot uphold the national standard, much less transmit the new law of the land to their children. The Arabized children turn against their mothers, as in-

structed by the government. Instead of the symbolic wedding sancti-
fied by the blessing of the national mother tongue between equal and
mature citizens of the nation, as imagined by Anderson, Algeria offers the grim picture of real internecine killings and rapes. Mohammed Boudiaf, a national hero of the liberation war and a short-
lived president of Algeria (1992) was the only president to address the
nation in dialectal Arabic, that is, in the language he learned from his
mother and spoke with her, with his wife, and with his fellow citizens.[20] He was not only respected; he was loved. And he was assassi-
nated.

Symptomatically, the situation has produced a cultural polarization around the figure of the mother, which resonates loudly
throughout Francophone Algerian literature. Kateb Yacine dedicated
his first book to his illiterate mother. In an article entitled "L'Algérie
sans la France," Rachid Mimouni speaks of expressing the "intimate
and secret being" in literary French.[21] Assia Djebar explicitly con-
ceives of her work as a transcription of the oral memory of Algerian
women. But how can these writers claim to redeem their cultural
memory in the language of the oppressor? There are at least two
ways: an Algerian Francophone literature did begin to develop long
before independence, at a time when French was the only authorized
written language. And French carried within it an old literary tradition that itself relied on established institutions and a solid infrastructure. With independence, the power relation between languages
was altered. Because standard Arabic, and not dialectal Arabic, was
politically constituted as the rival and replacement of French, and because this move entailed the suppression of dialectal Arabic, French
was constructed as the medium through which the repressed dialectal idiom was secretly reinscribed, in translation. Let us note that
Kateb Yacine, who wrote primarily in French, stopped writing for a
time after independence and then produced plays in dialectal Arabic.
The use of French as a secretly bilingual idiom puts the writers doubly at odds with the official national-monolingual ideology, not unlike the "mothers" they celebrate. In addition, it undoes the fiction of
belonging on which nationalism rests. For, their writing in French
proves, if it were necessary to prove, that French belongs no more to
France than they themselves do when they use it.

In a debate that took place within the framework of the conference
on postcolonial Algeria at Cornell University in 1996, Jacques Derrida reasserted precisely in these terms the theoretical and experien-

tial stance that is at the core of his "Franco-Maghrebian" book, *Monolingualism of the Other:*

> French does not belong to France. It belongs to the structure of any language that it belongs to no one. A language is exactly what I cannot possess. If one starts from this axiom—i.e.: that language doesn't belong—one will see that all colonial and nationalist violences are the enactment of a will to appropriate precisely that which is inappropriable [because it is inappropriable]. Violence is the sign of this impossible appropriation.

Following Derrida, let me add that the mother tongue, as the language of the mother, is no exception to this asymptotic relation between language and the speaking subject: the mother tongue belongs no more to the mother than it does to the mother's mother or to the children to whom it is transmitted. What founds one's relation to it, then, is not primarily the assurance (or anxiety) of possession but the enjoyment of what Anderson calls "love," provided, of course, that the mother, or whoever plays her role, "loves" her children, that is, speaks to them, and that they speak to her. To speak a language and to enjoy speaking it may indeed be the pleasurable reenactment—or reinvention—of the first love relation, whatever the language in which it took place. And this pattern of language learning can be repeated more than once in the course of a life. As Hélène Cixous, who also participated in the debate at Cornell, said:

> Algerians are not obliged to keep French. One doesn't choose the language(s) one speaks, at least initially. But can't one decide to choose again a language one hadn't chosen? I think that one speaks the language(s) one needs, the language(s) that give(s) us pleasure, which speak to us.

Let me add a last word on Algeria's strange "mother tongue," dialectal Arabic.

Like all languages, dialectal Arabic was originally a derivation. Like all languages, it was originally colonial, in at least two senses: first, its emergence was the result of a colonial process (the Arab conquest); and second, as the language of a particular, albeit local, culture, it is implicated in what Derrida calls, in *Monolingualism of the Other,* the "essential coloniality of all culture."[22] Is it what sociolinguists call a vernacular language? Yes and no. Yes, inasmuch as the word "vernacular" literally refers to the language spoken by the slaves of a domain, thus pointing to a hierarchical difference between the language of the slaves and the language of the masters. No, insofar as the same word suggests an opposition between the domestic and the public, which the Algerian leadership would indeed like to enforce, but which does not exist. Dialectal Arabic is as much the language of the streets as it is the idiom of the home. As a shamed language, it is also, like everything deemed shameful, the site of enjoyment of forbidden pleasures. In the midst of the terror and suffering the Algerians have endured since the beginning of the 1990s, a culture of jokes has emerged, all of them in dialectal Arabic. In this language, Algerians laugh at the powers that be; we know that laughing is a way of lifting or evading both conscious and unconscious censorship. Theater, which plays an important role in today's cultural and popular expression, is performed in dialect, thus giving dialect an institutional and public status. Theater actors and directors have been the targets of violence. Among others, the famous theater director and playwright Abdelkader Alloula was murdered. So was the director of the National Theater of Algiers, Azzedine Medjoubi.

Above all, dialectal Arabic is the language in which all the idioms that have made up the history of Algeria meet and mix. In dialectal Arabic, boundaries between languages are erased; political and symbolic hierarchies are dissolved. The language is full of words borrowed from Berber, Turkish, French, or Spanish and given a local turn. In this sense, as Alawa Toumi forcefully argues in "Creolized North-Africa" (2000), it is close to Creole, a linguistic formation that belies the naive view of the indigenous as monogenous.[23] Like Creole, this dialectal mother tongue exhibits the fictionality of monogenesis, the purity of origin. It is "impure" and overinscribed because it is hospitable (as opposed to conquering), open to the other and therefore to alteration. And indeed, it is constantly evolving, from heavily Gallicized in colonial times to "classicized" under the growing influence of standard Arabic. National institutions always aim to stabilize language, simultaneously ruling over it and teaching its rules, in the hope of reinforcing the identity of national subjects. In contemporary Algeria, dialectal Arabic is a reminder that identity and heterogeneity, past and present, inside and outside are irreducibly implicated in one another.

PART II
SYMBOLIC
VIOLENCE

[4]

civil war, private violence, and cultural socialization

Political Violence in Algeria (1954–1988)

OMAR CARLIER

IN THE SPRING OF 1976, a native of Algiers living in Oran went to the local police station and accused her neighbor of being "Moroccan." She hoped to claim the neighbor's apartment for her son. Almost twenty years later, in the spring of 1994, in the same city, at the market of Medina jdida, a teenager disemboweled a pregnant woman who had refused to let him steal her bag. He needed money, and the usual grab-and-run was not enough for him.

Denunciation, delinquency, and murder have existed in every place and in every time.[1] At first glance, these isolated events seem to demonstrate only their own singularity. In fact, however, they have all the pertinence of the miscellaneous news item (*fait divers*), which, beyond chance occurrences, almost always illuminates the nature and tone of an era, bringing to light tensions in social relations and mentalities. With nearly twenty years between them, these two, apparently distinct, events are connected by invisible, subterranean links; insofar as each poses the problem of individual and collective violence, material and symbolic violence, social and political violence, they both point to a transformation in people's relationship to social norms.[2] Nothing allows us to connect them to the murderous fury of recent times, nor to the nihilistic destruction

This chapter was translated by Whitney Sanford. A longer version of this article, written at the height of the violence that has recently torn Algeria apart, has appeared in French under the title "Guerre civile, violence intime et socialisation culturelle," in *Guerres civiles: Economies de la violence, dimensions de la civilité*, edited by Jean Hannoyer (Paris: Kartala, 1999), 69–104.

of that fury, its paroxysm and pathology. Yet among many other occurrences, these two help us reflect on and fill in the gap between
public and private violence, between ordinary offenses and the generalized disorder of behavior in times of crisis. These uncommon
acts, which accompany the rise of incivility, represent small-scale
delinquency but also new forms of violence visited on women (who
are sometimes burned with acid for not conforming to standards of
dress), and provide us with clues. In each case, an understanding of
these clues should be sought in the motivations of the agents and in
the context, but also in the multiform and discontinuous changes
that have been at work throughout Algerian society, at least in the
twentieth century. Departures from the norm and the increase in
these transgressions, are signs of a weakening of the social bond.
This weakening may indicate a redefinition of the possible and the
thinkable, or a breaking down of forms of regulation of the social
group and the individual subject by a third party, an arbitrator, judge,
or Father, whose name alone was enough to establish authority and
legitimacy (God, Law, the People).

In the first case, unthinkable ten years earlier, even in the midst of
the Algerian-Moroccan "sand wars," more than jealousy and sordid
self-interest were at issue. The solidarity during the war for independence, and neighborly conviviality, especially between widows of
shouhadas (martyrs killed in the war) dissolved in the face of the political orchestration of the national cause, appropriated in this case
for private purposes at the height of the quarrels between Maghrebian
independent states, at the time of the "green march" and the Polis-
ario.[3] This solidarity also began to give way to the pressures of the notion of consumerist well-being, which gained currency beginning in
1962 with the run on former pied noir possessions after a century of
humiliation and frustration, and was then revived with the oil wind-
fall after 1972, following a decade of austerity. In 1976, small-scale
betrayal went on side by side with large-scale denunciation. If, fortunately, the expulsion of Moroccans, and particularly the episodes of
children forcibly thrown out of school, shocked the moral conscience
of many in Oran, the memory of blood spilled in a common cause
was not enough to keep candidates for municipal elections in many
small towns in the west from sounding a xenophobic note as they
competed with one another. As for the murderous second incident, it
seems to suggest that the respect for mothers that had held back
delinquents had now lost its force. During the same year and at al-

most the same time, Abdelkader Alloula, an Algerian playwright and talented painter from the plebeian class in the same Oran neighborhood, was killed in cold blood by a fanatical student, who thought he was acting for the cause and in God's name.

Extreme violence is on the march. There are very contemporary reasons for it, as well as deep and ancient roots, which doubtless extend beyond the agonistic transition from a colonial to a national state. Violence culminates in the use of arms, but is fostered at all levels of economic, religious, and political social practice, and within every dimension of the human. Exploited by those in power, exacerbated by social and libidinal frustration, intensified by ideology and the terrorist buildup, violence between Algerians is inseparably public and private, individual and collective, sacred and profane. The sources of violence are found within the political conflict, within the harshness of social collapse, tucked away in the imaginary, in the most intimate recesses of being.[4] This complex origin has nothing to do with the biological or ideological determinism according to which Algerians would be violent by nature; it does have a great deal, if not everything, to do with civil and social war as it existed in the twentieth century, which, like any historical construction, is necessarily unique. The intricate causality of the violence, like its phenomenology and temporality, invite comparison and synthesis. All physical and psychic social modes can be found at work in this complex; these modes interact and exacerbate one another, forming a tragic continuum ranging from "irrational" violence (emotional, eruptive, and quick-tempered) to calculated violence (instrumental, cynical, premeditated, in a word, programmed).[5]

The Implosion of Civil Religion

The violence of the past decade's conflict, including its paroxysmal forms of expression and display, originated in great part from the conjunction of political and social fragmentation at a time when the Algerian economy was collapsing, which plunged the country into a decade-long depression.

THE FRAGMENTATION OF THE POLITICAL ELITE

In 1988, the crisis in the political order reached a level unseen since 1965, or even 1962. A coup d'état was expected, even under way.[6] Of course, the conflict at the top of the political hierarchy, like the cultural conflict at the grassroots level, stemmed from a complex set of causes that date from well before the October riots. Nevertheless, for the first time since 1967, if not since independence, the different factions of the politico-military oligarchy could not seem to settle their differences, which had come to light publicly in 1986. It is as if—to protect against the complete elimination of one camp by another, or of one clan by another, and at the risk of totally disappearing itself—the FLN-ALN[7] was settling its scores in 1988 by proxy, by means of social forces, without ever displaying itself openly or getting to the root of problems, while confronting new interests and forces, at stake in the division of oil and land revenues and the distribution of jobs and markets.

The accumulated tension released by the riots was thereafter displaced onto all the fissures that had formed in the previous two years between followers of Chadli and followers of Boumediene, proponents of state control and of the free market, democrats and autocrats, virtuous administrators and gangster-style godfathers.[8] But far from eliminating much older rifts between Arab speakers and French speakers, Berberists and Baathists, Kabyles and Chaouias, neo-Islahists and Islamists, pro-American, pro-French, and pro-Iranian tendencies, this tension exacerbated them.[9] Far from causing the disappearance of primordial local or regional solidarities, it reactivated them, to the point that, between 1992 and 1993, a Balkanization of the conflict was feared. Accentuated and accelerated by the brutal collapse of the oil market, the political crisis within the government widened the gap between state and society. The two no longer communicated except through rioting, under pressure from young people who were no longer in school but who had no jobs and no future. The most impoverished and humiliated of them, hostile on principle to the system itself, and failing to see that they were contributing to its continued existence, hesitated between violent crime, *trabendisme* (wide-scale smuggling) and Islamism, a hesitation that favored a concurrence of different modes of perception and action that seem incompatible at first glance. The crises at the top and at the bottom were fed by the definitive failure of the centralized economy of perks and kickbacks, by the cultural deprivation of the people, and by the mediocrity of the intellectual elite—the intellectuals and the ordinary people alike being fascinated by the enormous discontinuity between Hollywood and Mecca—but also by the persistent inaccessibility of the public space, at least in the audiovisual media, despite the euphoric liberalization of the written press.

At first, the confrontation between the president's circle of friends and advisers and the opposition within the FLN-ALN block was played out among the young people and the Islamists, who were both manipulated and manipulative. The Islamists were the big winners after the days of October, though they did not initiate them. They reaped the fruit of a decade's labor, whose foundations were even older (Carlier 1992). Afterwards, the battle continued with murders of third parties carried out on the basis of anonymous orders;[10] it culminated in the fight to the death between the armed branches of the state and the armed branches of Islamism.[11]

THE SYMBOLIC CRISIS

Behind the disrepute of the FLN and the army itself, which, since 1988, have been too closely associated with corruption and repression, the power of civil religion itself—as a mode of government, a state ritual, and a staging of might—was at stake. In fact, civil religion was not so much disparaged in principle, in spite of Islamist defiance, as it was criticized for the way it was practiced by the FLN leadership.

Since 1962, all Algerian governments have attempted to base their legitimacy on a presumed conformity to the ideals of the revolution, fidelity to the message of November and the memory of the *shouhadas*.[12] Like all modern states, and like its North African neighbors, Algeria continues to rely on a heroic national narrative, an epic, a political liturgy. But the patriotic religion is somewhat aggrandized. It originated in an inaugural act, the uprising of 1 November 1954, the annual commemoration of which emphasizes its founding power, like 14 July in France, which serves as a model to imitate. The culmination of the patriotic moment was 5 July 1962, independence day, which happened to occur on the anniversary of the 1830 convention that marked the beginning of the occupation after the landing of Louis-Auguste de Bourmont's troops at Sidi Fredj. The founding myth is particularly powerful since, in a way, it combines death, birth, and resurrection, but also American Independence Day and French Bastille Day, that is, political liberty and civic equality. From one commemoration to the next, the cycle of war is repeated, from the *ancien régime* to Revolution-Liberation.

Citizens remember, students imagine. Each stage of the struggle is marked by as many dates as are appropriate to commemorate the revolutionary calendar: 20 August 1955, recurrence of war; 20 August 1956, the Soummam Charter; January 1957, the battle of Algiers; December 1960, popular demonstrations in the streets. Each is at once a site of memory and a historical object, honored in stories and film. Every government except Ahmed Ouyahia's in 1997, began with a pilgrimage to the original site of the revolution in the Aurès. All film, theater, literature, and visual art were dominated for more than twenty years by the revolutionary epic. All historical scholarship was organized around the *exempla* of this sacred history, punctuated by the worship of heroes and martyrs. Of course, the genre is universal. Every nation yearns for its Lavisse and produces a Mallet-Isaac.[13] Socialist states all have their "vulgate" under the imprimatur of the Party.[14] Egypt celebrates Ahmed Urâbî and the revolt of 1882, Saad Zaghlûl and 1919, Nasser and 1952.[15] Habib Bourguiba assigned to no one but himself the task of writing the Tunisian nationalist movement's history, identified with his person and relayed in official historiography by the Party's strongman, who was strong only so long as he remained in the service of the *suprême combattant*. In contrast, there are few examples of a state's endeavor to write history that mobilized millions of veterans to build a pharaonic archive, although, in the end, this effort never saw the light of day; there are few history manuals intended for primary school students that begin with scenes of horror. Everywhere, in Muslim countries and elsewhere, the political calendar imposes its secular mark and its local rhythm on the religious calendar. But rarely does the liturgy of one compete with that of the other, as it does in Algeria, without some blending of the two at the top of the hierarchy, as, for example, in the celebration of the Moroccan monarchy. Rarely is the worship of the dead taken to such a level of commemoration, even on the day of the Aï'd, as a sort of competition with and displacement of the worship of saints, which is contrary to the teachings of Muslim orthodoxy.[16]

But it is this very worship that lost its power in the 1980s. It became routine and thus subject to erosion, in a sort of reciprocal torpor of the rite and its celebrants. In a way, the worship of the dead turned against the living. The political liturgy, though reinforced at school by patriotic songs and the flag ceremony, ceased to legitimate the government in the eyes of the younger generation—including, and perhaps especially, the children of the *shouhadas*. The former revolutionary fighter's past spoke for him; the present, his present, spoke against him. The mujahideen could no longer claim the status of *shahid.*[17] Yesterday's hero was both devalued and discredited, devalued as an ordinary individual when he was unassuming, relegated to anonymity by the powerful and to helplessness by the reign of money, disparaged by a large array of malcontents as a docile agent of power and constant solicitor of special privileges; but especially, discredited and disgraced when he became an arrogant, rich, and unscrupulous wheeler-dealer. For some, the November liturgy was nothing more than a performance that had lost the power of truth; for others, its invocation by the government was a veritable misappropriation of power. The founding myth was subverted from within the circle of power, when the self-proclaimed successors of Ben Badis appropriated this history: in the capital, at the heart of the university, from above and below. It was also subverted from outside the regime, or on its margins, by the unsupervised development of mosque networks. Young students in the 1980s easily believed that Sheikh Ben Badis, who died in 1940, was the great leader of the war for independence.[18] Accelerated by the collapse of Arab nationalism, of communism, and of Third World ideology, the loss of effectiveness of civil religion could be measured at least as much by the derision in the streets, protest in the sports stadia, and by the recourse to rioting.[19] Fathers and sons agreed at least on one point—the feeling of a rift between Larbi Ben Mhidi's Algeria and Chadli Benjedid's Algeria, between the historical FLN and the political FLN. Holy history turned against the regime that was exploiting it.

Socialization and Education

Three other interdependent aspects of this process also contributed to the paroxysmal forms of political violence.

First, from riots to terrorism, from the street to the maquis, the social and political violence that opposed the state, though not the exclusive domain of young people, was nevertheless linked to the powerful convergence of a generation, and a critical moment, composed of social disconnection and symbolic reidentification. As during the period between the two world wars, but in a completely different sociohistorical context, this convergence reflects an affirmation of adolescent identity, arising in this case from the conjunction of urban population growth and mass socialization in the new *école fonda-*

mentale, which awarded students a useless diploma. The affirmation of the young people was reinscribed within the social sphere of the neighborhood, while opening new transversal relationships between the local and the global. However, for a good many of the children of "r/urbans," this meant forsaking the *sha'abi* (popular) subculture, inherited from the 1980s, and especially the rock-raï synthesis of the 1970s, to reorient themselves toward Islamism, against Third World ideology, even as their elders divided themselves between Islahism and nationalism. Ten years apart—a valuable chronological and sociological index—two artists in particular felt the growing abyss between society and state. In 1980, Merzak Allouache filmed the malaise of the idle and impoverished *Hittiste* (literally, "he who holds up the walls"). In 1990, the humorist Fellag expressed the desperation of an entire generation, its hunger to leave the country, its desire for an elsewhere, in the fantasy of a "babor Australia," which was ultimately realized for some through a conversion to militant Islam and the rite of passage in Afghanistan.[20] Two years earlier, teens from the housing projects had targeted the symbols of the state and the Party as never before—its sites, its emblems, the words and signs of power and wealth. The youth of October created for themselves a mode of conduct and a language of display—both gestures and words—of theatrical aggression, so as to better denounce the contemptuous arrogance of the mighty and claim, from within the jungle of the present, everyone's right to an equitable situation. *Haqqi* (my right) became, in their parlance, the counterpart to *hogra,* the arrogance of the haves toward the have-nots.

Hogra and *haqqi* are two of the fetishized terms, the watchwords of this generation, but they are not the only ones. Other people were attracted to the "Islamic solution" and caught up in the exaltation of prophetic formulas, the "commanding of the good and the banishment of evil," as the French Orientalist Jacques Berque has put it. For them, the real *mujahideen* and the authentic *shouhadas* were henceforth to be found elsewhere, among those who defied the great American Satan and toppled red Moscow. The Algerian heroic model was no more, given that its proclaimed heirs were now illegitimate. Yet this model was more powerful than ever in the displacements onto external struggles it allowed. Resistance no longer stemmed from Arab nationalism, but from Islamism. It stretched from Sudan to Bosnia, from Morocco to Kabul. It restored prestige, confidence, and pride to those who felt humiliated and tricked. It reactivated, reformulated, and reinvented a memory of the war; it handed a new mirror to supporters of change in which they could seek their identity. In its most nihilistic expression, it drained off and channeled the delinquency of the poor, the malaise of the Hittistes, the trafficking of the *trabendistes*; it supplied men for the most violent renegades of the FIS.

Second, ideological displacement and critical investments found motivations and resources in the new school system. Very early on, there was a commitment in principle to mass education in Arabic from the primary to the university level, but it was established very slowly in practice. Around the time of Boumediene's death, it accelerated and was carried out harshly, without the support of any serious pedagogical concerns. At the same time, education gave rise to a movement of linguistic and cultural (re)socialization of astonishing magnitude throughout the contemporary Muslim and Arabic world. It proceeded in an atmosphere marked by the revenge of Arabic speakers on French speakers. This spirit of revenge and reconquest owes much to the marginalization of literary Arabic under colonization, to the sometimes arrogant domination of Francophones in the state and the university at the end of the war, to the pugnacity of former students of the Badisi schools (based on Ben Badis's teachings), and to the return to favor of the Ulema, well represented by Dr. Ahmed Taleb, beginning in 1965. This vengefulness was intensified by the configuration of the job market, where Arabic speakers were at a disadvantage, and thus found fertile ground in Arabized schools and administration. It was also reinforced by the diffuse tension between Arabophone rural areas and the Francophone cities, a tension that varies greatly from one region to another. School was the strategic axis of a veritable trench war that, unsurprisingly, was won by Arabic speakers, at the cost of decapitating the elite and incurring ongoing losses in the quality of education. Neighboring countries have not been spared their share of linguistic transformations accompanied by competition, and suspicion, but the conflict is much more intense in Algeria, particularly because of the low number of truly bilingual elites and their symbolic weakness; skilled practitioners of both Arabic and French were, moreover, quickly dismissed from important university posts (Arkoun, Merad, Bencheikh). Interdependent linguistic and educational issues fed on all the other conflicts, and stimulated them in return, in an escalation whose primary beneficiary was the FIS. Symbolic violence prepared the way once again for physical violence. It opened the path to the murder of Francophone intellectuals in a sort of collective letting-off-of-steam channeled by those who targeted the latter for elimination. The hatred that has taken hold between certain writers, for example, the justification of Tahar Djaout's murder by Tahar Ouettar (an Arabophone writer and proponent of total Arabization), is symptomatic of this ethical collapse.

The relationship of the schools to violence was not the result only of the clan war conducted in their hallways; it also resulted from a certain transmission of knowledge and an internalization of a system of values. At issue is socialization in the schools. Beginning in the 1980s, this socialization favored the emergence of a new corps of teachers, who were trained and who trained others in a new manner. Schools integrated religious education, which had until then been reserved for Koranic schools and Islamic institutes. In the inner city, the secular tradition of the training institutes for grade school teachers (Ecoles Normales d'instituteurs) remained strong, but elsewhere it lost ground. Schoolmasters introduced a new climate to classes: a state of mind, an ethos unfavorable or even hostile to the previous secular ethic. This was not a return to Koranic school, but a promotion of a neo-Islahist school system, oriented toward the sciences but moving the pedagogical model in a direction less favorable to individual and critical thought. A growing number of teachers—they populated the city halls won by the FIS in 1990—increasingly oriented the schools toward an Islamist discourse. The history textbooks lent support, by proposing an identity model that altered the Algerian's self-image as a Maghrebian, confirming the stereotype of the Arab on the periphery who is found perpetually lacking by comparison to the original nobility reserved for the Middle East.

Concern about parents' behavior with respect to religious observance was not unusual. One witnessed the advent of the characteristic reversal of totalitarian systems, which give children the responsibility for watching parents. School was no longer the potential hunting grounds of the JFLN (Jeunesse FLN, or FLN youth) or of the Scouts; it had become the spearhead of the Islamic revolution in the eyes of its champions. Along with the mosques, schools after 1988 became the privileged site of moral rearmament, of a veritable counterrevolution of morality, commensurate with the successes of the FIS, by now a powerful mass movement firmly rooted in society and with a tightening grip on the state.[21] The reorientation of education in the 1980s contributed to the popularization of Islamist discourse among young people, and to the emergence of a readership and an audience sensitive to the statements, agendas, and recorded tapes and disks of the FIS. Education was thus in keeping with the indoctrination conducted in Islamist mosques, and the establishment of utopian projects, whose charitable aspect was transformed into a veritable neighborhood social politics. School became a mosque, and the mosque acted as a school. Each brought society back to God's order, and gave everyone the means for recovering "true Islam." In this case, it is necessary to speak of a veritable cultural revolution, since mass education in Arabic made direct access to the Koran possible, following the example of the Protestant reformation, which arose at once from Martin Luther's translation of the Bible, educational progress, and the invention of the printing press. For the first time in its history, Algerian society, at least members of its younger generation, were in a position to read the sacred text in an individual and personal manner, even though a gap between the sacred language and standard Arabic remained—and even though knowledge does not prevent recourse to received ideas.

Third and finally, let us consider the effect of the schools on the actual structure and on the fantasmatic representation of gender roles, especially within the family. In the first place, mass education for girls gave rise to a generation of learned women. This movement, which began in the 1940s and greatly increased on the eve of independence, accelerated once more after 1962 and affected all rural areas in the 1970s. Thus, in less than twenty years, a thousand-year-old model of sexual differentiation, validated by tradition at least as much as by the Koran, was called into question. The road to public school was enough to give concrete form to a modernization that was often perceived as a Westernization of Algerian women. This large-scale innovation, grounds for pride for some, a source of concern for others, had little material effect on work structures, since women remained very much a minority in the "working population" (Alahite 1983). The level of anxiety of conservatives increased with the social and moral crisis of the 1980s, and expressed itself in official praise of the mother as caretaker of the family and pillar of society and its values, and in everyday masculine discourse. It was also and especially a problem for the family, since it is within the intimacy of the domestic unit that the female student tends to disrupt the usual order of things. Her emancipation, or her evolution, may or may not be integrated into the family model. When her qualifications lead to a career that confers both status and income, she becomes objectively a more important element of the household because of her salary, even when it is turned over, in part or in whole, to the father. Because of her education, especially in Arabic, she, like the boys, has at least potential access to the arena of religion formerly reserved entirely for men. She can flaunt her knowledge, even of "women's" matters—not only before her mother, which does not rule out complicity with her—but also before her father, the figure of male authority, the imam of the household, the "natural" religious leader of the basic social unit—which does not rule out respect or affection.

Nothing about these situations is a matter of course. An illiterate father may certainly maintain his authority over his medical student son, and even more so over his educated daughter, even if she is a school principal, all the while thanking God for this treasure sprung from his loins. However, many were disturbed by this upside-down world. An educated girl might wear the hidjab against her father's wishes, with the support of Koranic verses, or, on the contrary, might refuse to wear the veil as her father or brother prescribes, using a different argument from the sacred text. She might also marry against tradition, go out into the city as she pleases without a veil, or behind one, in the name of her right to be herself, out of respect for the righteous, Koranic path, or in the name of feminist or secular ethics. She may discuss, object, contest. In fact, the FIS, especially the "Afghans," have sought to limit girls' access to schooling and to bar them from employment, like the Taliban. If one is not careful, women might put themselves before men, daughters before their fathers, and might lead prayers.

Thus, mass education and mass Arabization each played a part in the economy of tensions and corresponding violence in the past decade, by redistributing sex roles in social and familial structures, which, here and elsewhere, were connected to the conflict between holism and individualism. Care for the self, personal opinion, a desire to lead one's own life, a rejection of imposed traditions, all of these found their way, to some extent, through contemporary Islamism, thus making it possible to look for an alternative to "Western-style liberty." The family-as-*faction* replaced, or superimposed itself on, the nuclear family. The former could very well circumvent, control, or break the latter. Yet that family-as-faction might be overwhelmed by the tension it had appropriated and intensified.

In any event, school played a role in individualizing the relation to family and religion, community and society. School also contributed a great deal to loosening the habitus of age and sex roles.

Fantasies of Kinship, Malaise of Identification

The loss of norms and the falling status of the guardians of norms in politics, law, religion, and family, the breadth of resocialization by the schools and of desocialization in the city, the revival of the contradiction between public and private space, prohibition and laxity, Hollywood and Mecca, individualism and holism, the rising tension between care of the self and social control in face-to-face encounters, the material and libidinal frustrations aggravated by the ever-widening gap between consumerism and poverty, hedonism and puritanism—these are the main reasons for the social and psychological violence at work in Algeria, for the intensification of social violence, its forms and the sites of its expression, within and beyond the immediate struggle for power or for material and symbolic market shares. The political struggle in the strict sense—between the state and civil society, between democrats and autocrats, "Occidentalists" and "Orientalists," the fight to the death between the army and the FIS, and finally, among the Islamists—is both cause and effect. We should, however, pay more attention to the historicity of the representations underlying this economy of tensions and passions. The transformation of the individual subject into a violent, oppositional, armed, and ultimately terrorist subject raises the question of what the violence between relatives and within the self means. This, in turn, leads us to question the resistance of the symbolic system, as well as its erosion, and the challenge to imagoes of sociality as they are formed in their most powerful symbolic structure: kinship.

THE BROTHER—EQUALITY AND PARITY

Over time, throughout the long twentieth century, which began in 1880, all of Maghrebian society, and Algeria more than its neighbors, has supported, rethought, and reinvented itself in accordance with the endlessly readjusted perspective of parity between brothers and disparity between men.

Parity between brothers in the tribe and in the mosque, between those of the soil and those of the Zaouïa (religious brotherhood), between men of arms and men of the cloth, between those ruled by '*orf* (custom) and those by Shari'a (Koranic law)—such is the dominant paradigm of a centuries-old solidarity that still had meaning for the newly drafted soldiers of World War I, already much sought after by the Young Turks and the Nahda. Parity is founded on proximity, resemblance, sameness: men of honor and men of faith, connected through the name of the family or brotherhood, are equal as sons of the father, in spite of the respect due the eldest son, and are thoroughly homologous as sons of Adam, in spite of the respect due the sheikh. This solidarity and endogamous parity, produced by kinship, reflects the immediate, corporeal, familiar, visible, and tactile proximity of blood and earth, nurtured within the framework of the village community. But it also opens on a larger dimension, the mediated proximity of the imagined whole, the Umma, invisible as such but already there, incorporated into the ritual of Friday prayer, and eventually represented and realized in the unique venture of the *hajj* (pilgrimage). *Djema'a* (assembly) and *jami'a* (mosque) meet, combining deliberation and invocation, in a sacrificial blend of the visit to the ancestor and the visit to the prophet, blood identity and religious identity, the little homeland (*watan*) and the great community of believers (Umma).

The power of the sultan or bey (*maghzen*), and the brotherhood's network (*tariqa*) provided a mediation between the different levels and forms of parity, kinship, and community. Beginning in the 1920s and 1930s, the ideas of nation and Nahda took hold, disseminated by the schools and by newspapers, and taught by schoolmasters and sheikhs at the instigation of the party and the *cercle*. They spread to rural areas with World War II, and acquired a sacred aura with the war for independence, reaching their peak in the 1960s. Yet, with the next generation, the nation (watan) was confronted with the globalization of consumer and spiritual goods, and with the reversal that pitted communist and Third-World "revolutionary" universalism, already on the point of collapse, against the Islamist reiteration of religious universalism.

The eternal disparity between men came to be added to the doubly threatened parity between brothers. This is not a simple disparity attributable to the irreducibility of the individual, inherent in the infinite diversity of human nature, and recognized in countless proverbs; it is the powerful disparity of social roles and status illustrated in hagiographic stories or fantastic tales, for example, in the evil or enchanted reversal of fortune of the fallen prince or the craftsman-turned-king.[22] In the Republic of cousins, tradesmen, and believers, at least six forms of legitimate disparity can be identified: that between believers and unbelievers, men and women, fathers and sons, masters and disciples, youth and elders, and *'amma* and *khassa* (elites and plebeians). The perception of the moral and material gap between *'amma* and *khassa*, which contradicts the ideals of justice, morality, and good governance, often puts the diffuse but meaningful criteria governing the legitimacy of distinctions to the test. In the precolonial Maghreb, crises of succession, successive bad harvests, and tax revolts were all moments likely to exacerbate tensions.

This model of balanced tensions, which twice underwent a crisis, was also twice reformulated, with considerable impact but mixed success. The first time was in reaction to the colonial state, with the rise of the Parti Populaire Algérien (PPA) and various components of the national movement, which were eventually grouped together into the FLN. The second time was in reaction to the national state, with the advent of the FIS and other proponents of the "Islamic solution." Both the FIS and the FLN invoked the ideal of parity, while maintaining legitimate disparities, resulting in the release of extraordinarily intense collective violence. This strategy was the translation of a populist discourse, a language of nationalism and Islamism both inherited from the past and invented in the present, and understandable to everyone.

In the first crisis, the FLN model promoted the equilibrium of a politico-military clan, not a parity of citizens. That model failed to alter former modes of disparity, including that between men and women. Hence the republic of cousins and puritans outlived the sacralization of the political. In the second crisis, a discourse of "brothers" attempted to achieve the ideal of social justice and channel it into a model of parity placed under the aegis of the "Islamic market economy," through a new combination of relations between market, religion, and gender roles, thus reinforcing—in the guise of reformulating—the old forms of legitimate disparity.

WOMAN AND SISTER—CASTRATION ANXIETY AND MODERNIST INVERSION

Relations between the sexes are truly at the heart of the current crisis.

Let us begin with the social relation between man and woman, and the personal relationship between husband and wife. The first factor is women's employment. Certainly, it progressed very little after 1962; the return to peace also signified a return to the home, except for a handful of activists, soon condemned to tokenism (Amrane 1991). However, the general trend toward salaried work by women advanced in the economic arena of the new Algeria, beyond the forms accepted during the colonial period (when women worked exclusively in the textile industry or as domestic laborers).[23] A significant portion of the male population, and the more sexist professions—not only the police, but also the legal profession—balked at giving women access to positions of authority. But the movement appears irreversible, and is becoming accepted, even though it concerns only a small minority of women. Already, its consequences are substantial, directly for those concerned, indirectly as a powerful example or counterexample.

Paid work, even in its most modest forms, conferred on the women involved a status and an income that spouses, in-laws, neighbors, and citizens in general, were obliged to take into account. The husband and father was no longer the breadwinner upon whom everyone depended. What is more, a woman who works is by definition absent from the home, subjected to a daily schedule and rhythm not necessarily convenient to her spouse. She goes into town, away from the constraints of the marketplace or the ritual of family visits or religious celebrations. As a result, men have lost part of their authority, though we must concede that he had always had to compromise with the mistress of the house in the domestic sphere. Women in education and civil service, who belong to the rising middle and upper classes, began to drive automobiles, bring their children to the beach alone, and go abroad for training. Parity, at least another sort of parity, was being constructed, this time not between brothers, but between husband and wife. The sociology of women's employment, the structure of the couple, and urban behavior evolved in concert. Between women professors at the university and hospital helpers, an entire range of intermediary situations took shape in the urban world. Along with nurses and primary school teachers, a mass of secretaries emerged. Many put off marriage to keep their salaries and their freedom while waiting for the ideal husband. These women were changing: they were different from their mothers, aunts, or older sisters; the city changed with them, even if men did not. More numerous, more active, and less restricted, they played sports when they were young, and "went to the gym" as they grew older. They read magazines, followed the fashions, went to the hairdresser, met in tea rooms. Women changed their bodies and within their bodies— you could see it in their faces, clothes, and walk. Some walked quickly without a glance at passersby, to dissuade men from proposi-tioning them, an activity unthinkable not so long ago. Others raised their heads proudly and confronted the new gender mix in the streets at rush hour. The Western model was widely internalized, though it still affected only a small minority of urban women.[24]

There are conflicting tendencies in this evolution. On the one hand, the contradiction between models, accentuated by the eco-nomic crisis and social disconnection, has increased the number of divorces and suicides. The trend led divorced mothers to depend all the more on their work, in the absence of a family to support them. Finally, all women were impelled to become more autonomous by going to school or finding employment if possible, otherwise by maintaining the household, an increasingly difficult task in cases of overcrowded housing, or by other means, including Islamism. For students or young salaried women drawn to Islamist discourse—con-cerned about the fate of the less educated majority excluded from the labor market—and for other young women without strong religious motivations but in search of an escape, the Koranic norm served as a resource against the masculine social order, since the Koran is in many ways more favorable to women than is tradition. In the context of a religious and puritanical backlash, a return to the moral order, which these women sometimes internalized, the *hidjab* became a so-lution, or at least a lesser evil. Henceforth, the struggle of women spread within Islamism, as it had in Iran. It is a paradoxical struggle viewed from the outside, but a rational one for many of the women concerned. In contrast, men's real or imagined loss of authority was experienced by many as an attack on their identity.

We now come to the virility syndrome—common throughout the Mediterranean world but particularly exacerbated under these cir-cumstances—which involves authority, desire, and the sacred. Woman is both desired and monitored more than ever. She is desired more than ever because she is more visible, more free, more beauti-ful, without becoming more accessible; and she is monitored more than ever because her reputation remains a principle of masculine honor for the men close to her; this is true for the majority of men, even in the city. But the woman is in the street, at the office, at school, at the market. Always seductive under the "haik,"[25] noticed for the quality of her veil and her shoes, but even more for her gait and gestures, she is even more tempting without the veil, whether her beauty is natural or artificial, whether her clothes are by Chanel, her hair by Jacques Dessange, her scarf by Saint-Laurent, discreetly perfumed with the bourgeois elegance of Paris, or whether her means are more simple, like the students who know how to personalize and play up clothes and hairstyles, wearing long skirts or jeans, Grace Kelly chignons or bob cuts, or like the young working-class women, who soon followed the fashions of U.S. television soap operas, adopting miniskirts and, even more provocatively, pants, and who also managed to spend next to nothing on their clothes. More than ever, in the early 1960s, springtime in Algiers and Oran was a celebration, as Tunisian, Moroccan, and even Parisian friends passing through often noticed! And Ramadan became a celebration, where the revival of faith was no obstacle to a joie de vivre verging on the carnivalesque. The hinterland, the rural world itself, was overtaken by the fever. Under the veil, in the village, or on visits to town, women saw themselves differently, and men along with them, not only in the street, but even more so in still images or on television. The 1970s was the decade of television, the 1980s that of satellite antennae. The many dreams of the fantasy woman were supplemented by the multiple faces of actual women—or men—in movies brought to the city, and, within the family, by Egyptian, Brazilian, or U.S. television series, especially for women. For men with satellite television, this even included X-rated movies, which they often watched among themselves during this period combining all imaginable opposites, temptations, and frustrations. Once again, the moral counterrevolution orchestrated by the FIS was on the same scale as the return to "Sodom and Gommorah." In 1910–14, 1930–35, 1944–45, 1956–60, and 1979–82, several forms of puritan reaction gained ground to varying degrees, in the sectors of society anxious about the collapse of morality, whether represented, as in the past, by alcoholism and prostitution, or, as in the present, by the inconvenient freedom of women. The debate over the veil keeps returning, as both a tangible sign of and a metonymy for women's status. But it was the promise of the supposedly orthodox family code that became one of the leitmotifs of the early 1980s.

A conservative reaction led by Islamist students in Algiers and Constantine took shape at this time, and was encouraged by certain sectors of the government. Some state ministers, party officials, mosque leaders, and members of the press put the emphasis on the pernicious Westernization of young people, and especially of Algerian women, as signs of depersonalization and degeneration. The economic crisis notwithstanding, the promulgation of the family code in 1984 revealed the buildup of a part Islahist, part Muslim Brother current within the FLN, and the search for a compromise between economic liberalism and religious conservatism similar to the *infitah* initiated by Anouar Sadate in Egypt. Then things changed during the period of economic crisis and widespread unemployment, which continued without respite beginning in 1985–86. At this time, the women, often more qualified than the men became formidable, "intolerable" competitors in the eyes of many men, even though this "threat" was in part compensated for by the value of a second income, which allowed many families to achieve a higher standard of living, which they wished to maintain. Things also changed with the rising political tension, the 1988 crisis, the conjuncture of democratic initiatives and ideological polarization, and the rising power of the FIS. Related through the very notion of creation to the unequal relation of man to God, the unequal relation of woman to man remains a major axis for representing self and world, an axis that endures when everything else has become fragmented. In any event, male privilege is what remains when everything else has been lost, or, at least, when nothing has been gained. The feeling of general decline in values easily leads many to see women as one of the causes, if not *the* cause, of all the rest, the ultimate threat. Loss of male authority, loss of female modesty—are not these the signs of an upside-down world, which ought to be set aright? The sign is eschatological, the response prophetic. The Islamic solution not only relies on a theologico-political discourse, it comes forth to reiterate an originary Word.

No one felt more deeply the governmental corruption, the social injustice, the loss of a virile identity, and the sexual frustration, no one felt more intensely the necessity of a radical alternative, than the recent graduates without prospects or the young unemployed adults, especially the downwardly mobile youth of the small towns and suburbs, condemned by their own account to delinquency and *trabendisme*. Like their fathers' generation, they sensed the general loss of masculine authority, but the ordeal concerned neither their wives nor their daughters. It began with their sisters, whom they were in charge of monitoring, as they had been told often enough, and their other sisters, the sisters of others, whom they were meant to seduce, as they had been cajoled to do often enough. But this double sister escaped them, the untouchable blood sister and the permitted but socially and culturally unapproachable seductress (*tchi-tchi*), in the streets. The romantic games of the past at familial and collective celebrations, the flirtations of the 1980s, now held only meager rewards. The weekly movie or the daily television series replaced them with the actress, the supermodel, or simply, the anonymous female body in advertisements. Second only to the Oedipal relation to the mother, the relation to the sister is the site of convergence of social and libidinal forms of conflict; thus we return to the two destabilizing modes of modernist inversion. The sister had become, in fact, the first competitor in the education and employment markets, where she was often better qualified than her brother, and the first female to protest domestic authority. She escaped her brother not so much because he lost his right to control her—a right that might have reassured him of his status—especially once she left the home, as because, with the rise of the new egalitarian figure of woman, he lost, in almost an ontological sense, his duty to control her. The sister is also the foremost intimate female figure, next to the mother. At least, she is the first one recognized and then experienced as such, as many interviews with doctors, researchers, and even journalists attest. The brother knows her body, observes her dress, and breathes her perfume, in spite of all the careful precautions and modesty, and the self-discipline characteristic of sensory inhibition. The irresistible disinhibition of the larger society's gaze, directed at the female body, including the sister's body, intensified the frustration of the younger generations and brought their libidinal drives and castration anxiety to a peak.

It is now clear why many young people won over to the cause of political Islam are susceptible to a radical internalization of conflict through a return to the lost values of virtue and male authority, to be guaranteed by the Shari'a. There is little doubt that the hardened puritanism of the various Islamic currents, and especially, the unleashed paroxysm of sexual violence in the GIA's abductions of women are commensurate with the tension between libidinal drive and libidinal repression. There again, the conscious use or infantile and ignorant internalization of religious references served to legitimate sadistic violence, when, for example, kidnapped women were explicitly treated like slaves after being seized and divided up as "the spoils of war" (*butins*).

FIGURES OF THE FATHER, IMAGO OF THE MOTHER

The Algerian political system never completely recovered from the symbolic conflict psychoanalysis calls "the murder of the Father." I hesitate to automatically reject the Freudian paradigm as ethnocentric, since the reference to the Father, if not the expression "murder of the Father," has been used so often by antagonistic "brothers" over the course of the Algerian conflict. From the 1930s to the 1950s, the head of the nationalist party was the "father of the party," and, by extension, the "father of the nation." Messali Hadj in Algiers and Bourguiba in Tunis fall into the same category. It is symptomatic that the cycle that began in 1954 with a Freudian murder of the Father, that of Messali, perpetrated in language by the sons of November, recurred as actual bloodshed by the heirs to the FLN, or at least a portion of the "revolutionary family," against Boudiaf in 1992, that is, at the end of the "revolutionary" cycle.

Indeed, these brother-heirs had in turn become fathers—collective fathers, since the FLN is the patronym of the revolution (*thaoura*). And they too had to endure the revolt of the biological and symbolic sons, either because they had given up struggling for an ideal, revived, then reinvested in the new revolutionary triptych of Boumediene's industrial, agrarian, and cultural revolutions, or because they had exchanged the mujahideen's burnous for the mujahideens' Mercedes. Even so, the revolt rose up against the revolution, all the more violently in that, ten years later, the actual practice of the fathers appeared to be suddenly turning its back on the parity model that had until then legitimated it. Universal education, free medical care, guaranteed employment, a socialist economy, inexpensive stores, a tax on products—all these had been signs that acted as confirmation, increasingly distinguishing Algerians from their Moroccan and Tunisian neighbors. Socialist Algeria had not forgotten the "circle of equality," the old ideal of justice and balance inscribed in the "Princes' Mirror"; it adopted this principle during the industrial period (Dakhia 1998).[26] The Algeria of four-year plans had thus reinvented the redistributive and unifying function of the Zaouïa, characteristic of agrarian society, all the while projecting the language of the

Koran onto the world of iron and steel. A sort of paradoxical populist aristocracy brought a new society of equals into the modern world.

In contrast, the 1980s, a decade increasingly characterized by the ostentatious display of wealth, was a time of mourning for this briefly glimpsed dream. In less than three years, between 1985 and 1988, the collapse of oil revenues laid bare the truth about prices and performance within the triumphant market economy and the reign of capital. Bouyali no longer masked Guizot.[27] "Freedom" was just another name for misrule, corruption, arrogance. The revolution had not been transmitted to the sons but turned against them for no reason; they were guilty of having been born too late. These sons seized on the revolution in the name of regaining their fraternity in opposition to a parity gone awry. In the eyes of the generations socialized by heroic films, school textbooks, and the memory of the dead, the shift from the historical FLN to the political FLN was experienced as a move from truth to lies, from the pure to the impure. It became increasingly intolerable. Mosques and schools used the words and symbols of the past revolution to transfer the heroic, populist, and messianic model of the fathers' generation to the generation of the sons, that is, the FIS's future troops and leaders. In this sense, the new FIS is very much the son of the FLN.

Against the deficient father, vanquished and renounced or arrogant and all-powerful, against the system of the fathers, the politics of the fathers, the sons devised a cult of ancestors, not to reestablish as such the family of days gone by and the prophet's medina, but rather to support a new public and private order where every brother might become powerful and equal, a male order of the Shari'a to which the family and the Islamic republic held the imaginary keys. Between the old-style patriarchy, which hearkened back to the tribe, and the new puritanism of the Muslim Brothers' Umma, the revolt against the fathers found resources in a fantasmatic call to the reassuring order of the grandfathers. But is not the search for support in the figure of a patriarch, even one who is a generation removed, really a reactivation of a new father image? The memory of the learned sage Sheikh Ben Badis was revived; posters and recordings allowed the population to project onto a terrible and inflexible old man, the ayatollah Khomeini. Abassi Madani and Ali Benhadj[28] a sort of father-son duet, owed a good part of their effectiveness to their power of mediation and symbolic recomposition, their ability to draw together the threads of the generations, their aptitude for remaking, for the most socially disadvantaged urban youth, an order of the father and the brothers, a national-Islamist order that conserved the best of the past and guaranteed the future in response to the decadence of the present. From the outset, the FIS played on frustrations and rewards in the name of a new political revolution. This revolution knew how to play on myths—that of the crusades, a model for the battle to be waged against the West, that of the hereditary enemy who has left behind his language (French) in the form of an internal enemy, and finally, that of the purity of origin as opposed to the *junta* of the corrupt and the corrupters. Confronting all these figures of Evil, the heirs to the FLN promised the social justice of a moral counterrevolution. Against the fathers, they reformulated a model of parity between brothers and reformulated a principle of disparity between believers and nonbelievers. The GIA would perpetuate the cycle of retaliatory violence.

Yet the castrating father and the profiteering brother are not the only parties at issue; the mother too is involved. The imago of the mother is a particularly active element in the resocialization of contemporary Algeria, and in the acute tension that leads to the mother's sons to kill one another. Mother Algeria is related to all other maternal figures: mother earth, the mother tongue, and the mother who nourishes with her blood and milk. This last mother refers back to the community of sons of the universal mother of faith, to the *umma islamiyya*. Language, land, and religion have indeed been the key terms in the confrontation and conflict since 1930 between Ben Badis's Arabic-speaking elites and Messali's French-speaking populists. The figure of Mother Algeria evokes the mother's womb and the motherland. Her name has been proclaimed, written, recited, and sung for almost a century. But it is an ambiguous figure, as the name itself indicates. In standard written Arabic, *El Djeza'ir* is masculine, but in dialect, *l'Algérie* is considered feminine, through an integration of the feminine French term into the Algerian form of dialectal Arabic. The locution *l'Algérie* is as common in songs as in daily life. "Algeria rahet" (meaning "she is vanishing, she is collapsing") was a common expression in 1988 and again in 1992. This ambiguity, connected to the imago of the bad mother, does not concern only the amniotic and symbiotic corporeality of the womb and of nursing. A "stepmother," the allegorical figure for France, continues to lurk behind the mother figure, though less in literary texts than in collective memory. Thus, a memory trace and an affective mark of two mothers remain: an always positive Mother Algeria, and a Mother France, about whom one never knows whether or when she will be loving or threatening. "Madame la France" is another common expression which, since the 1930s, has taken on every possible inflection, from real affection to the most scathing derision. Nevertheless, in Algeria more than anywhere else in the Arab world, the *umma wataniyya* (homeland) has been conceived as a bind between identification with the metropolis and detachment from it. Even in the past, this tension went far beyond the problem of acculturating a handful of Franco-phone Kabyle émigrés or readers of *La Voix des Humbles* (The Voice of the Humble, a journal of "indigenous" primary school teachers), and the interplay between four or five languages derived from the Arabic-Berber-French triad. This tension now goes well beyond the ordinary game of diplomatic relations between nation-states, or even relations between Francophones and Arabophones. Over the long term, it has raised issues of socialization by the schools, military service, work, wealth, and the state itself, not only during the colonial period, but among the leaders of the nation-state. It is related to the excessive and fantasized presence of the past, to the conflict between memory and history, to the endlessly reformulated tension between the same and the other, which is linked to the French share of Algerian identity, however stigmatized, and to the Algerian share of French identity, which is becoming more prominent every day. A parallel and shared history passes from one shore to the other, in both directions, through newspapers, novels, and satellite dishes. Relations between the two countries embrace an increasingly extreme principle of separation, yet they are characterized by intense forms of communication. The political problem of the mother is the problem of the reiterated separation from an adoptive mother, whether or not she was abusive, a bad mother; this problem surfaced in an exemplary and paradigmatic manner in Ben Badis's bald rejection of France in a 1936 speech, in his famous response to Ferhat Abbas.[29] A bygone past? Not in the least. Ever since the 1970s, the paradigmatic term for the enemy has been concentrated in the expression *hizb franza* (the side of France): This expression stigmatizes the foreigner, the enemy, the traitor, the Other, to such an extent that anyone from that "side" who was once recognized as a compatriot and fellow Muslim is now symbolically expelled. In 1988, and especially in 1992, there was a shift from the *takfir* manipulated by the FLN communitarians to the politico-religious *takfir* orchestrated by FIS dissidents and GIA emirs.[30]

As a colonial war, the Algerian conflict was dirty: summary executions, torture, exactions against civilians. It was accompanied by a war within the war among Algerians (and among the French). The war in present-day Algeria is even more complex. It is developing with the memory of the colonial war still present as a paradoxical nexus of amnesia and hypermnesia, but also amid the most extreme contradictions between the real world, ideology, and utopia. It takes on the appearance of a civil war, but of a particular kind of civil war. It does not pit ethnic or religious communities against each other as in Yugoslavia, Lebanon, or Ireland, where the foundation of the conflict is more social than religious. Nor does it pit militias against each other, again as in Lebanon, or two ideological camps against each other, or civilians against the military, as in Greece or Spain. Rather, there are groups heterogeneous to the army on one side, and to the civilian population on the other, as in Guatemala, and an internal religious specificity with international repercussions, as in Iran or Afghanistan.

The current paroxysm of violence between Algerians in Algeria cannot be explained solely in terms of a sadistic pathology, liberated and generalized by anomie, activated by anxiety and panic, or by the terrible pain of the cycle of retaliation. This violence requires a stronger explanation than that given by the killers, their commanders, and other perpetrators. It is related to a synergy of repression and release, in conjunction with a political, social, moral, and religious disjunction. It is related to the implosion of every form of consecration, to the weakening of all bonds: of nationhood, language, locality, social status, family, sex. It shows itself through the Islamic extremist's return to Koranic truth and the purity of the believer, through the army's attempted return to order, and, in society as a whole, through increasingly burdensome downward mobility. These lines of tension developed between 1930 and 1950 under pressure from the PPA and the Ulema as they moved north to the city, and were then federated and organized against the occupier in a violent manner, a violence that was finally both internalized and overcome by the FLN. By the end of the 1980s, the collective formula established thirty years earlier was inoperative. The old political class, which had either not noticed or not understood the importance of the growing and defiant new forces, wanted to change the institutions but still maintain the upper hand. It has persevered in the face of the claims and frustrations of new generations who speak a different language, surrounded by an ever-increasing tension between the constraints of the market and the demand for democracy. The traffic in arms and the aftermath of the murderous turn of events run the risk of leaving deep scars within a context of exacerbated social inequality. Delinquency and criminality, whether organized or not, are already feeding on this situation, and are not likely to disappear anytime soon. However, in Algiers, at the heart of the conflict and the center of the country, it seems that a new political formula is being elaborated, a formula whose true shape no one can yet define. Let us hope that it will move toward a reconciliation of unity and diversity, and will finally subordinate might to right.

[5]

the experience of evidence

Language, the Law, and the Mockery of Justice

RANJANA KHANNA

Given that all experience is the experience of a singularity
and thus is the desire to keep this singularity as such, the "as
such" of the singularity, that is, what permits one to keep it as
what it is, this is what effaces it right away. And this wound
or this pain of the effacing in memory itself, in the gathering
up of memory, is wounding, it is a pain reawakened in itself.

—JACQUES DERRIDA,
"Passages—from Traumatism to Promise"

Since they have dared, I too will dare. I will tell the truth, for I
have promised to tell it, if the courts, once regularly appealed
to, did not bring it out fully or entirely. It is my duty to speak;
I will not be an accomplice. My nights would be haunted by
the specter of the innocent.

—EMILE ZOLA, "J'accuse"

ON 8 MARCH 1995, that is, International Women's Day, a mock
trial took place in Ibn Khaldun at a hotel theater in Algiers, near the
offices of the prime minister. Although none of the accused were

My thanks to Martine Delacombre, Mme Fleuri, and the other helpful staff at Institut National de l'Audio Visuel (INA) in Paris; to Tamara Fernando, for her research
on the concept of the mock trial; and to Anne Berger and Srinivas Aravamudan for
comments on earlier versions. This paper was presented at a seminar at the Society
for the Humanities at Cornell University (1998–99); my thanks to the society, the
other fellows, and guests at the seminar (Salah Hassan, Nathalie Melas, Satya Mo-
hanty, and Marie-Claire Vallois) for their helpful comments and lively discussion.

present, Algerian women (for the most part, members of the Algerian Union of Democratic Women—Rassemblement des Femmes Démocrates Algériennes [RAFD]), along with some women from the international feminist community, staged a trial of Abassi Madani and Ali Benhadj, leaders of the outlawed FIS (Islamic Salvation Front); Anwar Haddam and Rabah Kebir, two exiled FIS leaders; the GIA (Armed Islamic Group), a branch of the FIS that has been responsible for the extraordinary level of real and symbolic violence against civilians; and former president of Algeria Chadli Benjedid. All were on trial for crimes against humanity, and Chadli was also charged with killing democracy by legalizing the FIS in 1989. The presiding judge was Leila Asslaoui, a former spokesperson for the government, and minister of national solidarity and the family, whose husband had been brutally killed two days after she resigned. The trial differed from earlier trials: Madani and Belhadj are already serving twelve-year sentences for "acts against the state." This mock trial was championed around the country at rallies calling for women's "right to life." (In Algeria, the expression is associated not with the abortion issue but with the human right to survive).[1]

What was the purpose of the mock trial symbolically held on International Women's Day? What was the purpose of women symbolically but anonymously taking the bench to pass judgment on these political figures? The performance aspect of the trial seems crucial. "Witnesses" gave their testimony on videotape,[2] or their testimony was dramatized, with actors dressed up as ghosts returning to haunt the halls of justice. These were women who had themselves been violated, or who had been widowed, had lost children, and frequently, whose loved ones had been "disappeared." Such "disappearance" affects the ability of the body to be represented.[3] In one sequence, women witnesses were dressed in white and splattered with blood; their faces were made up to look pallid. They spoke primarily in French, and stood up to condemn the torturers on trial, who defended themselves in Arabic. They too wore white, but, as if they were actors in a diabolical simulation of humanity, they had executioners' masks over their faces. The ghostly and pallid women in mourning figured as witnesses and as signs—gaps in language haunted by their desire to be represented and their traumatic relationship to the language and judicial system that had failed to represent them. These were women who had returned from the dead to bear witness to their own deaths for the sake of the living. Conscience could not be erased, and so it continued to manifest itself as a ghost, as a spirit that has both returned from the recent past and that carries with it associations with the war of independence. In that war, perhaps overoptimistically called a "revolution," the homogenization of the people of Algeria by the nationalists failed to take into account the inadequacies of the oppositional revolutionary discourse, which neglected the nation's heterogeneity. The ghost of that revolution hovers above the performance. There seem to be two important issues at stake in the mock trial—first, the use of a French legal model and the French language (the discussion that followed the mock trial was in French); and second, the use of symbolism and performance in the face of violence.

To conduct the trial in both French and Arabic in a country whose judiciary has functioned in Arabic at least since the mid-1980s was to respond to an imposition of Arabic with an act recalling an earlier oppressive cultural, political, and legal regime. Education in classical Arabic[4] and Modern Standard Arabic, rather than in the local popular Arabic that has always been spoken in Algeria, in Tamazight, in other Berber languages, or in French, which was seen as the language imposed by a foreign power and its legal system, has produced generational differences in one's relationship to language. For some, then, the French language, and indeed, the use of the French courtroom model, harks back to the tyranny of colonial rule, which spoke the language of citizens' rights while at the same time imposing on Algeria, an integral part of France from 1848 to 1962, the most complicated history of citizenship in the world, and therefore denying access to the very rights the French had proclaimed to be a basic human need.

What has characterized the violence over the past six years in Algeria, during which between 80,000 and 120,000 people have been murdered, is its spectacular nature. It is as if, then, in the symbolism of the trial itself, this spectacular violence had to be countered with performativity. There have been an extraordinary number of murders and rapes, particularly of intellectuals, journalists, and foreigners, women as well as men: throats have been slit inside mosques, decapitations, mutilations, rapes, and murders have been carried out deliberately in front of family members, including children. Decapitated heads have been thrown into the street through windows after being severed from already dead bodies, or have been placed inside bodies that have been sliced open.[5] Such incidents may bring to mind a people's war (in which the lack of arms against a much greater military force leads people to resort to "terrorism" and "torture"), but, in this case, they are considered by the Islamists in Algeria as acts of a jihad that began during the war of independence and has continued since then.[6] Following the logic of torture, where it is the threat of potential suffering that constitutes the deed, rather than the logic of war, which kills without drawing attention to the suffering, the viciousness of the recent crimes against humanity has instituted a reign of terror. The GIA has set itself up as a combination of a mystical and a military organization that acts on *fatwas*, which, for example, call for the murder of unveiled women or those speaking in French (see Mediene 1996).

The FIS, which has publicly condemned all terrorist activities, whether conducted by the GIA or the state,[7] has nonetheless called for control of women's activities along lines they associate with Islam; it is, however, by no means the only party or political group that has called for restrictions on women's rights.[8] Indeed, between 1978 and 1984 the family code was debated and finally passed by the FLN, the group that had most actively fought for independence and that ruled Algeria officially until 1992, then unofficially and under new guises following the change to a multiparty system in 1988. The FLN's family code reinforced what was constructed as *traditional* Islamic law, which concerned, in particular, women's status and access to the public space.[9] However, it is in the GIA's bulletin, *El Ançate*, which details the *fatwas*, that we find the murdering of women encouraged and assurances that the "terrorists," as they are called in Algeria, will "dine at the table of the prophet." The average life expectancy of a terrorist is, by some accounts, between five and six months.

The economic, social, and political reasons for the rise of fundamentalism in Algeria are beyond the scope of this article. Let me simply say that, when the FIS won the local elections in 1990 and the first round of national elections in 1991, it did so within a corrupt system, which led to a very low turnout for the elections. By contrast, when General Zeroual was elected president in November 1995, the turnout was over 80 percent. The voice of protest against the FIS, then, has been loud and clear even under the threat of violence. That voice, however, has appealed to a repertoire of images stemming from the struggle for independence, ghosts, in fact, that point to the failure of representation, political and linguistic. Zora Flici, who works for the Association for Victims of Terrorism, has spoken of the all-too-familiar pain inflicted by "terror": "We understand this pain, because we've already been through it once, and I think we understand it better than others" (see "Algérie" 1997). But these ghosts, we should add, are not simply a repetition of the past. As Benjamin Stora has written,

> The recurrence of war in Algeria and the repetition of words of war in France do not lead the historian to look for hypothetical "beginnings." The quest for correspondences allows us to see discontinuities, fresh appearances, and discordances. . . . Behind the frequency of vocabulary and old habits still in use, it is necessary to recognize singular silhouettes of new and different practices. (Stora 1995, my translation)

Hence, although it is true that the current discourse of politics and the media in both Algeria and France draws on the vocabulary of religious war and on that of the war of independence, the political scene cannot be understood without some sense of history, and particularly the history of colonial rule in the area—the Ottoman Empire, of course, but even more, the peculiar model of French colonial rule, which made Algeria three departments (administrative units) of France from 1848 to 1962.

Without a doubt, comparisons can be drawn between the oppressive political system of the French bureaucracy and that of the FLN after colonialism. After the rousing statement in the 1964 Algeria Charter that disavowed the colonial administration, some believe, the colonial bureaucrats were simply replaced by Algerian ones. Thus, the current struggle of the FIS is viewed as similar to that of the FLN during the war years. At the end of that war, when Arabic was proclaimed the national language, which at that point seemed to be a positive devaluation of the Gallicization of Algeria under colonial rule, Algeria's nationalism looked like a more resistant secular one, even though the country had proclaimed Islam the national religion. Socialism and Islam, in fact, were bound together in the constitution as complementary means for modernizing Algeria. Parallels have also been drawn between the violence of the French and that of the FIS—in this scenario, it is again national independence that is seen to be at risk. Similarly, the condemnation of the form of violent fundamentalism we see in the GIA, which has now been loudly condemned by the FIS, and of what some claim is the peculiarly Islamic nature of the violence, is seen as an attack on Islam in general, something once more associated with France and with the neocolonialism of the United States (Entelis 1997). And the use of the French language is considered to be a further devaluation of the many languages currently in use in Algeria.

This relationship to the language in which many Algerians are most proficient, raises interesting questions regarding the manner in which testimony can be given, whether legal testimony in a court of law or some other kind of performance—"testimony" without any intention on the listener's part to produce evidence, based on the communication of "what actually happened." The court of law is one place where we call on language to act as if pure referentiality were possible, where the information conveyed through language is supposed to be least ambiguous, and where, as a result of this transparency of language, firm evidence can be given and justice can be served.

Interestingly, in two cases where women organized a collective protest against state torture—in the mock trial I have described, and in Gisèle Halimi and Simone de Beauvoir's committee for Djamila Boupacha, which called for a fair trial on behalf of a victim of torture, the relationship of legal language to referentiality is foregrounded, in a manner that reflects a changing attitude both toward the legal system and toward the French and Arabic languages predominating in Algeria (Beauvoir and Halimi 1962a and b). These cases represent a shift in the concept of the relationship between referentiality and justice, and in that between referentiality and politics. This shift could not have happened without three historical occurrences: the revolution, when a call for independence, glorified since in national memory, intentionally ignored the nuances of the "Algerians" it claimed to represent; the war against civilians in Algeria, from 1993 to the present, which has often worked to destroy memories of political violence;[10] and the changes in international feminism during the decolonization period.

I would like to address three central issues. First, how can transnational feminism be practiced effectively at this time, given the thorny colonial politics during the war and at present? Although decolonization and cultural loyalty have at times led postcolonials to reject international intervention or commentary (as Boupacha herself did, though she may have been manipulated by the FLN),[11] more recently, some feminists in Algeria have called for both feminist activism in the Arab world (thereby avoiding some of the significant problems of modern colonialist interactions with the First World) and outside it.[12] This means considering some of the work that seems to have been effective, at least in bourgeois circles, perhaps the only arena where women can take advantage of what the law has to offer while simultaneously questioning its very ability to provide justice.[13] Second, what is the relationship between language, justice, and the law, and in what way might the mock trial constitute a recourse to justice? This involves analyzing the differences and similarities between designation and arbitration—terms that are often used interchangeably within the context of representation. And third, how does the politics of language in contemporary Algeria intersect the other two concerns? The first two questions appear to lead in opposite directions: the practice of transnational feminism is a pragmatic problem, the relationship between language, justice, and the law is, in my analysis, a philosophical question that contains a tension within itself, between a messianic and pragmatic understanding of justice. In making the claim that French is at this point (and possibly only at this point) the only language in which recourse to justice is possible, I do not want to reify any of the other languages at issue. Obviously, at one level, the pragmatic and pertinent appeals, such as Hélie-Lucas has made, to other feminists in the Arab world, presumably, in Arabic, may pose a vehement challenge to this claim and with some justification, since, at a pragmatic level, justice sometimes seems to be served, the guilty are sometimes convicted and the innocent acquitted, and this may occur in principle in any language, whether or not one is against the politics associated with that language. Similarly, as Amilcar Cabral has argued, on the borders of political centers, resistant cultures may emerge that embody cultural counterhegemonies (see Cabral 1970). In making this bold claim about the status of French in the mock trial, I do not want to suggest that any language can rid itself of its colonial history, though it may become a quite different language in another context. I also do not want to posit *justice* as something pure and accessible within the French language. Rather, in my analysis, access to justice is *virtual* and is enunciated in a language haunted by the specters of colonialism. The notion of *virtual justice* I want to formulate describes simultaneously the possibility of justice and the mockery of that very concept.

To use the term of my analysis of Simone de Beauvoir, my argument functions metonymically to represent this moment of transna-

tional feminism, and, inasmuch as it takes the law and justice as its
themes, it establishes its transnational connections along fairly bourgeois lines. Like Djamila Boupacha, who went on to become a
spokesperson for women's causes in Algeria, the women who participated in the mock trial were not subalterns, but they nonetheless
performed the very problem of women's representation (and perhaps,
by extension, of representation more generally, which happens to be
foregrounded in discussions about transnational feminism) (see Halimi 1978; Lippert 1987, 209–32). The political work performed by the
mock trial, and understood through the concept of a haunted virtual
justice, causes a rupture in the conventional notion of public space,
which we may associate with justice and the law, and places the concept of repression at its very heart.[14]

A brief consideration of the changes in the politics of language and
of the legal system in Algeria will allow us to understand how these
linguistic ghosts now manifest themselves, and how ghosts may paradoxically be the only recourse available to what we are calling "virtual justice." Since Algeria's first constitution went into effect in
1963, language as a nationalist issue has been at the forefront of juridical consciousness in that country. At that time, Arabic was supposed to supplant French as the language of the nation, even though
government work continued to be conducted largely in French, and,
for all practical purposes, Algerian elites (the politicians, the upper
class, and the intelligentsia) remained bilingual. Which Arabic? And
what of the languages other than French and colloquial Arabic that
circulated in the Algerian state? What of Tamazight and other Berber
languages, which are spoken by a large portion of the population? The
power of language was recognized not only as a force of potential national cohesion, but also as a force of law, and alternative control.
The language named in the 1963 constitution was classical Arabic,
and no mention of Tamazight or any Maghrebian dialects was made.
As part of Ben Bella's promise of "education for all," Modern Standard Arabic was the language of school instruction. Although some
efforts were made to employ teachers to assist in the transition, these
were rather weak. After a lull in the enforcement of Arabization in
the 1970s, the mid-1980s saw a massive resurgence, and the judiciary
system was Arabized in 1986.[15] From that moment on, and particularly since December 1990, what had been an unenforced, and unsuccessful, statute of the constitution became an occasion for violent
civil unrest.[16] Not only has freedom of speech been effectively oblit-
erated in Algeria with murders of tens of thousands of civilians, a

large number of whom were from elite or bourgeois backgrounds, writers, journalists and feminist activists who often worked and spoke in French. In addition, Arabic is also achieving the status that French once had in the region—the language of power designed to obliterate local cultures, often for corrupt political ends. The recent establishment of English as Algeria's second language is further evidence of the attempt to demote French, ending its literary, political, and legal hold over the Algerian imaginary. As John Entelis (1981) remarked, "the government's official policy of Arabization, Algerianization and Islamization gives additional expressive and symbolic meaning to Arabic language used by all concerned."[17]

The idea that occasioned the change of national language may be too obvious to repeat here. The politics of language had become an urgent issue in Algeria with the institution of a language policy in colonial education. Under French colonialism, the rationale for teaching French was articulated quite differently than the rationale for teaching English under British colonialism. The British in India, for example, did not demonstrate any particular desire to assimilate the natives of India culturally or linguistically, and seemed content to enforce power without hegemony. Famously, Thomas Macaulay's minute called for the education, in the most British manner, of an elite who would mediate between the British ruling class and the people, with their various local cultures and languages. In that way, British economic and political goals could be more effectively achieved.[18]

In the case of Algeria, however, the policy of assimilation dictated that, in principle, the French language be taught to all inhabitants of Algeria, which, after 1848, became three departments of France (see Betts 1961; Ageron 1991). According to some, however, what occurred was the gradual destruction of Algerians' literacy in any language (Lazreg 1994). At independence, an astonishing 80–90 percent of Algerians were illiterate, as a result, some say, of the systematic eradication, during the first forty years of French rule (1830–70), of local schools teaching Arabic. Gradually, the difficulties of establishing a French colonial education system produced a lack of infrastructure for effectively teaching French, a lack that belied the claim to carry out the *mission civilisatrice*. From 1870 to World War I, France established and consolidated its schools and its economic and political hold. That hold would be vigorously challenged in the postwar period, with the reestablishment of local schools.

The drive to educate that came with the early colonial policy of as-

similation was justified by French scientific studies of the region,
which had developed from the same roots as those policies. The need
to educate in the French system was articulated as early as 1831 by
the Institut National de France, and Pierre Genty de Bussy quickly
established three schools for Europeans in his first months in office
as chief governmental representative in Algiers. Discouraged by
France in his effort to establish a French school in a mosque in Algiers, he quickly established Arab-French schools, which were initially bilingual in instruction. Their numbers, however, diminished
drastically after 1870. Thus, although integration seemed a possibility at one time, this effort quickly foundered for lack of funding and
because the policy of secularized education was interpreted to mean
that French instruction should be established in the schools. Far
fewer women than men were educated in the colonial system. The
colonial endeavor did not merely reinforce educational differences
among boys and girls, it actively shaped them, and placed new pressures on social gender dynamics. Without the resource of a colonial
education or of indigenous schooling, women became increasingly
unskilled. And the French colonizers frequently attributed this
deskilling to "Islamic tradition" rather than to the particular dynamics of the political context. Although pockets of cultural resistance
still formed, they were largely invisible to the center and thus were
only partially effective in offering a challenge to it (see Lazreg 1994;
Cabral 1970).

The status of spoken language, then, was inextricably bound up
with the status of the colonial regime, and its political, military, and
juridical power and abuse of power. Indeed, even some religious practices, despite the status of the language of scripture, were recast in
Catholic French. This was a result of both the education system and
of the legal system. Both British and French colonial law had to deal
with local legal systems in their colonies, the legacy of which continues today. In India, for example, separate local courts dealt with family law, whereas criminal law was administered by the state.[19] Even
the Shari'a, in its various local forms, transmitted orally, put particular pressures on colonial legal systems. In Algeria, some efforts were
initially made to maintain the local legal system with its accompanying law schools (which were in the mosques), to avoid disturbing
the system and thereby giving rise to insurgency. Even though the
schools were initially maintained, however, the status of the law
changed considerably. Local variations of Islamic law were subsumed

under a more centralized system that began to resemble the system more familiar in France. Some have even called the system a "romanized . . . qadi justice" (Christelow 1985, 8–9). The Shari'a became a highly codified written law associated not only with the state but with divine law. The peculiarity of the relationship to codified French law actually led to the replacement of a two-tiered concept of law (the Shari'a and divine law) with another two-tiered concept (Islamic law and French law), which effectively forged a stronger relationship between the Shari'a and divine law, blurring the distinction between the two, which has had serious consequences for contemporary Algeria. In addition to recourses to the newly codified Shari'a, appeals could always be made to the "higher court"—the French court. Thus, not only did the nature of local law change, in ways that secularized it and in others did the opposite; the law was also formalized and subordinated to French law. In the 1880s, an effort was made to remove the local courts entirely and put both French law and Muslim law in the hands of French judges, but this met with great resistance, and the French were obliged to back down. After 1919, in rare cases when an Algerian was eligible for citizenship, he had to renounce the Shari'a.

The clash between the two legal codes had many consequences including, for women, impoverishment. For example, they were no longer awarded alimony by the Muslim court in case of divorce; and, in the nineteenth century, changes in the land tenure system often meant that property negotiations were conducted by the head of the family with the colonial masters, to the detriment of women's interests.

Although, in retrospect, it is possible to identify a history of resistance and insurgency against the French language and the civil code, the power of those codes persists in postindependence Algeria. The status of the French language during the colonial period had become sufficiently normalized, that is, sufficiently hegemonized, to make it a desirable acquisition, even though, for many people, it did not seem to be their own language. That is, it was not a mother tongue.[20] For our purposes, a mother tongue is one in which we believe we can represent ourselves linguistically, and even psychologically, politically, religiously, and legally as well.

It is exactly these complications in representability that arise in Halimi and de Beauvoir's committee for Djamila Boupacha.[21] In 1960, Gisèle Halimi asked Simone de Beauvoir to assist her in publicizing, in France, the case of one Djamila Boupacha, a young woman who had been tortured by French police officers in Algiers to extract information (that is, testimony) about those involved in "terrorist" activities during the war of independence (1954–62). Halimi (Djamila's lawyer, of Tunisian descent), and de Beauvoir had a central aim: to achieve full legal representation for Djamila in a court of law in the French metropolis. Despite the fact that it was the law that had brutally tortured this woman—and rationalized it in the name of justice (as information retrieval needed to counteract "terrorist" activities planned by the FLN and ALN)—these women embraced the law as an instrument of adjudication.

In 1961, de Beauvoir and Halimi decided to compile a book about Djamila Boupacha, then a political prisoner. Most of the book was written by Halimi, who describes her encounters with Djamila, and recounts, in narrative form, her first contact with the case and the trajectory it followed. Halimi's text is incomplete but it takes us up to Djamila's hearing. The remainder of the book consists of an introduction by de Beauvoir, her article from *Le Monde*, testimony by Djamila's father regarding the events leading up to Djamila's arrest and to his own, and their subsequent torture at the hands of the French military forces. It also includes Djamila's civil indictment, various "testimonies," articles written by French intellectuals concerning torture in Algeria by French forces, drawings of Djamila by Pablo Picasso and Robert Lapoujade, and a painting by Roberto Matta.

The book was compiled by Halimi and de Beauvoir as a document for the Djamila Boupacha Committee, which was headed by de Beauvoir at Halimi's request, and was formed to introduce Djamila's torture, her private suffering, into Parisian public discourse. Although the function of the committee was ostensibly to bring the case to a court in the French metropolis, the torturers were ultimately granted amnesty. The English translation of the book begins with a statement that might have been obvious to French readers, but came into effect after the book's publication in France:

> Since this book was completed, the Evian agreement has come into force. It was signed on the 18th March, 1962 and on the 20th an amnesty was declared for all Moslem political prisoners, to take effect between 18th March and 8th April.

Djamila's family were consequently released in early April, and Djamila herself on 21st April, but under the terms of the amnesty her torturers also gain immunity. No further action will be taken against her for her activities in support of the FLN, but she will be unable to proceed with her case against General Ailleret or the Minister of War. Nor will she be able to take further steps to bring her torturers to justice. (Quoted in de Beauvoir and Halimi 1962b, 7)

In a sense, then, the book presented itself as the only recourse to justice, given the impossibility of legal recourse. The book granted justice *virtually*, as a record that haunts the manipulation of the language of law, and as a text that moved beyond the apparent referentiality of that language. This pressure of the virtual foregrounds both the force of circumstance and the very impossibility of succumbing to that force when considering justice. Against the impossibility of law, we see justice maintained as an impossible yet discernible ethics.

De Beauvoir agreed to head the committee and to have her name appear on the book, primarily so that she would share responsibility with Halimi were there to be any legal repercussions. Although the book was her idea, she refrained from contributing very much, and we are obliged to turn to *Force of Circumstance* (1965), the third volume of her autobiography, and to her letters to Nelson Algren (de Beauvoir 1998), to get her impressions of the event.[22] The purpose of the project is to appeal to metropolitan French citizens to save themselves from the disease of apathy and from the normalization of a corrupt and "infected" legal and governmental system. The call for a fair trial is, in a way, a medical call—a call to heal the psychological illness of the French people and a sick legal system that was failing to represent Algerians (both in the sense of allowing them to speak and to be heard, and in the sense of giving them legal representation).

For de Beauvoir, the work for the Boupacha committee satisfied another need as well. She needed to find a way to do something for the Algerian cause that was quite different from what Jean-Paul Sartre was doing. She writes: "I wanted to stop being an accomplice in this war, but how? I could talk in meetings or write articles; but I would only have been saying the same things as Sartre less well than he was saying them. I would have felt ridiculous following him like a shadow" (de Beauvoir 1965, 382).

She also wanted to continue her work on women, demonstrating that there was such a thing as gendered violence, whose repercussions on women were often less visible. She was, in this regard, taking a double stand against Albert Camus, who had not only disappointed her in his war efforts, but had also trivialized her feminist work. He had dismissed *The Second Sex,* she tells us, "in a few morose sentences," accusing her "of making the French male look ridiculous" (de Beauvoir 1965, 200).

Camus, of course, was equally disparaging of Sartre's efforts during the Algerian war, accusing him of adopting a naive attitude, as if a simple condemnation of colonialism in grand terms addressed the particular difficulties of any nation undergoing decolonization (Camus 1960).[23] Camus's unwillingness to condemn his fellow French colons came from his feeling that it had always been the French of the metropolis who stood to gain the most from the colonial enterprise in Algeria, in contrast to the relatively less wealthy colons. It was easy, in his estimation, for someone like Sartre to condemn the colons and the colonial army's actions in Algeria, and indeed, Camus also condemned the violence on both sides. But perhaps Camus saw Sartre and de Beauvoir as two people who were making up for their lack of sustained activity in the French Resistance during World War II. And Camus too was (wrongfully) accused of inaction during the Algerian war.

De Beauvoir's language actively works to resist any connection made by the French to World War II and the Vichy period, condemning those who rationalized torture as a disease. When de Beauvoir, Germaine Tillion, and other members of the Boupacha committee went to request that Djamila's case be tried in France, Edmond Michelet, the minister of justice, used the disease metaphor to describe the army in Algeria, an interesting analogy, given that many of the perpetrators of violence were doctors, who were on hand to keep patients alive and to administer the torture (Fanon 1965, 121–47; de Beauvoir and Halimi 1962b): "It's terrible, this gangrene the Nazis have bequeathed to us. It infects everything, it rots everything, we simply aren't able to root it out. Roughing up is one thing—you can't have a police force without it; but torture! . . . I try to make them understand; the line must be drawn somewhere. . . . It's a gangrene. . . . Fortunately it will all be over soon" (quoted in de Beauvoir 1965, 515–16).

Similarly, M. Patin, the head of the Committee of Public Safety, speaks of "a canker in our midst," adding with relief that Djamila was raped vaginally with a bottle and not penetrated "per anum," as was the practice in Indochina (quoted in de Beauvoir and Halimi 1962b, 14).

De Beauvoir, however, does not allow this "disease" to serve as an excuse, as if there were no agency involved in enacting violence, and as if torture were something distant, a Nazi tropical frenzy, in which those in the Hexagon had no complicity. She brings the sickness back home, expressing both her disgust at her compatriots, and even at herself, speaking of a "tetanus of the imagination," which she feels on looking again at the documented descriptions of torture. At the time (in 1957), she said, she wished simply to push aside the vivid description in disgust (de Beauvoir 1965, 379).

By the time de Beauvoir wrote the article for *Le Monde* in 1960, however, her style had changed. Reproaching the French public for their complacency, she transferred the "gangrenous" torturous mentality inherited from the Nazis back onto the inhabitants of metropolitan France, to show that the tetanus of the imagination was also inherited and had persisted since the time of the Nazi occupation. The sickness of complacency becomes iconic—a threatening metaphor of the memories of occupied Paris, rather than a rationalizing displacement. She now framed it as a scandalous abdication of responsibility.

In his introduction to Henri Alleg's *La question*, Sartre speaks of the "annihilation of the colonized." He continues: "We have wiped out their civilization while refusing them our own. For most Europeans in Algeria, there are two complementary and inseparable truths: the colonists are backed by divine right, the natives are subhuman" (Sartre 1958, 31–32). This internalized divine right, which, according to Sartre's logic, leads to a lack of humane treatment on the part of the French, can also be seen in the report of the Committee of Public Safety. De Beauvoir cites the article in *Le Monde* in *Force of Circumstance*: "Acts which in other times and in normal circumstances might appear exorbitant are perfectly legal in Algeria" (de Beauvoir 1965, 392). She remarks with horror that "this narrative— [related in the case against Ben Saddock] of hangings, beatings, torture—was read out in stony silence; not one gasp of surprise or disgust: everyone knew already. My heart froze inside me as I once again faced the truth: everyone knew and didn't give a damn, or else approved" (de Beauvoir 1965, 393).

It is this shocking complacency that de Beauvoir seeks to address in her article in *Le Monde* on 3 June 1960. It begins, "the most scandalous aspect of any scandal is that one gets used to it," and concludes, "such an abdication of responsibility would be a betrayal of France as a whole, of you, of me, of each and every one of us" (de Beauvoir and Halimi 1962b, 197). She paints a picture of a France that has already lost control of its army in Algiers, reports that Djamila herself cried out while being tortured that de Gaulle had outlawed torture. In response to Djamila's plea, the army officer responded: "De Gaulle can call the odds back home but we are masters here" (de Beauvoir and Halimi 1962b, 197).

Between this threatening vision of an army run amok and a French people indifferent to the tortures being meted out in its name, we read a vivid description—which we later learn was taken from the text of Djamila's civil indictment—of the torture perpetrated on her body: she was illegally imprisoned in a detention center where she should not have been held, was kicked in the chest by a group of soldiers, and had a rib permanently displaced; she had electrodes affixed with transparent tape to her nipples, legs, face, anus, and vagina, and was given electrical shocks; she was burned with cigarettes; and she was "deflowered" with a beer bottle. De Beauvoir includes the voices of the victim and of the assailants at this point, as if her own words cannot do justice to the horror: "Several days later the men interrogating her said: 'You won't be raped, you might enjoy it.' Djamila Boupacha herself states what in fact took place: 'I was given the most appalling torture of all, the so-called "bottle treatment." First they tied me up in a special posture, and then they rammed the neck of a bottle into my belly. I screamed and fainted. I was unconscious for the best of my knowledge for two days.'" De Beauvoir adds in parenthesis: "She was a virgin" (de Beauvoir and Halimi 1962b, 195).

De Beauvoir leaves out one of the tortures described by Djamila, "the bath treatment," where the victim was "trussed up and hung over a bath on a stick, and submerged until (she) nearly choke(d)" (de Beauvoir and Halimi 1962b, 191). At the request of M. Gauthier from *Le Monde*, de Beauvoir reluctantly replaced the word "vagina" with "belly" but would not omit the statement regarding Djamila's virginity.[24] De Beauvoir alludes to, but does not describe, the tortures experienced by Djamila's father and brother-in-law. Halimi, in her narration of the case and of her experiences as Djamila's lawyer, speaks extensively of the water-hose torture, where the victim is filled with water by placing a water hose in the mouth and is then jumped on so that water is expelled through the orifices.

Vivid depictions of torture abound in this book, and the exactness of the legal language, which entails a precise description of the instrument of torture, becomes a necessary means for representing pain, as if, in fact, this description of the instruments conveyed the pain. The internal pain and humiliation of the rape is the only torture that is represented by speechlessness—by a literal loss of consciousness, which points to an epistemic and cultural gap, whereby a particular type of sexual violence cannot be articulated in a description of the instrument of torture. Language describing pain will always be inadequate because pain is characterized by its irreducibility to language. In a courtroom, the victim is asked to recognize instruments of torture. Household items such as bottles or water hoses, or more specifically engineered instruments, were introduced as evidence. If the victim recognized their function, they became indexes of her pain. The attempt to describe pain through such indexes restores language to the victim, but fails to represent pain. It is language that is undone through pain, or, in Elaine Scarry's terms (1985), unmade. Articulating pain in the language of courtroom testimony gives it shape or structure. It fails, however, to acknowledge the undoing caused by the infliction of pain. World War II changed the nature of war by introducing the possibility of absolute genocide through the creation of atomic fission: this was genocide without index, and the inverse of the "people's war", being waged in Algeria.

The possibility of complete annihilation, and the failure of political and legal representation, or indeed, the failure to recognize that Algeria and France were at war, produced in Algeria what Sartre called a "people's war," a new form of war that emerged in the colonies following World War II. In some ways, this was a civil war—or, to use a term employed for the current unrest in Algeria, *a war against civilians*—and the only strategies that could be used, given the lack of arms, were "terrorism, ambushes and harassing the enemy" (Sartre 1968, 65; Limqueco, Weiss et al. 1971, 350–64). The form of justice employed, then—torture as trial—assumed that a war was not taking place. (That the French also employed terrorist tactics against civilians is a point, of course, not without its contradictions.)

In her article in *Le Monde*, de Beauvoir depicts Djamila's case as unexceptional in itself. She was arrested, along with her father and brother-in-law, in her home in Algiers. It is alleged that she planted a

bomb in a university canteen, which was defused before it could ex-
plode. Boupacha admitted she was a militant FLN activist, but did
not admit planting the bomb until she was illegally detained and
cruelly tortured, at which point she confessed. When she did so, however, she also confessed to crimes for which other people had been
imprisoned and executed. In this confession, she recognized herself
as a symbol for the humiliated French military—a woman who had
fooled them to advance the independence struggle through whatever
means necessary, an Algerian to whom they could attribute military
action. For the French army in Algiers, then, she became a metonymy for "terrorist" activity—a substitutable signifier of the threat to
the French public—whether she committed the crime or not, she admitted to being a militant FLN member, which means that she might
commit a crime of this sort and could therefore be condemned on
suspicion.

What betrayed her, then, was not so much the "information" she
agreed to give under torture, than her symbolic and rhetorical position. It is true that the demand for information points, like that of
testimony, to a referential use of language. For the type of information requested and delivered in court (or in police chambers) is supposed to establish facts, to produce and support material evidence,
not to refer one back to something as allegedly subjective as "experience." Yet, confession, in this case, is obviously proof of nothing
other than the pain inflicted through torture.

In *The Body in Pain: The Making and Unmaking of the World*
(1985), Elaine Scarry speaks of the language of the body being tortured and enduring war. She refers to the separate spheres that the
sufferer and the witness occupy, suggesting that "to have great pain is
to have certainty; to hear that another is in pain is to have doubt" (7).
The imprecision of the language of pain, the difficulty of articulating
the intensity and mechanisms of pain, cause the sufferer and the witness to resort quickly to analogy—"it feels like"—and, in the case of
torture, the victim often describes the instruments and the physical
marks as a means not only to describe the pain but also to externalize
it. For the witness to that pain, or for the jury that hears the account
of that pain as testimony, the mechanism works quite differently. For
the legal discourse of the courtroom, where proof is the central concern, the mechanism of suffering indeed has to be testified to through
external signifiers. Halimi writes that she is anxious for Djamila's
case to be tried before the electrode burns have faded from her skin.

Similarly, the officials who verified the evidence needed to be sure that she recognized the *gégène*, one of the instruments of torture; they almost cruelly insisted that Djamila identify the instrument, the sight of which caused her terror, as if she were identifying the perpetrator of the violence, as if, indeed, the instrument itself had agency. The witness, then, always doubts, precisely because the pain itself cannot be communicated.

In Scarry's terms, the externalization of pain through language can be a mode of human making that documents the process of unmaking (the infliction of pain), and it can also be a means by which an analogy is produced for the benefit of the witness. For Michelet, who speaks of a gangrene overtaking the army in Algiers, the metaphor of physical incapacitation is displaced from Djamila to the army, through an invocation of Nazi-occupied Paris. Camus, who in 1955 had proposed a "civil truce" in response to the despair he felt at the slaughter of the French in his homeland of Algeria, called for attacks on civilians on both sides to be outlawed (Maran 1989, 163; Camus 1960). In war, then, according to Camus, civilians on either side of the conflict can be substituted for one another. Sartre, of course, would take issue with this idea: the people's war leads to certain kinds of combat that become necessary in the face of the threat of genocide. To focus on civilians is to suggest their lack of agency in a violent war. Each victim, then, is generalized: the immediate conflict is set aside and the victim becomes a synecdoche for all "innocent" victims of war. Camus's own sense of the horror of occupied countries, so vividly described in *La peste*, on this occasion leads him to see an equivalence between the two sides of this war, a view that was to lead to his split with de Beauvoir's and Sartre's circle, who were adamant that the FLN be supported in their struggle for independence. In spite of his support for the FLN, Sartre recognized the complex human rights issues confronting the French at this time, while also acknowledging the importance of supporting the victims:[25] "Appalled, the French are discovering this terrible truth: that if nothing can protect a nation against itself, neither its traditions nor its loyalties nor its laws . . . then its behavior is no more than a matter of opportunity and occasion. Anybody, at any time, may equally find himself victim or executioner" (Sartre 1958, 14–15).

This crisis of humanism is taken up quite differently in de Beauvoir's work. All French people, according to de Beauvoir, are guilty of complacency unless they speak out against the torture of Algerians.

All French people are guilty if they fail to acknowledge that, for Algerians such as Djamila, her father, and her brother-in-law, speaking out against their torture is practically impossible unless they have the *public* support of a Parisian lawyer. Djamila refuses to speak when her lawyer is not present, perhaps realizing that the eloquence of her silence will protect her more than words ever could, or perhaps because she has little access to her own pain, a possibility that seems to be compounded by her loss of consciousness for an astonishing two days. The loss of consciousness enacts a traumatic and illocutionary breakdown of the access to pain at the moment it occurred, and for as long as the trauma remains traumatic. "She would stay mute," Halimi informs us (de Beauvoir and Halimi 1962b, 81). But the refusal to speak also suggests something else, which may undo Scarry's opposition between the victim's and the witness's access to pain. Although Scarry quite pragmatically advocates a linguistic code for measuring the unmeasurable—that is, for expressing the types and degrees of pain, she assumes that victims always have access to their own pain and fully understand it. Work in trauma studies, whether it draws on psychoanalysis or on the psychological works of Pierre Janet, has taught us something quite different, however. Pain, especially when it is traumatic, cannot always be expressed, is not always known, and is likely to produce faulty memory and flawed testimony that differ from what we may discover actually occurred.[26] This is certainly difficult to take into account in the courtroom, which is why de Beauvoir insists that all French people are guilty if they fail to recognize how the French military and governing bodies in Algeria make the political representation of Algerians very difficult. Gisèle Halimi, for example, was on many occasions denied the proper visas allowing her to stay in Algiers so that she could gather information, prepare her case, and represent Djamila. Djamila's words betrayed her—in torture, she confessed. In other words, the mechanisms of war—acts of violence, which, according to Scarry, rely on injury but deny the rhetoric of injury in favor of the rhetoric of strategy and politics, generally understood to exist in the realm of public discourse—force us to understand the torture of Algerians simply as a part of the rhetoric of "information gathering" so important to war strategy. However, for Algerians, torture, although occurring in the public context of war, is, through the enforcement of silence and the threat of more torture, confined to a private sphere of suffering; this is the psychological consequence of a "people's war."

Instruments of torture and marks on bodies cannot bring about the articulation and externalization necessary for the public discourse of law on a victim's private pain and suffering. As Simone de Beauvoir says, "the exceptional thing about the Boupacha case is not the nature of the facts involved, but their publication" (1962b, 10). Indeed, exactly for this reason, Halimi's narrative of Djamila's torture and of her own experiences as her legal representative slips between the registers of the discourse of personal exchange and that of information extraction for the purpose of public testimony. The personal trauma of the young Muslim girl who lost her virginity (described by Halimi as "a kind of amputation") indeed intrudes into Halimi's narrative (de Beauvoir and Halimi 1962b, 75). And yet, there is no room for personal trauma in the public discourse of the courtroom. For the French, however, the personal humiliation they feel because Djamila has dressed in a coquettish manner, like an *évoluée* who wears European clothes, does have a place within public discourse. Their humiliation is in itself attributed to an act of violation on her part (de Beauvoir and Halimi 1962b, 84).

For Djamila Boupacha, speaking about the signifiers of torture—its instruments and its marks on her body—becomes a means to externalize her own pain and to transmit the private discourse of torture as the public discourse of war, through her lawyer, Gisèle Halimi. Without her, and without her legal expertise in the specific context of the discourses circulating about the Algerian war, Djamila's creation of terms to designate her pain—her description of her "unmaking"— would remain within the realm of the private. For Djamila, torture becomes a metaphor for her existence—she externalizes what is specifically internal—pain through the instruments that threaten to unmake her again if her speech is found to be inappropriate by the French military. For her, torture becomes iconic. Halimi's narrative account of Djamila's case demonstrates the means to measure silences. For her, the language of torture has to gain credence within the public realm of the courtroom. As Scarry says, "under the pressure of this requirement, the lawyer, too, becomes an inventor of language, one who speaks on behalf of another person (the plaintiff) and attempts to communicate the reality of that person's physical pain to people who are not themselves in pain (the jurors)" (Scarry 1985, 10). Halimi's testimony must demonstrate the deliberate and systematic attempt to silence the whole affair, by showing the mechanisms of corruption. In that sense, the instruments of pain, and indeed

Djamila herself, have to become, in the courtroom, metonymies (indexes) for the system of corruption. They are therefore brought into the public discourse of a corrupt war—a war in which even militants have their agency stolen from them by torture and the discourses surrounding it.

To make her feminist intervention (though it is not articulated as such), de Beauvoir has to use a different form of influence, which makes her use of metonymy and metaphor quite different from that of Halimi, Boupacha, and indeed, from Michelet, Patin, Camus, and Sartre. To cure the French public of this "tetanus" of the imagination, she must make Djamila an unexceptional figure—a metonymy for the suffering of Algerians. "The most scandalous aspect of any scandal is that one gets used to it" (de Beauvoir and Halimi 1962b, 194). Here is yet another case of torture. De Beauvoir must also make an appeal to France's humanity: "Such an abdication of responsibility would be a betrayal of France as a whole, of you, of me, of each and everyone of us" (de Beauvoir and Halimi 1962b, 197). Djamila's case here becomes a metaphor for the "unmaking" of France. It also draws on another unmaking—the memory of a previous "unmaking" of Paris under the Occupation. It draws, in fact, on that iconic anxiety— the gangrenous violence inherited from the Germans to which Michelet refers. De Beauvoir also individualizes Boupacha, citing her testimony—giving her a voice—but not leaving her with the impossible task of speaking alone. She thus recognizes the impossibility of both linguistic and legal representation. The worst torture for Djamila was her "deflowering" with the bottle. The pain externalized through the description and cited in de Beauvoir's article is characterized as an outrage. The private horror of pain lives through de Beauvoir's article, which places the private discourse of torture at the very heart of the public discourse of war. Her work stands in sharp contrast to Sartre's work on torture during this period, because what we see in that case is a highly virilized discourse of combat, "the torturer pits himself against the tortured for his 'manhood' and the duel is fought as if it were not possible for both sides to belong to the human race" (Sartre 1958, 23). He pays very little attention to the silences—the unspoken and perhaps unspeakable, trauma and pain of the victim,—which de Beauvoir carefully describes in a manner that is empathetic but also very conscious of the function of her own writing and of Boupacha's political commitment, which enables the generally tough-minded Boupacha to emerge as something more than a victim, but as traumatized nonetheless. What we begin to hear in Boupacha's language, and the manner in which it is represented by de Beauvoir, is the emergence of phantoms that foreground the unspeakable and that acknowledge that, although the pragmatic language of the courtroom (or indeed of the code Scarry calls for) may be necessary, it also performs a demetaphorization of language. The language of law assumes that justice can be fully done, that the phantoms emerging from one's own repression and those that remain in one's language from the generations of colonial violence could be laid to rest by a verdict, or that the work of healing can begin after the judgment. "The fantasy of incorporation reveals a gap within the psyche; it points to something that is missing just where introjection should have occurred" (Abraham and Torok 1994, 127).

The Djamila Boupacha committee, whose most vocal members were women, allowed de Beauvoir to make a transnational feminist gesture that demonstrated the importance of a discourse using both the indexical and the iconic, and the necessity of understanding the performative context of discourse. This gesture had a specifically pedagogical aim: to save the French from themselves. The performativity of both legal and journalistic writing, under the guise of absolute transparency and with a belief in that transparency, makes possible a strong political gesture in the face of a crisis. De Beauvoir is also attentive to the particular problems of violent sexual behavior that accompany a military conflict, behavior that is, at worst, exacerbated, and, at best, ignored, by a conception of torture as a battle for masculinity.[27]

What is interesting is that, in spite of de Beauvoir's commitment to the Algerian cause, there is very little evidence in the text of her overall view of Algeria. She confines her remarks to the case at hand, the horror of a war crime performed in France's name. Her aim is to "prevent the crime of silence," to cite the title of another attempt at virtual justice (Limqueco, Weiss, et al. 1971), the reports of the Russell War Crimes Tribunal for Vietnam (in which Sartre, de Beauvoir, and Halimi played an active part). She also aims to acknowledge and be sensitive to the form of that silence and the failure of language, which, in the legal context, is understood to be merely referential. The particular problems of making the courtroom a viable place for Algerians seeking justice (these problems have been recently documented in Jean-Marc Théolleyre's *Juger en Algérie 1944–1962* [1997]), require that the ghosts from World War II that de Beauvoir invokes be included, and indeed, that they bear witness. These ghosts challenge the language of justice and empowerment and establish the inability to represent.

Camus, speaking of the need for justice, for a condemnation of terrorist and other violent activities in Algeria during the war, and for a civil truce, criticized those who reproached the French nation by "endlessly going back to the errors of the past." "It is dangerous," he wrote, "to expect that a nation will confess that it alone is guilty and condemn it to perpetual penance. . . . Problems must be seen in relation to the future" (Camus 1960, 120). Of course, we will never know what would have happened had there been no violent uprising in Algeria, in which 100,000 Frenchmen and approximately 1,250,000 Algerians were killed. We will never know whether the French would have continued to hold on to a colony that was not financially lucrative, and Camus to some extent acknowledged this. His "Appeal for a Civilian Truce" offered concrete plans for a future that would acknowledge that the age of colonialism had passed; his inability to consider that the two sides were unequal placed him firmly, as he himself says, on an ethical ground that is not political and cannot really take into account the political situation. His ethical quandary transcends but also falls short of the task of dealing with the political context. In fact, his language transcends the referential. Consider Camus's comments on the relationship between ethics, politics, and justice:

> Such a spirit of equity, to be sure, seems alien to the reality of our history, in which relationships of force outline another sort of justice; in our international society there is no good ethical system except a *nuclear ethics*. Then the only guilty one is the vanquished. It is understandable that many intellectuals have consequently come to the conclusion that *values and words derive their meaning altogether from force*. Hence some people progress without transition from the *fait accompli* or the cruelest party. I continue, however, to believe with regard to Algeria and to everything else, that such aberrations, both on the Right and on the Left, merely define the nihilism of our epoch. If it is true that in history, at least, values—whether those of the nation or those of humanity—do not survive unless they have been fought for, the fight is not enough to justify them. The fight itself must rather be justified, and elucidated, by

those values. When fighting for your truth, you must take care
not to kill it with the very arms you are using to defend it—
*only under such a double condition do words resume their liv-
ing meaning*. Knowing that, the intellectual has the role of distinguishing in each camp the respective limits of force and
justice. The role is to clarify definitions in order to disintoxi-
cate minds and to calm fanaticisms, even when this is against
the current tendency. (Camus 1960, 120–21, my emphasis,
with the exception of "fait accompli")

A purely referential language, stripped bare of any *living meaning*,
is a language that responds to the loss of meaning—nuclear holocaust—by undoing its very potential. Through total annihilation, language's referential function is of course destroyed. But countering
this with a kind of absolute referentiality, a language stripped bare, is
another form of annihilation that makes of language a law of absolute
referentiality. The *nuclear death* of language as meaning is thus
countered by another form of killing, making language exist in a very
limited sense, as if direct communication were possible, as if, in effect, language could be transparent and could simply denote. Justice,
understood as only virtually available, is possible only with a living
language that produces meaning because it is haunted, but which is
not simply referential. If we contrast this to Sartre's comments on the
"people's war" (from his essay "On Genocide," presented at the Russell War Tribunal as a commentary on Algeria), we find that, for him,
the people's war is the flip side of a nuclear ethics in which meaning
is lost. "Terrorism, ambushes and harassing the enemy" (Sartre 1968,
65) are, in a way, justified politically in Sartre's argument (and perhaps in my own); Camus, however, believes that language can live
again only through an ethical position that he believes "can spare
useless bloodshed . . . in the solutions that guarantee the future of a
land whose suffering [he shares] too much to be able to indulge in
speech making about it" (Camus 1960, 112). And what does it mean
for language to live? It means that language recovers the "simple reason" that allows us to move into the future, without the ghosts of injustice hanging over us. Nevertheless, we know that "simple reason," language, and the law have betrayed and alienated. If we are to
give life to language, we would surely have to hear the ghosts that
language bears within it, to see, in other words, what exceeds (but
does not rule out) both its referentiality and its reason. The language

of pain, or rather, the unmaking of language in pain, has already forced us to consider this, and the pain we have encountered is not abstract but the concrete pain of a people's war.

To be fair to Sartre, I should add that, in 1948, when he published *What is Literature?* and *Black Orpheus,* he made an exception to his claim that literature should be politically referential and that poetry should be rejected in favor of prose, which draws less attention to the performativity of its own language. In *Black Orpheus,* he calls on black (male) poets to rise up "spermatically" and create something new from a language that has alienated them. He thus argues that re-fashioning language and allowing it to perform is itself a political act. But, at the moment of revolution, he might consider such work inappropriate, and he might be right. Even if, at one level, he were realistic in his sense of political efficacy, would that mean that a sense of being alienated from a language and a legal structure would be beside the point? Would it mean that one had to assume that the only form of justice is that dictated by *nuclear ethics,* as Camus argued? And what sort of ghosts would that erasure of meaning and performativity, which transcends the revolutionary moment, produce? Although Camus may have been blinded by a colonialist ideology when he spoke of a "re-establishment of the necessary justice" (Camus 1960, 124) ("establishment" would have been the more appropriate term), "justice" is a necessary ideal to hold on to. And, in this situation, justice must entertain the possibility that a performance of language exceeds referentiality, but that, in its performativity, language inevitably maintains an attenuated relationship with the political context, which leaves behind its ghosts, or, we could say, its phantoms, which are incorporated but not introjected.[28]

At the Russell War Tribunal, Sartre recognized the problems of making judgments about war crimes from a particular political position. Because no government sanctioned the tribunal, and because it did not take place after the war—as was the case with the Nuremberg trials—when the victors can identify the war crimes of the vanquished, Sartre claimed that the tribunal could function free from political pressure, precisely because it could not pass judgment, and could not, therefore, enforce its findings. To some extent, this is the case for any international war tribunal, because, in spite of the Geneva Convention, it is difficult to enforce international law. In that sense, the tribunal was a kind of *mock* trial—a performance of justice that can only exist as such outside the political realm.

De Beauvoir invoked ghosts of inactivity during World War II, to force Algeria into French consciousness; she forced the French to remember what may have been haunting them. And, for the then future of Algeria, that is now Algeria's present, we see another haunting, a sense of a war repeating itself. It is that haunting that occasioned a mock trial, in which political opposition took the form of a lament. It might be more appropriate to call that trial, which took place on 8 March 1995, International Women's Day, a mock tribunal.

What the trial mocks is the availability of recourse to justice through the law, and through the language of the law, which demands referentiality in the form of evidence.[29] In doing so, however, the mock trial performs a kind of justice in the face of the inadequacy of the law. Justice exceeds the structure of law, and the performance of ghosts—signs that haunt language as much as politics—demonstrates the very nature of justice as an *impossibility*, as an ethics that haunts the law. The use of the French language in the trial made possible a performance of that haunting. French was now demoted from its status as the language of law, to a language that potentially performs the very difficulty of claiming and enforcing a national language. The use of French, in fact, highlights the complex way in which all the languages of Algeria have become haunted by a politics that expresses the very difficulty of representation in the postnuclear, postcolonial period. This is foregrounded in the fact that even the FIS, while calling for Arabization, wrote its manifesto in French.

Intellectuals from Algeria, such as Assia Djebar, and Benamar Médiene, as well as intellectuals from France who grew up in Algeria, Jewish Franco-Algerians such as Benjamin Stora, Jacques Derrida, and Hélène Cixous, speak of their memories of the tyranny of the French language—and not just any French language, but that of Parisian intellectuals, the Académie Française, and of a French spoken *without an accent*. In other words, not only is this the French associated with the law through the Declaration of the Rights of Man; it is also a French that is reconstructed as Law, in relation to which one can only be other. The unrelenting attempt to reproduce and be attune to the cadences, rhythms, and intonations of the language has left some of these authors with such an uncompromising, and perhaps pathological, sense of the *purity* of the language as they surrender to the law of the Other that the result is a handicapped memory of anything beyond monolingualism. Although this is certainly a symptom of the repressive nature of politically enforcing the use of French, it has led to a radical change in the status of the language. Although the FIS appeals to its authority when it writes its manifesto in French, the very act of writing a call for a jihad in French places law and culture in a strange relationship. After all, Arabic is also inextricably associated with the law, bound to both divine and civil law since the years of French colonial rule; and it is that language that is now taking over as the uncompromising and absolute law, as the Other. The consequences of speaking any other language but Arabic are violent, which makes the French language, paradoxically, not only the language of an elite but also a language of protest.

Why, then, has French been adopted by some of the very people who have recently been the focus of the violence of political Islam? It is surely not from a naive notion of democracy, which views French, and the legal system associated with it, simply and unproblematically. Memories, though handicapped, are not that short. But French paradoxically becomes the language of protest even as it carries within it the ghosts of the past. Perhaps the uncanniness of the language—its paradoxical status as the language of the Other and, simultaneously, as an elusive mother language that provided opportunities—has become the only viable alternative, however haunted it may be by its own colonial specters. Language as Law, once associated with French, has undergone a displacement to Arabic. If, in precolonial times, the distinction between divine law and civil law was clear, and if, in the colonial period, that distinction began to erode because of the preeminent status of French law, in the last few years, civil law has become more closely associated with divine law, first, because of concessions the FLN made to Islamic traditionalists, and second, because of the confusion about who is perpetrating which acts of violence, and about whom those acts are attributed to. In a sense, French has become decolonized, creating a virtual lingua franca, in which the hauntedness of that language is revealed at the very moment of its performance, which is an alternative to the attempt to institutionalize a highly politicized and centralized Islamic law.

In the mock trial, as in much Franco-Algerian intellectual writing, French has lost its taboo and has become the language of the performative possibilities of the future—a language in which protest is performed in a manner that exceeds the law, as a way to find a form of justice that dramatizes the very impossibility of its full realization in language, but nonetheless the centrality of its impetus. The repetitions of and associations with an earlier moment have produced a kind of mockery of the power once associated with French at a time when that power, and a violent reign of terror, are now the domain of Arabic. The association of both languages with the law forces French to reveal its own ghosts just when, tragically, Arabic is becoming associated with absolute power. If justice can be performed, it is only virtually. The trace of French linguistic and legal injustice is present in a form both material and immaterial. The specters of the dead are present in this trace and demand that justice be done. They therefore put pressure on the present. The pressure on language from the post-nuclear people's war calls for a recognition of both the impurity of all linguistic performance and the shortcomings of ignoring language's extrareferentiality, its ghosts. The performance of these women in pain, who have little recourse to representation of any kind, becomes, in effect, the sign of singular traumas that are not dated but that carry the wounds of war and give life to language. Legal speech, which bears the traces of trauma, is ultimately speech without a legal end, and this may be why it performs some recourse to justice, in the very impossibility of justice. The illocutionary failure that is foregrounded in the women's laments articulates both justice as impossibility and the difficulty of inhabiting the language of law and sovereignty, when it is the state and religion that make the recourse to justice impossible. The phantom that appears in virtual justice negotiates between the law and ideal justice, between the material and historical on the one hand and the mystical on the other.

Virtual justice includes a simulation of justice that is not simply false justice (though it may be that as well), but a justice that actually enacts the failure of the law to do justice, understood as an ideal form, as something pure. Justice cannot be served, though it may perhaps be bequeathed. Although the law fails to do justice (even when it may seem that justice has been served—remember that many of the accused had already been condemned in courts of law), justice requires that the law exist so that it can be bequeathed. Although the law may fail to do justice because it is inevitably tied to the immediacy of the political dynamics (to the state-machine), justice must rely on the law to lodge the possibility of its existence. It cannot simply float freely, as if it bore no relation to the law or as if it were not bound by the history of legal discourse. Hence law may be a *simulation* of justice, and therefore a false or diabolical version of the truth, but it also sustains justice. Justice, however, is not free from the

snares of the law machine. And virtual justice is not simply a simulacrum of justice—as opposed to the simulation of the law—that is,
an imitation of justice somehow purified by virtue of its departure
from the law, freed from referentiality and legal or political responsibility. Such a notion of justice would give it little traction and would
probably remove it completely from the realm of the material.

Virtual justice is haunted by specters of traumas impossible to introject. Haunting is a constitutive part of virtual justice, not just to
the extent that the performance of a simulacrum—or, indeed, a repetition or a citation—is haunted by the fact of its displacement.[30]
Rather, that language itself bears the traces of particular phantoms,
particular historical events, and particular traumas. Therefore, although, in the case of the mock trial, the women assume roles, the
words bear within them not simply a displacement from one mode—
the traumatic—to another—the performance of the traumatic. The
continuity between the law court and the hotel theater and between
the law court and other arenas of cultural production, allows the
mock trial to be something more than simple mimicry. That is why
justice may be bequeathed but not served.

The concept of the bequest of trauma as it emerges in the haunting
of specters raises a set of questions within the context of colonialism,
since it is hardly possible to assume a first or last term, the ultimate
cause of a trauma, in a single historical event. To bring the concept of
trauma into the study of colonialism also requires a particular concept of forgetting and remembering as at times repression, at other
times a new and conscious fabulation or testimony. One could say,
for example, that the South African Truth and Reconciliation Commission performed justice through narrativizing trauma. This was
done in the service of national cohesion. It is as if national cohesion
could only be achieved by "remembering to forget" the violent divisions within national history, to use Renan's famous formulation in
"What is a nation?" (1990), whether the source of the violence was
hegemonic or counterhegemonic. But this kind of performance is
slightly different, at least potentially, from the kind I am considering,
because of a difference in the mode of testimony. It is not simply
that, in the case of South Africa, the testimony is in the service of the
state and could therefore be subject to the same criticism that Sartre
made of the Nuremberg trials; in addition, the commission functions
precisely as a recourse to justice through the narration of a traumatic
history. Although it is possible that such testimonies could still be

haunted by what cannot be thematized or articulated, by what is not bound by referentiality, or by the bequest from a previous generation, it is likely that such hauntings will be ignored in favor of choosing to forget what is already conscious, or what has been identified as the trauma of a people.

Trauma introduces a notion of temporality into justice, which challenges our understanding of the latter term as a simple reparation or restitution for events in the past. It makes possible the thematization in language of specific acts of cultural repression, which emerge at particular and contingent moments. The traumatic events of colonialism, or indeed, of slavery, are quite different from those of the Holocaust, for example, since different notions of historical event and traumatic event are at issue. In the first place, although certain events under colonialism may produce traumatic responses, and which we may acknowledge to be horrifying—a massacre, the death of a significant person or loved one, torture—we cannot speak so easily of a single defining traumatic incident. (The same might be said about the Holocaust, however. Although it is considered an event, it obviously lasted for years, and the buildup to the actual Holocaust included a number of anti-Semitic, antigay, and antigypsy occurrences.) It is far more difficult to think of colonialism or slavery as events, perhaps because it is the very structure of the modern that was built on colonialism. In contrast, we could say that, the event of the Holocaust brought about the destruction not only of a people but of the very structure of the modern, which posited the knowability of the event. How one responds to an event, that is, whether it becomes traumatic, depends on a completely different set of relations and variables. The thing is not traumatic in itself; it becomes traumatic when we fail to assimilate it into our histories, when we fail to introject it into the (national) ego. In that sense, the historical event is not the same as the traumatic event, which can continue throughout a lifetime and can manifest itself in our language across generations, without our even being aware of the repression that has taken place. I would suggest that this form of repression, which manifests itself as trauma, haunts language as a kind of disjuncture, particularly when the history of the languages themselves have been so fraught with political and cultural aspirations, disappointments, suppression, and repression. The accumulation of incidents that are not introjected but that leave an incorporated trace haunts the language, and, at particular moments and for particular reasons, causes a phantom to appear.

This form of haunting as a bequest from one generation to the next, which seems so apt for the analysis of colonialism, is not simply a postmodern questioning of master narratives, nor is it restricted to the postcolonial era. This counternarrative bears the weight of history even as it questions that history's temporal structure. It has co-existed with the discourses of European modernism, not as a response to it but as a constituent part of it, or, we might even say as a shadow, a phantom, a *virtual modern*.

[6]

the scheherazade syndrome

Literature and Politics in Postcolonial Algeria

LUCETTE VALENSI

Then King Shahriyâr said to himself:
By God I won't kill her
before having heard the end of her tale.

— *The Thousand and One Nights*

THIS BRIEF SURVEY of Algerian literature originated in the deep impression left on my mind by Rachid Mimouni's first novels, *Le fleuve détourné* (1982) and *Tombéza* (1984). They struck me as a powerful statement about the author's country.[1] Here were works of fiction about Algeria after the French and without the French, about the Algeria of the Algerians. Here were works that demystified postcolonial Algeria. After its independence, that country, more than any other in North Africa and the Middle East, benefited from a high degree of sympathy and admiration because of the long war the Algerians had sustained against the French.[2] It enjoyed lasting prestige as the Mecca of Third World regimes, as the enemy of all forms of neoimperialism, and as a refuge for exiled political activists of all kinds. The Algerian state and the FLN party developed a monolithic and dogmatic discourse on national liberation, social justice, and equality, combined with a Soviet-style approach to industrialization and modernization.

This text was published in a slightly different form in *Avenirs et avant-gardes en France, XIXᵉ–XXᵉ siècle. Hommage à Madeleine Rébérioux*, edited by Vincent Duclert, Rémi Fabre, and Patrick Fridenson (Paris: La Découverte, 1999), 177–96. Press files on Assia Djebar and Rabah Belamri were kindly provided by the Algerian cultural center in Paris.

Suddenly, Mimouni's novels blurred the images of national heroism. Twenty years after independence, the national epic was transformed into a bloody tragedy. And it was through the medium of literary fiction that social disillusionment was expressed and the critique of Algerian society elaborated. For myself, travel in Algeria in the 1960s and 1970s left me with no illusions, and I was not alone in that. But, with Mimouni, the denunciation originated with an Algerian, and unexpectedly, came in the form of novels, not (or not yet) political action, or studies by Algerian political or social scientists. Several years before the riots of October 1988 revealed to the entire world the Algerian regime's failure to keep the promises made after independence and its inability to respond to social expectations except with empty rhetoric (*langue de bois*) and tanks, it was a novelist who demystified Algeria's politics and official discourse.

The questions raised by Mimouni's novels were the following: Is literature the locus for social criticism in a situation of political oppression and totalitarianism? When it comes to grasping social tensions, is the literary imagination superior to other forms of intellectual activities? Is Rachid Mimouni an isolated case, or do other novelists share his enterprise of demystification? Such questions in turn raise the issue of Algerian literature and its relationship to Algerian society. Who were the writers of postcolonial Algeria; what was their status? What kind of discourse did they develop, and for whom?

Postcolonial Literature: A Heterogeneous Field

Postcolonial Algeria has produced a remarkably large number of writers, whether poets, playwrights, or novelists. If we consider only the novelists and compare them with their counterparts in the neighboring countries of Tunisia and Morocco, we find that Algerian novelists are not only more numerous but are also more varied. There are a number of women novelists (thirty-seven between 1947 and 1991, versus ten each for Tunisia and Morocco) (Déjeux 1994); there are expressions of regional identity in the Berber-speaking area of Kabylia, which has produced scores of "Berberist" writers.[3] There is a specifically Algerian brand of literature generated among North African immigrants and their descendants in France (the so-called Beurs). There is also a wide range of novels written by Algerian-born Frenchmen—including Algerian Jews[4]—who are excluded from most anthologies of Algerian literature, even though their source of inspiration is Algeria;[5] Muslim immigrants to France, on the other hand, are still counted as Algerian.

Among Algerian novelists, however, a large number never wrote (or published) more than one novel. There are many as well who published their only book at their own expense or entrusted their work to small publishing houses, lacking adequate means for broad advertising and distribution. This abundance of "short-term" writers is in itself a symptom. To write a novel is to perform an act that was unusual in the Algerian tradition. A solitary, silent form of expression, novel writing is not necessarily a form of protest.[6] But it might be an act of individuation, an assertion that the writer has something to say for her- or himself and wants to say it outside the normal environment, that is, the family network. It is true that the purpose of quite a few of these one-time writers is to bear witness regarding their native town or region, to be the memorialist of their segment of Algerian society. When this is the case, the "I" speaks for a "we" and remains embedded in the primordial group. With others, however, the act of writing a novel is a sign of individuation, of liberation from traditional forms of literary and social expression.[7] Ironically, the failure to have their books published by established publishing houses threw the authors out of the market and back to the friends and family members to whom they could give their work as a gift.

Algerian novelists are also more productive than their counterparts in the two neighboring North African countries. To mention only those I shall consider at length in this article, Rachid Mimouni published seven novels between 1982 and 1992, Tahar Djaout five in approximately the same period, Assia Djebar a dozen since 1957, Rachid Boudjedra the same number since 1969; finally, Rabah Belamri was the author of several novels as well as collections of tales and short stories.[8]

As was the case in Morocco and Tunisia, the first cohort of novelists in Algeria coincided with the last stage of the liberation movement. Published during the 1950s and 1960s, their novels contributed significantly to popularizing the liberation movements against French colonialism. Authors such as Kateb Yacine, Mouloud Mammeri, Mouloud Feraoun, Malek Haddad, and Mohammed Dib, published in French and in France, made the public in that country more sensitive to the social and political issues of Algeria. Theirs was a literature engagée (committed), nationalistic in its orientation, and ethnographic and realistic in its form (with the exception of Kateb Yacine's works). Unlike Tunisia and Morocco, however, Algeria displayed a discontinuity, a marked gap, between this first generation of writers and those of the postcolonial period. Novelists of the first generation either died before their time or fell completely silent or moved on to other activities. Mouloud Mammeri turned from literature to ethnography, Kateb Yacine abandoned novels for theater, and Malek Haddad abandoned all creative writing. The two notable exceptions are Mohammed Dib and Assia Djebar, who continue to have successful literary careers.

Many of the writers who emerged after independence developed an Algerian form of socialist realism. A flood of official literature idealizing the heroic resistance to French colonialism and the power of Algerian popular culture contributed to building a national identity. Even some talented professional writers jumped on the bandwagon and contributed their share to the national, populist, and official culture. A case in point is Rachid Boudjedra, who wrote the screenplay for the government-sponsored Algerian film *Chronique des années de braises.*[9]

Simultaneously, in the two decades following independence, a prevalent public rhetoric condemned the use of the French language or cast a veil of suspicion on those who published in France. The Arabic language, in its modern standard form (the Algerian mother tongue is generally disqualified as a "dialect" or *parler,* a spoken language), was imposed as a symbol of national culture. Along with Islam, its "function was not only to protect the Algerians from foreign influences but also to generate unity among them" (Harbi 1992, 22).

Although the official politics of language are a long story, let me simply describe the position of Algerian writers.[10] They were generally caught in a torturous relationship to both the French and the Arabic languages. As the language of the colonizer, French had to be rejected and professional writers advocated its rejection as part of decolonization. In a gesture of self-negation, even, at times, of self-hatred, they apologized for their own use of French and stigmatized it in the most violent terms. Kateb Yacine spoke of having thrown himself into the wolf's gullet. Unable to use standard Arabic, he devoted the remainder of his career to theater, writing and producing in the vernacular language. As for Assia Djebar, she has revealed that, between 1965 and 1978, her aim was to become an Arab writer, but in 1984 she confessed that her relationship to the French language had become "clearer": "If I write in French, it is because I chose this language, not because I am a colonized person." Yet, one year later, she added: "To me the French language is a stepmother, this language in the past was my people's sarcophagus, I carry it as a messenger who would carry the folded message ordering his condemnation to silence or to confinement."[11] Like Kateb Yacine, Djebar never mastered standard Arabic, and did not publish any novels for several years, turning to television films, *La Nouba* and *La Zerda*, which were performed in Algerian Arabic. After *La Zerda* appeared, she spoke of her "happiness" ("here defined by my physical settling down into the Arabic language, or rather, into the music of the Arabic language") and the role this had in allowing her serenely to accept her own bilingualism.[12]

By the 1980s, however—partly because of the excesses of the official discourse on Arabic, partly because the writers had been recognized by the public in France, in Algeria, and internationally, and partly because the Algerian readership remained unexpectedly attached to the French language—Algerian writers reversed their stance on the political use of language. They asserted more openly their use of French as the language most appropriate to express their feelings and thoughts and to describe Algerian "reality." They openly criticized standard Arabic for being as alien to the Algerian public as French. They criticized the attitude of Algerian writers toward official cultural policy after independence as a "failure of the intellectuals" (see Gafaïti 1985). And finally, they characterized their own use of French as an act of transgression, and, as such, as one important, subversive aspect of their literature.

As for Arabic, in spite of repeated invocations of its beauty and richness, of its ability to be the bearer of Algerian authenticity, most Algerian writers were not at ease with it. Only a few of those who wrote in Arabic, such as Tahar Ouattar and Abdelhamid Benhedouga, emerged as recognized novelists. For those writing in French, Arabic literature was mentioned in the most general way, with almost no reference to any specific author. It was sometimes used for quotations inscribed at the opening of a novel, as a token of political correctness, whereas the background of most Algerian writers was in

Western literature, from Fyodor Dostoyevsky to James Joyce and William Faulkner, and primarily in French literature. Without admitting it, they ignored or held in low esteem their fellow novelists from the Middle East. In a book-length interview on his work, Boudjedra praises Arab authors from the classical period, while dismissing modern Arab literature as mediocre (Gafaïti 1987, 55). In a more recent interview, he could not conceal his contempt for the modern Arab novel, singling out Naguib Mahfouz's writings as the prototype of this second-rate literature, a symptom of his profound ignorance of modern Arab novelists (Gaudemar 1991).

Let us return to the literary landscape of Algeria after independence: until the middle of the 1980s, all publishing activity was state-controlled. Two successive "national" companies were in charge of selecting the manuscripts, publishing and distributing the books, and importing and distributing books from abroad. As a result, some manuscripts languished in desk drawers for years. One remarkable example is Mimouni's first novel, *Le printemps n'en sera que plus beau*, which took seven years to be published. Others were rejected: *Le fleuve détourné* was simply returned to Mimouni, who then published it in France, where it received instant acclaim. Even after it was published in France, the novel was not distributed in Algeria, nor was it exhibited at the national book fairs. It was not translated into Arabic, though it appeared in many other languages. Nor were Mimouni's early books reviewed in the Algerian press (Gafaïti 1985). When they were finally reviewed, the response was ambivalent, since the reviewers regarded recognition in France as a sure sign of the French manipulation of Algeria.[13] A similar phenomenon occurred with Rachid Boudjedra. For twenty years, his books were not reviewed in the national press; subsequently, they received bad reviews. At the same time, Boudjedra was a prominent columnist in the official journals *Révolution Africaine*, in French, and *Al-Shaíb* in Arabic.[14] Meanwhile, other authors, who remain unknown outside Algeria to this day, were published by the national companies and received generous royalties. Writers of Arabic—such as Abdelhamid Benhedouga and Tahar Ouattar—were honored for giving the most authentic expression of the Algerian people and were promoted to the role of censors.

During the period when publishing was a state monopoly, the technical work of editing and producing books remained mediocre and unprofessional. Censorship hampered the publication of accepted manuscripts. Given these unfavorable circumstances, it is difficult to speak of a literary field in Algeria. Nevertheless, an impressive number of fine writers found their way to the public and, paradoxically, most of them wrote in French. Almost all those I shall deal with reached adulthood and began their publishing careers after Algerian independence. Several of them did not attend French schools, nor did they pursue their higher education at a French university. Some, such as Belamri, came from illiterate families, and some did not spend any significant part of their lives in France (Djaout, Mimouni). Yet, except for Boudjedra, who, after publishing in French, made an attempt to shift to Arabic, all these authors chose to write in French. This was already remarkable in the atmosphere of ultranationalism and violent rejection of the legacy of the colonial period that has prevailed in Algeria since independence. Writing in French was stigmatized as a symptom of cultural alienation, of dependence on French culture and the French market; it was seen as a sign of contempt for the local audience and as an elitist attitude. It is true that, for Algerian writers, France remains the only place to find legitimation. My assumption, however, is that, confronted by a blank page, these writers who were producing their first novels were not thinking primarily of how to reach the French publishing market; rather, they breathed French and wrote in the language they felt was most adequate to the expression of their thoughts and feelings. Weaned on Western literature, most of what they read was in French; they responded to it in the same language. In doing so, they addressed those Algerians who could read French, and willy-nilly, their work paradoxically became part of French literature. But that was not their primary goal.

In my view, the very act of writing in French was in and of itself subversive. It was an acknowledgment that—as a result of colonialism, of permanent contacts with France, and of the experience of temporary emigration to France by large numbers of Algerians—Algeria remains a bilingual society (trilingual, in the case of Berber-speaking people). In effect, French is one of its vernacular languages. Such a de facto acknowledgment is rarely articulated by Algerian writers, however, who most often have to take a defensive position (or choose to apologize) for their use of the French language.[15] One exception that deserves to be underscored is Rabah Belamri, who strongly asserted his untroubled relationship to the

French language and the total legitimacy of what is generally called "littérature algérienne d'expression française" (Algerian literature in French).[16]

Incestuous Cannibals, Les cannibales incestueux (Kateb Yacine)

The study of Algerian literature as a locus for social criticism does not require an exhaustive reading of all literary works published in the past three decades. Because of the volume and heterogeneity of literary production, the forest may hide the trees. I chose to focus on a few major writers of this period because, in my view, they succeeded in "taking the maquis," both in the sense that they adopted a subversive stance, and in the sense that they have, through their work, dominated the literary field in their country.[17] I have selected five French-language novelists, and will mention a few others for comparative purposes: a woman, Assia Djebar, born in 1936; and four men, Rachid Boudjedra (born in 1941), Rachid Mimouni (1945–95), Rabah Belamri (1946–95), and Tahar Djaout (1954–93). My reading of their work is quite close to the narrative level, and, as such, does not do justice to the diversity of narrative devices and verbal innovations these novelists introduced. This approach does not question the value of literary critical methods, but is justified by the relative transparency of Algerian novels and the exegesis Algerian writers themselves provide for their own work.

Even a superficial reading of these authors yields recurrent patterns and characters. Among the recurrent characters, we encounter the commissar, the policeman, the governor, in short, every incarnation of official authority and brutal force, with whom any discussion or negotiation is simply impossible. The relationship between such individuals and ordinary people in the novel (most often, the narrator him-or herself) is a relation of power in which the subject has almost no chance to be heard. When a protagonist is not defeated, it is only by chance, and his success will inevitably be counterbalanced by the suppression of someone else. Let us take the example of Djaout's Les vigiles (1991): the narrator, a young teacher, has invented a new device and struggles with the local bureaucracy to patent his invention. He fails. Eventually, his invention receives an award in an international exhibition. The narrator's situation is thereby reversed. But now, a culprit has to be found in his town, to assume responsibility for not having recognized his talents at home: an innocent man, a former fighter in the national movement, is designated as the scape-goat and driven to commit suicide.

The characters, the action, and the ambience of the novel are strongly reminiscent of Kafka. Indeed, Kafka haunts Algerian litera-ture. (The same is true for two other novelists more directly con-nected with Algeria, Albert Camus and Kateb Yacine.) But the Kafkaesque situations we find in Djaout's writings and in other nov-els are distinctly Algerian. Their location, the words and action of the protagonists, are historically and socially situated in present-day Al-geria. This is already an interesting contrast with the earlier cohort of Algerian writers, who had generally chosen an ethnographic, realis-tic, populist mode of storytelling (except, of course, for Kateb Yacine, whose work stands apart from all the others) rather than a satirical or ironic mode.

To unravel the mediocrity, the incompetence, the silent, blind vio-lence of local bureaucrats is not, however, a difficult exercise, nor would it shock the reader: *Ça ne dérange personne* (it doesn't bother anybody).[18] What is less expected and more upsetting is the recur-rence of a lonely narrator in the novels—men in the case of the male authors, women in Assia Djebar's novels and short stories. This is both surprising and paradoxical, because, traditionally, family is the pillar of Algerian society; there is no room for loners, except for asce-tic, saintly figures, who are by definition out of the ordinary. A close relationship is supposed to connect the members of a family and community. Similarly, the idea of contemporary Algerian society conjures up images of cramped living spaces in urban apartments and neighborhoods, and of groups of young men everywhere. Finally, the official, nationalist discourse has relentlessly exalted, in the Algerian historian Mohammed Harbi's words, "the community at the expense of the individual" (Harbi 1992, 24). Yet characters in Algerian novels move in lonely spaces, either literally, when they are confined to a single room, a jail cell, a hospital bed, or a pit in some cave, or sym-bolically, in spite of the physical presence of a wife, a nurse, or fellow passengers on a dark bus. Most often, there is no verbal communica-tion between the protagonists. Dialogue is not common in such nov-els. Long, at times delirious, monologues are the common mode of expression.

For example, in Boudjedra's *L'insolation* (1972), the narrator is a young professor detained in a psychiatric hospital, and his text is a hallucinatory monologue.

In Boudjedra's *L'escargot entêté* (1977), the hero is a monomaniacal civil servant obsessed with his job, which consists of exterminating rats in the city. An invasion of rats in a city? Here we find the third ghost of most Algerian writers, after Kafka and Kateb Yacine, namely, Albert Camus. Yet there is no question that the setting is present-day Algeria. Again, the appropriate mode for monomania is the monologue.

In Boudjedra's *Le désordre des choses* (1990), the monologue is that of a young doctor. He has an alter ego, his twin brother; but the relationship between the two is one of mortal hatred.

In Boudjedra's *Timimoun* (1994), the narrator, a bus driver on a route between a large city and the Sahara, produces a long monologue on his family and childhood memories and on his inability to love.

Assia Djebar's *Ombre sultane* (1987a, translated into English as *Sister to Scheherazade*, 1988), concerns the parallel solitude of a woman and her shadow, another young woman whom she has imposed as a second wife on her husband.

In Rachid Mimouni's *Le fleuve détourné* (1982), the main character is a man who was considered dead, killed by the French army during the war of liberation. When he comes back after several years of suffering from amnesia, he fails in his efforts to reconnect with his village, his family, his wife, and even to recover his own name and identity.

Mimouni's *Tombéza* (1984) is the silent speech of a man in a coma. The narrator is condemned to loneliness from the day of his conception, since he is the product of a rape and his mother dies in labor. Then his grandfather refuses to acknowledge his existence and to name him. A bastard, an orphan, a handicapped child left to himself, he is—when the novel begins—caught in silence and loneliness after what may have been an accident, but seems to have been an attempted murder.

In Mimouni's last novel, *La malédiction* (1993), the main character is a lonely doctor who ends up being killed by his own brother.

The deluge of words and violence one finds in Boudjedra's novels, for example, is absent from Rabah Belamri's. There is a kindness there that is missing from other male novelists' work; eroticism is poeticized, spoken of euphemistically, kept at bay. Characters and motives are inspired by folktales. Yet the protagonist of *Femmes sans visage* (1992) is a hunted man, threatened first by his father and later by his comrades-in-arms, who sentence him to death.

In Tahar Djaout's *Les vigiles*, the main character has a girlfriend but lives by himself. The man who is ordered to commit suicide has a wife, but no verbal communication with her.

More recently, Abdelkader Djemaï's *Sable rouge* (1996) consists of a lonely man's thoughts on an ordinary, yet fatal, day.[19]

This leads us to another common pattern in Algerian novels—the perversion of human relations and the disorder prevailing in the interaction between individuals. The text that inaugurated this theme is clearly Boudjedra's first novel, *La répudiation* (1969). Here we encounter the entire gamut of family disorders: adultery (by the narrator's father), incest (by the narrator himself, who has intercourse with his father's second wife, then with a half-sister born from his father's affair with a Jewish woman), pedophilia on the part of men and women, homosexuality, in the case of the narrator's brother, and an overall obsession with castration and menstrual blood. The dust jacket blurb explains that the novel was intended as a critique of traditional Algerian society. With the passage of time, however, and when viewed in relation to the other novels published in the past two decades, it can be read quite differently.

Similar themes occur in Boudjedra's other novels, more specifically, in the aptly named *Le désordre des choses* (The disorder of things, 1990). There is disorder in the relationship between twin brothers; between wife and husband (the husband accuses his wife of adultery, without any basis for the charge, which leads to the wife's slow descent into madness); between the father and his sons; and so on.

The perversity continues in Mimouni's, Belamri's and Assia Djebar's fiction.[20] The standard mode of human interaction is violence and aggression. In one of Djebar's recent books, *Vaste est la prison* (1995b), the setting for the story is a hammam, a community bathhouse, traditionally described as the place for women's sociability and sensuality. Immediately and spontaneously, women speak of *ëadu*, the enemy, that is, their husbands. This is the fundamental divide, the segregation between men and women, a relationship based on violence; there is a dual and contradictory obsession among men with the virginity of their women on the one hand, and with their violent defloration on the other.

In all these novels, we are confronted with a reversal of the most basic values. The only absolute rule, it seems, is to transgress all the rules, in the domestic space, in the workplace, in the public sphere. One rarely encounters party leaders, ministers, or high-ranking decision makers as characters in these novels. More eloquently, it is the ordinary members of an ordinary society who are placed on stage and set in motion.

A key term that passes from one author to the next is "disillusion." As one might expect, disillusion comes from observing the powerful: their greed for material wealth and imported goods, their appropriation of national companies and public wealth, their consistent corruption, their exclusive appropriation of power combined with their complete incompetence, their cynicism toward the very people who are supposedly the center of public concern, namely, "the Algerian people," "the Algerian woman," "the Algerian peasant," the youth, the poor, and everyone else. But what is occurring at the higher levels of the hierarchy is equally occurring at lower levels: there is a constant misuse of position, a constant misappropriation of resources, a permanent perversion of people and of human relations. Nurses use their positions to steal food and medicine from their patients, male nurses to disseminate information about women patients; teachers use theirs to sexually abuse their students, civil servants to abuse female employees. The victim of this social game, usually the narrator in the novel, is described as disoriented (and indeed, there is an unusually high rate of madness in Algerian novels), dispossessed (of his home, her land, his identity, her life). *Désemparé, déboussolé, délogé,* and *dépossédé* are the attributes of most characters in these novels.

Finally, the transgression of the most basic values takes the form of homicide. Although none of the novels mentioned is a thriller, all recount at least one violent death. Infanticide occurs in Belamri's novels, Djebar's short stories, and in a recent novel by Abdelkader Djemaï (*Sable rouge,* 1996); suicide, in Boudjedra's, Belamri's, and Djaout's works; fratricide in Mimouni's and Belamri's, or, as a substitute, the elimination of a comrade-in-arms;[21] and finally, uxoricide in Belamri's fiction and Mimouni's *Le fleuve détourné.*

Setting is an important element in Algerian novels, and the authors frequently make it clear that the place is a metaphor for their country. It is often a closed, airless, threatened space: a room where the narrator is confined, surrounded by enemies; a bus; a work camp;

and, in several novels—too many to be coincidental—a hospital. The hospital is not a place for giving birth or recovering from illness, but a place where people suffer and die. Finally, the desert, that is, a place defined by Kateb Yacine in *Les ancêtres redoublent de férocité* as "la morgue intime" (the intimate morgue), provides the locale for some Algerian novels.

Death is not a natural phenomenon in Algerian novels. It is not part of the plot, as in detective stories. It is the essence of human relations. As a matter of fact, very few detective stories and thrillers have been written in Algeria. To my knowledge, there are only two or three. Reading one of them, *Mimouna*, by Salim Aïssa, I was taken by surprise by two of its qualities. The first is the humor and tenderness of the narrative, unexpected in that literary genre and absent from authors such as Boudjedra or Mimouni. The second has to do with the plot itself: most characters are petty criminals, just out of jail, trying to survive in the big city. They become suspects in a crime they did not commit, the burglary of a bourgeois household and the murder of a handicapped teenager. Indeed, the real murderer is the victim's father, an elegant, eloquent, well-mannered gentleman, "au-dessus de tout soupçon" (above all suspicion), who thought he could hide his crime by hatching a plot that would direct all suspicion onto the petty criminals. Unexpectedly, this thriller confirms the rule of the Algerian novel.

A Ransacked Society

In Algerian literature, society is lethal, social justice homicidal, and Algerian men are cannibals. How can we explain this?

At the individual level, at least in Boudjedra's case, *l'enfance saccagée* (his ransacked childhood) made writing a form of therapy. It would be interesting to know whether the other novelists had similar experiences.

At a more general level, traditional society in Algeria was ruled by various symbolic systems, the most important of them being the ethos of honor and the rule of direct vindication. Ironically, it is one of the minor novelists who reminds us of this fundamental rule. Introducing his short stories, set in Kabylia at the time of colonialism, Boukhalfa Bitam explains:

In the place and at the time where these events occurred, there was no recognized law (it was custom that ruled), no police, no courts enjoying any legitimate authority. Colonial justice was not justice for our forebears for whom it appeared instead as the consecration of the law of the jungle (*la loi du plus fort*), its main goal being, in effect, to establish and confirm the victor's domination.

Almost everywhere, however, councils of wise men used to arbitrate those conflicts that could be arbitrated according to ancestral habits, that is, those based on some material disagreement that could be evaluated and settled.

As for offenses against honor, they were frequently resolved by killing. There was no court before whom they could be brought. (Bitam 1986, 6, my translation)

In such a system, to avenge an offense by killing is not to commit a murder, but to do justice. Traditionally, such "justice" was the responsibility of the kinship group. Vindication could be delayed, however, or negotiated by different means: the mediation of a marabout or of the village council (in Kabylia), or some transaction between male members of the two families in conflict. I suggest that, once the lineage system has been destroyed, once the confrontation between segmentary lineages has ended, once the village (or tribal) institutions of mediation have collapsed, the ethos of honor and the principle of direct "justice" nonetheless remain, albeit under a different guise: The person who feels offended is the self-designated judge and jury and perpetrates violence to vindicate his honor. If this is the case, Algerian literature has succeeded in underscoring a blind spot of standard sociology, namely, that it is at the very center of the family that the blight of violence makes its home (Mahe 1996).

The other symbolic system at work in Algeria is Islamic. One of the principles by which Islam acts to regulate society is the *hisba*, the injunction for every believer to command the good and forbid evil. Although Islam is conspicuously absent from most of the novels mentioned in this article, it remains implicit in most, and the principle of hisba is at work and constantly enforced.

Reflecting on the history of the national movement and the building of national institutions after independence, the historian Mohammed Harbi makes an important but unexpected statement: Although the Algerian political regime is authoritarian, a political machine but not a state has been created since independence. "The absence of a state is a constant feature of political life since 1962. Instead, there is a political machinery. Institutions are empty shells." As he emphasizes, the result is "the inexistence of the necessary conditions for a social pact" (Harbi 1992, 199, 29). If we accept Harbi's analysis, there is no available avenue of recourse for solving conflicts other than direct action, and no action other than violence.

Be that as it may, two verses in a play by Kateb Yacine (*Les ancêtres redoublent de férocité*) now read like a prophecy: "Toute vraie guerre nous remémore / Les cannibales incestueux" (Any real war reminds us / Of incestuous cannibals).

Writing in Algeria is a transgressive act. Writing in French is subversive. Writing about Algeria constitutes a vehement denunciation of Algerian social values and actions. It is not only a denunciation of the state and its agents, which has been acknowledged by readers and professional critics, but also a condemnation of ordinary people in their most ordinary interactions, a diagnosis that has been more often concealed than made explicit.[22]

In many respects, Algerian literature is less reminiscent of the literatures of other North African and Arab countries than of art and literature in totalitarian states. With reference to similar cases of fiction and art under oppression, I have coined the term "Scheherazade syndrome." Authors such as Varlam Chalamov and Vassili Grossman in the Soviet Union and a painter such as Zoran Music, who survived the Nazi extermination camps, embody this process. Confronted with lethal danger, the storyteller comes forward and delays the sentence. In the face of deadly threat, she not only postpones her own death but also keeps the killer hostage to her own voice. It is through the medium of the tale that she challenges deadly violence. It is through a poetization of a brutal reality that she unveils it to the public and to the protagonists. In the case of Algeria, as in similar cases in our time, the sad end of the story is that the storyteller does not have the last word. Tahar Djaout was butchered; Rachid Mimouni, Abdelhamid Benhedouga, and Rabah Belamri died prematurely. It is as if the sin of speaking out had to be punished by death.[23]

PART III
WRITING IN
OTHER(S')
LANGUAGES

diglossia

ABDELKEBIR KHATIBI

In memory of Kateb Yacine

WRITING IS NOT speaking; such would be the internal bilingualism of every language.

I would like to demonstrate, as well as I can, the validity of this proposition for Maghrebian literature. In the Maghreb, actual bilingualism or multilingualism did not originate in the colonial situation; it preexisted it. The war between languages, between idioms, has always played a role in the formation of nations and states. A language policy, whether declared or indirect, is always involved in this moment of formation.

Well before the French and Spanish colonization of the Maghreb, there was a double idiomatic discontinuity between, on the one hand, classical Arabic and what is called dialectal Arabic, and, on the other, Tamazight (Berber) and the Arabic language in all its diglossia.

We know that the Tamazight language was preserved orally through its popular literature and songs. Although rarely written, it has been set down with the help of an ancient sign system, the *tifinagh*, and transcribed into Arabic script, but it also appears in Latin characters in French Orientalist literature. The fate of *tifinagh* shows the very uncertain status of writing in pre-Islamic North Africa. It is Islam that imposed on the Maghreb the idea of the unity of language and religion, a notion founded on the principle of the unity between language and sacred text. This notion constitutes both a politics and an eschatology.

We must add to this first idiomatic discontinuity a second, introduced by the French language during the colonial period. I use "colonization" here to refer to three languages in a dissymmetric hierar-

This chapter was translated by Whitney Sanford.

chy, where one dominates the other two. This conflictual situation may be either latent or overt, and has yet to be elucidated. It cannot be so long as the Maghreb does not take charge of the active plurality of its utterances.

Borne by its shadows, Maghrebian literature "of French expression" inscribes itself all along this double fissure. But the gaps and ruptures are themselves an initiation into writing, into all writing. They bear with them imagination and dissidence. It is in this historical churning between peoples, between civilizations, that we may glimpse writing as it bursts forth, strong and free, as a historical event.

Such is the schematic background upon which I would like to overlay a few propositions:

First proposition: A foreign tongue is not added to the native tongue as a simple palimpsest, but transforms it. When I write in French, my entire effort consists of separating myself from my native language, of relegating it to my deepest self. I am thus divided from myself within myself, which is the condition for all writing inured to the destiny of languages. Dividing myself, reincarnating myself—in the other's language. Henceforth, little by little, my native tongue becomes foreign to me. Bilingualism is the space between two exteriorities. I enter into the telling of forgetting and of anamnesia. Henceforth, "I am an/other" in an idiom that I owe it to myself to invent—a limit experience inherent in this situation.

Second proposition: This Maghrebian literature is a translation from French into French, and not, as one tends to think, a transcription of the native language into French.

A curious paradox, a scandal for some, an anomaly or aberration for others. But everything is translation, since, between voiced emotion and the written word, it is the body that sets the rhythm, the body that casts the writer toward the absolute outside.

Third proposition: Maghrebian literature is a radical experience and experiment of autobiography.

Yes, the Maghrebian writer tells of the self in telling the tale of languages. He searches for the vernacular foundation of his word, a foundation transferred, deported into the language of the other.

Veiled by this transfer, the writer is a scribe of melancholia, of loss, of the loss of a secret shared with (kept from?) his kin.[1] A tragedy of guilt, tinged with betrayal. When I write in French, I am taken hostage.

Tradition sanctions an autobiography of confession, of avowal, of self-construction, of self-justification in the face of lurking death. Autobiography finds itself destined for the hereafter. But the (Maghrebian) writer must not be content to vindicate himself before God and men, but instead must return meaning to the lost language, to literature, reanchoring it in absolute alienation and dissidence.

The magnificent Kateb Yacine says:

> Never, not even in those days of success in the eyes of the
> (French) schoolteacher, have I ceased to feel deep within me
> that second rupture of the umbilical cord, that internal exile
> that no longer brought together the schoolboy and his mother
> except to wrest them, each time a bit more, away from the
> murmur of blood, from the reproaching shivers of a banished
> language, secretly in an agreement as quickly shattered as con-
> cluded . . . Thus I had lost at once my mother and her language,
> the only inalienable treasures—and yet alienated, the only in-
> alienable and yet alienated treasures.[2]

Commenting on this passage, I have written:

> I have suggested—and Kateb has clearly stated—that the Arab
> writer in French is caught in a chiasmus, a chiasmus between
> alienation and inalienation (in every direction of these two
> terms): this author does not write (in) his own language, he
> transcribes his transformed proper name, he can possess noth-
> ing (insofar as we may appropriate a language), he owns neither
> his mother tongue, which has no written form, nor written
> Arabic, which is alienated and given over to substitution, nor
> that other learned language that calls upon him to disappropri-
> ate himself and fade into her. Irresolvable suffering when the
> writer does not assume this gashed identity in a clarity of
> thought, which lives on this chiasmus, this schism" (from
> *Maghreb pluriel*).[3]

A few years after his country's independence, Kateb was tempted to "return" to his native language. Impossible. His vow of silence—silence in the other's language—was in vain. He had his plays translated into dialectal Arabic in order, he thought, to stage for the people their liberation. How then can one forbid oneself to write in one's only written language? Is such a thing likely without madness and the withering of one's roots? Writing rips us from the origin, it produces a dis-identification whose suffering we can hardly stop or magically turn back. Kateb became a hostage to his own silence. A blank silence, a white silence. Sinking into the denial of a self writing in the language of the other, he faced the impossible. Like Rimbaud, his brother in revolt, he fell quiet, took ill, and died in progressive loneliness, without symbolic protection. His death was stolen from him. But whether he wished it or not, he remains among us, emblematic figure of dissidence, from one language to another. And his work vouches for him and for the invention of a new literary idiom in the Maghreb.

[8]

multilingualism and national "character"

On Abdelkebir Khatibi's "Bilanguage"

RÉDA BENSMAIA

IN A PASSAGE FROM his journal dated 24 October 1911, Franz Kafka made the following remark:

> Yesterday it occurred to me that I did not always love my mother as she deserved and as I could, only because the German language prevented it. The Jewish mother is no "Mutter," to call her "Mutter" makes her a little ridiculous ("Mutter" is not ridiculous by itself, since we are in Germany). We give a Jewish woman the name of a German mother, but forget the contradiction that sinks into the emotions so much the more heavily, "Mutter" is peculiarly German for the Jew, it unconsciously contains, together with the Christian splendor Christian coldness also, the Jewish woman who is called "Mutter" therefore becomes not only ridiculous but strange. Mama would be a better name if only one didn't imagine "Mutter" behind it. (Kafka 1948, 111)

Closer to home, in 1945–46 Bertolt Brecht meditated in an open and unfinished letter to "an adult American" on his relationship to the "standard American" language that his exile in the United States enjoined him to learn:

> I should say right away: I have no hope of ever learning this language. It's not that I wouldn't like to, not that I lack oppor-

This chapter was translated by Whitney Sanford.

tunities, it's something else. I've tried for some time now to express myself like the natives of the country. I must say that,
during a discussion, I do not say what I want to say, but what I
am able to. It's not at all the same, as one can easily imagine.
One assumes that it has something to do with a confused but
temporary state, one that longer studying will fix. This is, unfortunately, false. It is not simply a question of vocabulary or
syntax. Let us speak rather of a certain *habitus* that I don't see
myself acquiring. With a little more tenacity, I would perhaps
be able to say in American phrases that in certain American
paintings the sky and the trees give the impression that they
are wearing makeup, as if worrying about their sex appeal more
than anything else. But I wouldn't be capable of taking the correct attitude necessary to express these things without shocking. I would need to learn how to become a "nice fellow."
(Brecht 1970, 229–34, my translation, my emphasis, "nice fellow" English in the original)[1]

In his recent book *Amour bilingue* (*Love in Two Languages*), Abdelkebir Khatibi gives a new and contemporary twist to these half-
disillusioned, half-tragic reflections. Indeed, we can hardly fail to be
struck by the muffled yet insistent presence of a set of problems that,
here and there, a situation of "exile" from the mother tongue renders
unavoidable. Can one love in a foreign language? Can one think,
write, dream, sing in a foreign language? Can one find the "right
tone"? These apparently trivial questions have endlessly haunted the
consciousness and thought of Maghrebian and African writers (both
Francophone and Anglophone) since the period of independence.
What is striking in Kafka and Brecht, however, and in Khatibi as well,
in a very original form, is the recurring and well-ordered "traits" that
characterize the problems caused by the confrontation between two
languages—in the form of diglossia. For each, the "question" of bilingualism, or more precisely, the question of the domination of one language by another, is never posed in the abstract psychological terms
of *expression,* but always in the concrete (vital) terms of *Umwelt,* territory, "ways of *being in the world,*" Kafka's "feeling" and Brecht's
habitus.

It is true that Kafka's situation was different from Brecht's; his
"exile" was internal, brought about by his situation as a writer and
Jewish intellectual living in Czechoslovakia, who was obliged to

speak Czech (or Yiddish if possible) and *write* in German. Kafka brilliantly analyzed this "impossible" situation throughout his works. He also left behind some lovely comments in his diaries—No, *Mutter* in German, don't you see, it's not possible, it's ridiculous and it "sounds" wrong! Something else has to be found! Something else has to be invented! The basso continuo of German humming "behind" the mother tongue, the reverberation behind the Czech (and Kafka is one of the rare Jewish writers to speak it fluently), or behind the Hebrew or Yiddish (the language "that frightens," as he says), which Kafka learned with great fervor: all that must cease. We know the "rest of the tune" as François Rabelais, another "master in foreign languages," would say. At the intersection of several languages, Kafka depicts the inaugural impossibility of his work as a cataclysm, writing while burning what he writes as he advances, writing as a "war machine" and not as a "mechanism of expression." It is no longer a matter of finding equivalents of *Mutter, Vater,* and so on—of sending language "to the nursery"—but of patiently destroying all the elements of this primal scene (of language). There is no more "Mommy-Daddy," but an unprecedented "deterritorialization" of the cultural anchor of Papa Goethe's German, the production of "vanishing lines" in whose wake "words," "cease to be representative in order to tend towards their extremes or their limits,"[2] or "to be like a foreigner in one's own language," "to slowly, progressively carry language away into the desert. To use syntax to scream, to give a syntax to screaming" (Kafka 1948, 48). Schizophrenia and language!

Brecht's situation, given its contingent and temporary nature, may have been easier. After the war, he returned to Europe and was "relieved" of the problem. During his brief exile, however, he was immediately able to define its most contorted aspects, revealing the fissure that a certain bilingual—or as Khatibi says, "bilanguage"—situation introduces deep within the speaking subject. In any case, it is remarkable how Kafka seems to tone down the "untimely" character of his comments—*Mutter* is not ridiculous "by itself" *since we are in Germany,* he says, with some ambiguity. Brecht makes no bones about it: losing the use of one's native language brings on a veritable *conversion,* entailing at least "becoming a nice fellow," which does not leave the "subject" intact. I might say that the sky and the trees give the impression that they are wearing makeup, like beings worried more about *sex appeal* than anything else, but I cannot go any further.

These two texts allow us to situate what is at stake in *Amour bilingue*: first, the impossibility of writing in French without ado, and, at the same time, the impossibility of simply returning to Arabic or Berber; second, the necessity of "going beyond"—even at the risk of madness—the dualism of the "first order" languages (French and Arabic), and of defining a new space for writing and thought, without falling into the obligation of becoming a "nice fellow," that is, one who "speaks well," who "writes well," who "masters" the colonizer's language better than the colonizer! For Khatibi, the task at hand is entirely different: above all, the writer must begin with the fact that he is not French and that, as Antonin Artaud might say, "behind" the language used for the purpose at hand there will always be a "language under the tree."[3] This means bringing out a "rhizosphere" to counter the logosphere, which tends to pull you under the rule of signs or levels of "expression," which always lead you to a "black hole"—the loss of "identity," the search for "authenticity," and other figures of colonial "entrapment." At issue is how to create instruments that will allow him to say what he *wants* to say, and not only what he *can* say in the language of the former colonial powers— in short, to escape from the "prison house of (colonial) language."[4] Surely this is a "translation" problem if ever there was one, a problem Khatibi has patiently clarified and marked with his poet's talent. Indeed, one of the most crucial problems dominating Maghrebian (and, more generally, African) thought after decolonization was how to define a national entity or "character," which necessarily entailed redefining the geolinguistic space in which work was produced. It became urgent to decide among the different languages occupying the terrain: Arabic, promoted to the rank of national language; French, which has long been the "vehicular" language and dominant language of "reference" (in North Africa at least); and the many vernacular languages that, from a certain point of view, were also "frightening." For most writers, the Gordian knot had to be severed; some stopped writing altogether, others opted for one language or another, and others switched languages in the end, but none of these decisions ever solved the problem. Nor have "internal" and "external" conflicts ever ceased to haunt Maghrebian consciousness.

What is striking in Khatibi's works—and especially in *Amour bilingue*—is that the *Kampfplatz* that the question of (two) languages represents in the Maghreb suddenly looks like a story about the past. In other words, with Khatibi, or rather *after* Khatibi, it seems we are confronted with something like a *before* and an *after* in the history of North African writing and thought. The intervention or inscription of *Amour bilingue* in the history of Maghrebian literature in French thus constitutes an *event* that it is absolutely necessary to follow attentively if we are to understand the upheaval that has occurred on the contemporary Maghrebian cultural scene. On the eve of the "euphoria" that was to drive him to "madness," Nietzsche said that his Zarathustra would "split humanity in two" (see Klossowski 1969, 304 seq.). *Amour bilingue* is a book of the same kind; it splits the history of Maghrebian thought and being *in two*. Not into two camps or clans or parts—that has already happened and will doubtless continue to happen—but into two "periods," a *before* and an *after*. Khatibi makes this split not to produce (greater) beauty or to demonstrate "artistic" or "stylistic" genius (always contingent reasons), but essentially, to call into question the false transparency of the problem of bilingualism.

In other words, with Khatibi (and this is what is at stake in his unique book), the dilemma is no longer whether he should write in Arabic or in French, whether doing one or the other is necessary or contingent, politically right or wrong: the dilemma is to make visible an "other" (infraliminal) level of writing and thought, which renders obsolete the dualistic opposition that has dominated North African production. Khatibi, an "agonistic" thinker who engages in "class struggle after the Taoist fashion,"[5] immediately rejects duality in order to consider, and to bring to the fore, a space that has remained unthinkable, where the two languages—Arabic and French in this case, but this move does not exclude other languages, such as Berber—meet without merging, confront their respective graphic movements *without osmosis* and without a reconciling *synthesis*. If, then, we can speak of a "translation," it is one that does not return to the *same*. The originality at work here—an originality that is not answerable to any mundane value judgments—can be attributed to the fact that, for the first time *in such a radical and concerted manner*, the question of belonging to (at least) two languages erupts in practice and in theory in a scriptural space that had previously been dominated by a Manichaean vision of language and identity (cultural, ethnic, religious and national).[6]

What is striking in Khatibi's book is that, although he seems to start from the same premise as Kafka and Brecht—bilingualism, the intersection of at least two cultures and three civilizations—he radi-

cally overturns the dualistic framework of that premise. In forging
his notion of "bilanguage," Khatibi presents himself as the fortunate
writer who can (only) love, think, and delight (*jouir*) in the interval
generated by the necessity from the start to hear, see, and write in
two languages *at once*.

> Bi-langue? My luck, my own individual abyss and my lovely
> immediate energy. An energy I *don't experience* as a deficiency,
> curiously enough. Rather, it's my third ear. Had I experienced
> some kind of breakdown, I liked to think I would have devel-
> oped *in the opposite direction*, I would have grown *up in the
> dissociation peculiar to any unique language*. That's why I ad-
> mire the *gravity of the blind man's gestures* and *the desperate
> impossible love the deaf man has for language*. (Khatibi 1990,
> 5, my emphasis)[7]

We will return to the specific nature of the "gesture" and the
"love"—desperate, impossible—that such a move implies. For now,
let us simply note that, while the bilanguage may cause forgetfulness
or anamnesis, the narrator's ability to see, hear, and write *double* is
never a source of anxiety, ruin, or loss of identity. The narrator always sees double, that is all: one/many, speech/writing, the body/lan-
guage, the same/the other, Arabic/French. "From that moment, the
scenario of the doubles was created. One word: now two: it's already
a story" (Khatibi 1990, 5).[8]

Let us point out right away that, with this gesture—it would be
preferable here to use the French *geste* in the feminine, to restore its
theatrical and carnivalesque dimension[9]—with the stroke of a pen,
Khatibi cancels out all the guilt a North African writer still feels at
the need to write in French, to "translate" into French her or his local
or regional context. In exposing the target language (French) to a process that turns it upside down, the bilanguage writer is no longer *subjected* to the use of French. Rather, s/he urgently needs it as a means
to an ends, to delight in it (*en jouir*) of course, but, at the same time,
to draw out what might never come to pass without it: to spell, to
translate, "the nameless and the groundless" as Khatibi says, which
follows in the wake of a nonmundane approach to the bilanguage:

> I baptised you: bi-langue. And now pluri-langue. To sum up, a
> question of translation, to be deducted from my sleepless

nights. I spelled out the no-name and the no-foundation as elements of my ordeal, everywhere where the incommunicable
held me close. Then I passed through the innocence of things,
the confusion of tongues and every preceding language of reve-
lation. (Khatibi 1990, 101)[10]

We might expect to see Khatibi, beginning from such premises, involved in a writing process tending to subvert the target language's
syntax and vocabulary. In other words, we expect him to refer repeatedly to Arabic, to "dialect-ize" or "Maghreb-ize" French in order to
force it to render what it has tended to eliminate from its sphere.[11]
However, no such process is apparent in *Amour bilingue*. Khatibi's
style is "classic." He does not mix languages. On the contrary, while
affirming his relation to two cultures, his preference for both languages, Khatibi seems at first to give French every chance of perform-
ing with the greatest possible transparency: "A certain unity of language was achieved in her body. Her moods, which changed from day
to day, were limpid, considerate, prodigiously unexpected. Was the
great suffering ended? How about renunciation? Affirmation, there
was only affirmation" (Khatibi 1990, 107).[12]

So, no suffering. No heartbreak and no renunciation, nothing but
affirmation. In fact, we do not see any of the "techno-narcissistic" devices that have characterized so many so-called modern Francophone
works. Nor will we see any typographical coquetry, all-purpose
words, conspicuous lexical or syntactical contortions. The text is
opaque at times but always "smooth," "flowing"; it never becomes
ensnared in the games of syntactical displacement or lexical innovation that characterize so many contemporary European and African
texts: "Tout était blanc. Clarté palpitante du jour!" And yet, when
reading or rereading the text—a single reading is naturally inadequate—we cannot help but hear a grating noise that constantly short-
circuits the French words in some way, haunting the vocabulary and
making the syntax of the French language vacillate to a rhythm
whose "reason" remains undecidable. Something is moving, constantly shifting and interfering with the text, though the reader cannot assign this shifting to a (geographical or rhetorical) "place." A
"mouvement de déport" (dislocating movement), in Roland Barthes's
expression, troubles the reading and makes access to the text difficult; at every moment, we have the feeling that we have changed languages, switched from one to another, but it is impossible at first to

say *in what respect,* by what trick: "this time he closed his eyes before paying concentrated attention: he felt a presence there, invisible,
inaudible. No hissing, no sound, but presently a silent music, a song
within the sea" (Khatibi 1990, 31).[13]

At this point, a question arises: have we changed languages or
haven't we? Is this simply a new mode of "translation"? We might
take what Khatibi says about an author he liked to read as a clue to
his own writing: "Once I read a peculiar author. in order to get rid of
his master, he changed his language. Such a rare switch was a stroke
of genius" (Khatibi 1990, 14).[14]

Perhaps it is more economical to say that Khatibi has *changed languages,* but with a breathtaking movement that consists not in a
reterritorialization of Arabic or an "Arabization" of French, but in
the continued use of *French.* At the same time, it consists of making
French *see double, loucher* in the active sense of peering at, eyeing,[15]
by subjecting French to a *system* that puts it in a position to *translate
the untranslatable,* to express the inexpressible. In a word, he radically tears it away from the meta*physical* and pre*critical* space where
the language was supposed to be only the *secondary* instrument for
expressing a single or unified mind, culture, or subject. Among other
things, Khatibi wants to make language *loucher, look cross-eyed,* to
make language *louche,* shifty. A *louche* is also the tool of a turner, a
lathe operator, used for widening the holes already begun (*Littré*).

Khatibi's project is to write like a "turner" (of foreign languages)
and to make French a frightening language. Once again, he does not
do this by tampering with typography, or even by manipulating syntax or vocabulary, but by putting French in the position of the *supplement,* that is, by giving it a dual movement that definitively tears
it away from any metaphysical or expressive co-optation, first, by
pulling the French language toward calligraphy, the grapheme, the interval—sending it back toward the "spacing" that its "normal" mode
of operation usually excludes;[16] and second, by making us see and
hear the other language (Arabic) in the *between-two-languages,* in
the breach created by this very spacing, without ever bringing about a
simple return to origins.

Such an act of translation is far more revolutionary and effective
than those that make the language "howl," by putting it in a state of
exhaustion.

I would like to explore this hypothesis with an analysis of the page
layout, the elements that are to be read and seen before the "narra-

tive" in the strict sense begins. On the binding—visible, readable, only when the book remains closed around its secret, sitting on the library shelf—we read *Amour bilingue* and *Abdelkebir Khatibi* in large black print. Nothing remarkable draws our attention. However, as soon as we take an interest in the cover, it is impossible not to notice a number of features that slow down our reading: first, the layout, or rather, the even *distribution* of proper names and titles (the "credits," as we would say of a film). ABDELKEBIR KHATIBI is in *black* capital letters; then, just below, in thick, blood-red letters, AMOUR BILINGUE appears; then, even farther down, is an elegant interlacing of Arabic letters—*unintelligible for the monolingual reader*—an "arabesque," which the bilingual reader can decipher as a translation of the title: "*Ashk Ellisanaïn*". The vowels are absent from the calligraphic transliteration of the title into Arabic. However, the dots that allow us to distinguish between a *kaf* and a *fa*, for example—and which are part of the system that determines contrasts and makes each unit a discrete character in Arabic—are marked in red, the red of the French title. A metonymic displacement opens the play of vertiginous shifts that, from one language to another, endlessly refer to a "spacing" that does not *legitimately* belong to either language. This exercise in translation constantly calls one language into the "courtroom" of the other, signaling, now the discrete elements, now the gaps, the distinguishing intervals, in this case, through the color of those "distinctive" traits.

What is even more striking is that this complex process of generalized translation or anamorphic (nontautological) transformation sweeps along in its fury even the proper name of the series in which the book was published. Indeed, if, in some cryptic way, the sign (illegible for the monolingual reader), positioned as a supplement, is nothing other than the deferred or displaced translation of the title, there is no significant reason that we should not also read the publisher's name (FATA MORGANA)—inscribed on the cover in the same font—as a coded "translation" of the author's name: *Abdelkebir Khatibi = Fata Morgana.*

Morgan le Fay, or the Castle of Morgan le Fay is the name given to the *mirage* on the Italian coast, where castles, palaces, cities, and so on seem to appear over the sea.

Etymologically, M. de la Villemarqué proposes to interpret the Celtic name as the Breton *mor*, very strong, and *gan*, brilliant, in Italian *Fata Morgana*, a mirage.

Morganatic is an adjective used in Germanic law. A morganatic marriage is a *marriage of the left hand,* a marriage in which a man marrying a woman of inferior rank gives her his left hand in the wedding ceremony (see *Littré*).

The courtroom appearance, then, is the celebration of a "morganatic" marriage between a language of inferior rank, a "minor" language, and a language of superior rank, a "major" language. At this wedding, the writer marrying a foreign language gives it his left hand.

It is striking that, from the outset, a certain economy of the signature and of paternity is profoundly challenged by the metonymic circulation of proper names: ABDELKEBIR KHATIBI—FATA MORGANA—MIRAGE. The mirage of the proper name and of (the transparency of) origin is forever double, always already entwined with the other, with *its* subversive other, "the mirage of androgyny," as Khatibi puts it so well.

In fact, after the brief epigraph that opens the book, we find this vital remark in parentheses:

(This beginning of a text seemed to consume the storyteller, who read it ceaselessly. Each time he approached this beginning which excluded him: a story with no protagonist: or if there was one, it was the story itself, which heard itself utter the lone command: Start over.) (Khatibi 1990, 5–6)[17]

This appears on page 12, page 4 of the narrative itself, since three pages are taken up by the epigraph, which begins on page 9 with this phrase, which, Khatibi says, "composed itself":[18] "He left. He came back. He decided to leave definitively. The narrative should have stopped there, the book should have closed on itself."[19] This might be an invitation to a journey and its peregrinations, a sort of how-to of reading or an initiation into the text that Khatibi proposes. We too have begun reading as if there were nothing to it, discovering, at the turn of a page or with a turn of phrase, the need to return *to the beginning,* running the risk of seeing the *book* close upon itself this time. Now we have been warned; at any moment the text may slip away from the reader, may *retreat* because of our blindness to its mode of operation, or because of our "deafness" to the rhythm that constantly unmarks and re-marks the slightest sign. *Fata Morgana!* A morganatic movement of temporalization or temporization, of delay and retreat, but also of eternal return, prohibits any drowsiness on our part and calls for a new way of reading.

Let us repeat once again: from the outset, any transparency between word and thing, between name and being, between the signifieds of one language and those of another is "barred" or blurred, as is any impulse to relate the spacing of the constitutive elements of the book to a simple origin. Given the nonsymmetrical (anamorphic) reflexivity at work in each signifier, the self-presence of the enunciating subject is called into question, along with that of the addressee. If each "word" always sends us back to a *double* that transforms it and transports it "elsewhere" (into another language, another writing, another culture), *what becomes of the present* (of reading), *the future* (of interpretation), and the *past* (of a forever-*deferred* sense of belonging to a culture or a language called "originary")? This is pure reflection, dissemination *as far as the eye can see*, "permanent permutation" as Khatibi says, with no hope of dialectical co-optation or reterritorialization. Hence we better understand the reason for this attempt at writing *with the left hand*, why this immoderate attempt to "mix it up" with what Khatibi calls "bilanguage"—and the double scene it presides over—necessarily implies a constant detour through the figures of death, emptiness, and dream. We cannot decide to be bilingual; rather, we are caught by surprise in that position, "seduced" by the bilanguage and the destructive dissemination on which it depends:

> He didn't forget that in his own lexicon, the word for "seduction" (fitna) is a homograph for both the word for "war" and the word for "seduction" itself, for that knightly passion celebrated by those who go off alone into the desert, a passion for the unknown beloved.
>
> In this respect, seduction carried them to a dual stage, delighting in language's sensuousness. What could they know? What was she looking for in him? Some child's notion of an oriental paradise? A forgotten desire? How to determine from the smallest word, the least deed the order of mortal law—or its disorder? Death: and to find a way to live in this word, it was necessary to go over all the bi-langue's power of destruction. In his mother tongue, death is a child's idea of heaven, a celestial hereafter. It was his duty to reseed himself not with

this charming reminder but rather with the illusion of invisible angels, thereby glorifying every loving encounter. (Khatibi 1990, 11)[20]

The love of language necessarily sends the narrator back to a *double scene* that enchants him, but which, in its *fitna*, its seduction and war, leads to nothing less than death and emptiness. The morganatic book is a desert topography.

Thus the book has never begun (to be read); in any case, it is obvious that whatever approach is used—monolingual or bilingual, for example—the book has always already embarked on the notions of beginning, middle, and end. If we are inattentive for even a moment to the play of permanent transformation and translation, we risk finding it closed (to any reading). To start *Amour bilingue* is always to start over. To decipher a word, an expression, is always to translate, that is, to transport the reader into another space, another place. Can we, then, consider ourselves quit of what the "monogram" of the frontispiece indicates regarding the perpetual displacement whose disseminating mark appears on even the slightest sign? In other words, can we ever open or close a book that seems to propose that we read it as deferral and difference? To answer this question, let us open the book anew and return to the beginning(s). New mirages await us there.

After the blank or white page, the book opens with a half-title page, on which only the two words, *Amour bilingue,* appear, this time in smaller (black) type than the red type of the cover. The rest is blank. When we reach the fifth page, however, one element can hardly fail to attract our attention: except for two or three details, page 5 is a replica of the cover. But, this time, although the format and color of the ("proper") names "Abdelkebir Khatibi" and "Fata Morgana" have not changed, the title, located in the same place as the cover title, is black on white, a mirror image. The monogram punctuated with red has disappeared, replaced by the name *Abdeslam* GENOUNI (the calligrapher) and the word *Calligraphies*. There are two calligraphies in all: the one on the cover, and the one on page 7, which occupies practically *all the available space,* haunting with its shadow or figure the vacant spot left by the suppression of "ASHK ELLISSANAIN," which appears only on the cover.

I do not think I am giving in to interpretive delirium by insisting on the fact that such an arrangement of textual elements is not fortuitous. It constitutes a *mise en abyme* that foregrounds the text's mode of operation. They mark the place of a difference, or more precisely, of a *différance*, which only a patient reading may—not domesticate or co-opt—but perhaps simply make perceptible or possible. In brief, let us say that Khatibi's text has a "third ear," an ability not only to read *between* the lines but also to read *through* the lines and even *through* the pages, the power to fade in and fade out, the skill of passing through the pages and *revealing*—in the theological or theophanic sense, not in the sense of revealing "what is hidden *behind*," like an X-ray—what, until that moment, had escaped the (expressive) naturalist and instrumentalist vision of language.

Let us not jump ahead, however, but rather let us restate the question. What does page 5 propose for us to read? What does it propose for our rereading? Apart from the colors in play (and the appearance of the calligrapher's name), page 5 proposes only that we "read" an absence, that we "see" a blank—the empty space left by the disappearance of the monogram *Ashk Ellissanaïn*—which is immediately overtaken by its magnified shadow. (It may be worth reminding the monolingual reader at this point that the monogram "Ashk Ellissanaïn" means "love in two languages.") As it happens, in fact, printed in thick calligraphic characters—but can such metaphysically loaded notions as "character" and "discrete line" still be used in this case?—the new "form" of the Arabic translation of the title cannot help but show through the large blank space produced by the appearance/disappearance of the monogram on the cover. This aspect of things is not without consequence, of course; even as it overcodes the *visible* dimension of the *readable*, because of its very absence, the transparency of the monogram designates, while canceling out, what should remain unapparent: the blank/white space, the irreducible gap that separates and divides *each letter* of the other language, the silent difference without which language could not happen. We might point out that it is this "supplemental mark"—which, in its very evanescence, brings blankness, nothingness, to light and "opens" the text—that constitutes one of the fundamental processes of the Khatibian text.

Like Mallarmé's fold, wing, feather, page, or veil, as Jacques Derrida describes them in "La Double Séance," the "excess of mark" and the "margin of sense" of the monogram that opens Khatibi's work "is not one valence among others in the series [of Arabic words transcribed and translated in French, in Khatibi's text; (my addition)],

even though it is inserted in there, too." *(Dissemination* 1981,
251–52). Because the monogram "translates" without returning us to
the same, because, due to its appearance/disappearance, it brings out
blanks and gaps that the target language obliterates, it constantly alludes to that which *exceeds* any language, *all the while designating*
the "law" of its mode of operation *in an atopical cipher (chiffre
atopique).* Henceforth, the writing machine of the bilanguage will
take charge of putting this impossible "logic" to work. Blankness,
then—and after that, what?

> Everything was white with the day's thudding brightness. He
> felt extremely tired. Only a little while before, sitting silently,
> an open book before him, he was meditating or dreaming. The
> slide of light: as the day wore on, he had the impression that
> the pages he turned were blank. . . .
>   He began to read again. His glance passed over the letters, so
> much that he grew dizzy with the blackness of each word.
> (Khatibi 1990, 39)[21]

To begin reading the book, perhaps we should first have folded the
cover in two, obtaining a figure something like a Rorschach inkblot,
if the images were symmetrical after a simple "fold," and if the colors
mixed and mingled. However, the *"morganatic" projection*—left-
handed or "gauche"—from the upper to the lower half of the cover
does not return to the same; the "morganatic" projection mixes neither colors nor languages. As a "geometry" of these two heterogeneous languages, the projection means that the color of one—the
color that adorns its blinding expression—re-marks the pertinent
characteristics of the other, that is, makes it *pertinent.* Thus the
"Book" (of writing) is a morganatic "test," an apsychological, atopical text of the bilanguage.

That is where we were when we began the book. But now (on page
5) we are faced with a lateral translation, not a fold of a page onto itself on the basis of an unlocatable center, but rather an impression, a
double exposure of an entire page in tinted laid paper, a deforming
trace or magical block. Anamorphosis. Fold upon fold; between-the-
two (pages), another blank page. *Fata Morgana!* It appears clearly that
the monogram, even if it is in permanent withdrawal or retreat,
overdetermines the text by forever postponing any attempt to drive
the text toward a single sense or theme, or toward a unified space

(here and now). At every moment, *and due to the very fact of its initial appearance,* "all positions are shattered" (K. Yacine). There is no longer any self-presence (of the narrator or of the reader) but there is also no longer any correspondence between the text and its signs. There is only infinite permutation, endless reverberation, and the play of blinding mirrors. It is true that this aspect of things concerns (only) the arrangement of the first seven pages, after which no calligrams appear to haunt the text with their intrusive presence.

What of the text itself, then? That is, how can it be claimed that the text is overdetermined by the irruption of a monogram that *all in all only appears twice* and moreover is not "legible" to a monolingual reader? But we should pay less attention to the frequency of a word or sign than to its *syntactic* status in the general economy of a text, in the *code* at work. As Georges Bataille has said, we must attend to the "toil" of words. With Khatibi, we must give our undivided attention to the "toil" of signs and their "disposition" within the general economy of the text.

What happens at the text's opening is part of a complex (metonymic) mechanism of displacement—a veritable *trans-fer(ence)*—of the differentiating power from the monogram to the foreign language. One of its major effects is to restore the foreign language—transformed by this very operation into the target language—to the original spacing that silently deployed discrete signs, semes, and punctuation marks, and consigned them all to the "symbolic."

To illustrate what I have just stated, let me refer to a characteristic passage from *Amour bilingue*. In the scene depicted in the epigraph, it is dark, the narrator is at home in bed. Perhaps he was sleeping and was suddenly awakened by a nightmare or an illumination:

> It was then that the words fluttered in a parade in front of him, then they came crashing down on top of one another: language was mad.
> Get up? He couldn't: instead of the fragments of a word, there was room for nothing visible: the sea itself had sunk in the night. And in French—his foreign language—the word for "word," *mot,* is close to the one for "death," *la mort;* only one letter is missing: the succinctness of the impression, a syllable, the ecstasy of a stifled sob. Why did he believe that language is more beautiful, more terrible for a foreigner?

He calmed down instantly when an Arabic word, kalma, appeared, kalma and its scholarly equivalent, kalima, and the whole string of diminutives which had been the riddles of his childhood . . . klima. . . . the disglossal kal(i)ma appeared again without mot's having faded away or disappeared. Within him, both words were observing each other, preceding what had now become the rapid emergence of memories, fragments of words, onomatopoeias, garlands of phrases, intertwined to the death: undecipherable. The scene is still silent. (Khatibi 1990, 4)[22]

I needed to quote this passage at length because it so marvelously stages what I have called the "transfer" from the monogram to the text. Khatibi recounts the "deciphered" version, spelling out word for word the disseminating logic of this phenomenon of destructive contamination of the foreign language's transparency. Yet this time, not only are the blanks that the foreign language had to repress in order to express itself exhibited, but language becomes crazed as it comes out of the morganatic test, since *in French the "mot" (word) is always close to "mort" (death)*. "Behind" it all—but still transparent— is that which forever disappears, that which appears *in the holes already begun,* yet another sign, another word from the other language. The effects of the turner's tool again? In what sense?

The monogram displays the invisible by erasing itself, by withdrawing; the blank, the margins, the folds, the gaps that were insignificant moments ago now haunt each word, or more exactly, the slightest interstice of the foreign language, which begins to signify between the lines, or *to open between the lines.* As Khatibi says so eloquently, *"le mot* is close to *la mort,* there is only one letter missing." Such is the power of the monogram's irruption between the lines, letters, and transparent pages on tinted vellum. The monogram is always about to surface at the intersection of the characters of the foreign tongue; its mode of appearing is by definition unpredictable and uncontrollable. It may, *at any moment,* cause one or several "figures" of the "inferior" language to loom up *in the blank spaces it clears.* Like the syncategoreme '*"between"* analyzed by Derrida, the monogram cannot be reduced to a purely syntactic or semantic game. Even better, "beyond its syntactic function, through the re-marking of its semantic void [a re-marking that is illegible for the monolingual reader and redundant for the bilingual reader (my addition)], it in fact begins to signify. Its semantic void *signifies*, but it signifies spacing and articulation; it has as its meaning the possibility of syntax; it orders the play of meaning. *Neither purely syntactic nor purely semantic*, it marks the articulated opening of that opposition" (Derrida 1981, 222) between two languages, or more precisely, between two systems of intervals that forever return to the void, the breach, and the blank that are the condition for their appearance. In typographical terms, the monogram can be categorized as one of the blanks and it determines a strange, an "other" writing practice, in Khatibi's words. We are now in a position to name this practice, referring to a sphere that *Amour bilingue* has never ceased to secretly seek out—the "hidden art" of typography.

"When it is necessary to move one line away from another, or to separate, as with footnotes, a more important from a lesser text, it is with a lead, or blank lines composed of quads, that we increase the spacing. This is called 'BLANCHIR' [to white out] or 'JETER DU BLANC' [literally, to 'cast white']" (Claye 1874, 21, my translation).[23]

If this text had never existed, a "friendly reader" of Khatibi's would have had to invent it, to account for the kind of writing *Amour bilingue* inaugurates. What makes for the force and beauty of Khatibi's text is perhaps, most of all, the art of "casting white," of "whiting out"[24] the French language he loves, and through which he tells of his love (otherwise "inexpressible") for the other (language), *his* other language. He *whites out* language not only in the simple metaphorical sense of the term—for example, by wresting it from a history where it had become synonymous with *de*culturation or with *accul*turation—but also in the *most technical* and *formal* sense. Since his project is to *separate* one language from another and to *detach* the (previously) stronger text from the "lesser," Khatibi invokes the disruptive power of Arabic calligraphy *in a French linguistic context*; by "increasing the intervals" of the "foreign" language, he clears an unprecedented space where what is called the "mother" tongue can make itself heard. In a way, it is as if he were "sideswiping" the French language to make it exhibit what, in its customary usage, remains completely choked: on the one hand, its own system of blanks and gaps, but also, more importantly, the repression and exclusion that French has represented for the Maghrebian (or other African) Francophone writer. "Casting white" at the French language consists of *relieving the guilt* inherent in using this "paper language" (Kafka) that French represents for the Maghrebian, but also of making it the instrument of a new psychic topography, what Khatibi calls an "other thought."

It is now easier to understand in what sense the calligram is never a simple "translation" of the terms of another text or language; to pursue the metaphor a bit further, we might say that Khatibi makes the Arabic calligram play the same role as quads in typography:

> Thus there are, besides the characters, diverse kinds not apparent after printing, that are part of the blanks; these are quads, em quads, the spaces we have just mentioned.
>
> The spaces separate the letters; they come in many strengths and thicknesses. The em quads go at the head of the line, and the quads at the end of the line, when the line is not completed by the text itself.[25]

Morganatic writing, that is, the staging of the bilanguage in *Amour bilingue,* consists of adding one more quad to the array of the writer-composer (in bilanguage), but a quad—a space—that this time would not merely intervene between words or mark the empty spaces from one line of the text to another. Rather, this other quad, though not apparent in the printing (of the text in the strict sense) and confined to working in the margins, would subvert the entire economy of the foreign language—in short, would make it do and say the impossible. It would almost make it speak Arabic, pidgin, the language of the pied noir, and so on. Having "whited out" French, Khatibi now finds himself in a position to claim for himself the words Kafka attributed to Madam Kluge, with a one-word difference "You see, I speak all languages but . . . in French!" *Il se calma/Kalma/Klima/Kal(i)ma.*

Let us return to the text we set aside a moment ago, which explains the necessity and the work of the calligram:

> He began to read again. His glance passed over the letters, so much that he grew dizzy with the blackness of each word, with the magnificent folios of the book. Instantaneously and at the same time, it seemed to him that although he understood and could decipher what he read, nevertheless at the heart of his reading was an intangible word not in the text. Worrisome intangibility which with one blow destroyed pages, words, lines,

and punctuation, through the agency of a black spot floating between his eyes and the book.

Soon, the book would light up around this word he still couldn't make out, this word which left the book to seep away from its pages and to mark by its passing the squint his glance produced so that the sign of the night would shine before him. Night entered and exited the book, somehow erasing the white with the black. Still, he could not tear his eyes away. (Khatibi 1990, 39)[26]

Signifying the spacing, the fold, the interval opened by the "whiting out" of French, the calligram makes use of a logic of the bilanguage *no longer accessible to a purely statistical analysis*. As Jacques Derrida has said, the "between," strictly speaking, does not exist; it is by nature plural, pluralizing *and* disseminating, itself disseminated. Therefore it is pointless to subordinate the effective power of the monogram to the frequency of its appearance. Whether or not Khatibi was the "designer" of the book layout changes nothing. The reference to the calligrapher, the repetition of the calligram after the blank page, and the particular distribution of the elements, which I described earlier, are all summoned by the text itself as much as they summon the reading and cryptic writing of the text they "order." Let us also note that, although Arabic letters, written by hand or typeset, are always *joined*—"entwined to death," as Khatibi says—this is only rarely the case of typeset French, where the "discrete" nature of the letters reappears whenever the manuscript is published in the usual manner. Hence it is surely the intra- and interlinguistic gap between the two languages that determines the rule for a (new) game with language. At stake in this game is not only the narrator's life and death, but also his psychological or sexual identity, and his national or cultural sense of belonging. This is the paragrammatic dimension opened by "whiting out" language and bringing the bilanguage into play.

"He calmed down instantly when an Arabic word, kalma, appeared, kalma and its scholarly equivalent, kalima, and the whole string." This example, chosen from many others, plainly shows that the *ana-* or *para*grammatic interplay at work in *Amour bilingue* is neither contingent nor "illusory." "Separating" the letters of the foreign tongue is always a dangerous game in that, even within its "mad" gesture, it still "touches" on a "Reality":[27] that of *ho-mophony*. Where the monolingual writer or reader can and must hear and see nothing (between the lines or letters), the bilanguage writer watches (the whole economy of) language collapse. "That's why I admire the gravity of the blind man's gestures and the desperate impossible love the deaf man has for language," says Khatibi. This demands a veritable "mutation of thought."

It is here that the alteration of time, which becomes a *temporization* and a forever-deferred gesture, can assume its full meaning. Indeed, if the "whiting out" of French hollows out the word (*mot*) and there traces the "death" (*mort*) that lives within it because it gives the narrator (always mirrored by the reader and the scriptor) the ability and dexterity to always see double, as he plunders the words under the words, this movement also determines a new relation to time in general, *and to the time of reading in particular*. Reading is sometimes *slowed*, sometimes greatly *accelerated* by the telescoping effect of letters and their accompanying phonemes; the bilanguage thus becomes a matter and an instrument of speed, a god of *word processing*! Writing-and-reading, but with two hands, "listening," but with a "third ear.": in this case, writing or reading is not only stereophonic or stereographic, but, above all, *stroboscopic and strobophonic*, a reading or writing *between* the lines, *between* phrases, in the margin.

> Nostalgia he liked to think about and pronounce in Arabic:
> hanîne, anagram for a doubled pleasure [*jouissance*]. He broke
> the word down into its elements: "h," an aspirant from the
> pharynx, then a murmured "a" before the "n-î-ne," modulation
> sustained by the long "i." Pronouncing this word, repeating it
> was a breath of a kiss in his throat, a regular unbroken breath.
> A vocal ecstasy, a euphoric call, for him alone a song, endlessly
> whispered to the absent beloved. (Khatibi 1990, 7–8)[28]

Khatibi's anagram, like the calligram that is the condition for its appearance, shows itself to be ambiguous; as Jean-Claude Milner writes: "On one hand, the anagram tells of how homophony belongs to language, but on the other hand, it also tells of how it is inassimilable" (d'une part, il dit *l'appartenance de l'homophonie à la langue*; mais d'autre part, il en dit l'inassimilable, 1978); or, in Khatibi's ter-

minology, it tells of the "intractable difference." Always necessarily
constructed with (at least) two languages, two graphic systems that
are deaf and blind to each other, occurring only in a place that exceeds all language, the Khatibian anagram is always a manifestation
of a dehiscence (in the being that speaks or writes), of an "even more"
as Milner writes, that will always take the breath away, cut off
speech: "Bearing the weight of an invisible god, a single gesture: to in-
terrupt him, render him speechless" (Khatibi 1990, 24).[29] From this
the necessity arises not only to invent another way of writing, to create a new "style," but also to cross the barriers that separate the
different modes of writing, the different literary genres, precisely by
mirroring writing in another writing—forever two languages, two
writings, two thoughts working *at once*:

> Later on I learned Braille and the languages of the handicapped.
> Perhaps I'm capable of writing only for bilingual cripples: in
> any case, it will be too late to get back together with me. Did I
> lose you before I ever met you? I must definitely have my story
> translated into Braille before the computer has swept up every-
> thing into the communicable. (Khatibi 1990, 24)[30]

It is all a question of speed, but in a relative sense, since "handicapped bilinguals" can always choose to read faster (or more slowly)
Their favorite place is the one the monolinguals miss because the latter do not possess the formidable time and space exploration engine
of the bilanguage and its gift of double vision.

In immediately inscribing the figure of the dissolving calligram as
an act of anamorphic translation, Khatibi has undertaken not only to
undermine the domination of one language or culture by another, but
has also dedicated himself to an even more revolutionary task, that of
founding an "other thought," that is, in his own terms, "a (thought)
that is essentially that of a minority, fragmented, incomplete."[31] In
short, the task is to found a mode of thinking of the *milieu* (the
middle, the background, the between) that is not "neutral," or "a
(thought) riddled by its marginality, displaced, and full of silent questions" (*Maghreb Pluriel*, 1983b).[32]

"The thinking of the 'us' we strive toward does not locate itself
within the circle of (Western) metaphysics nor within Islamic theol-
ogy, but at their margin. An increasingly evident margin" (1983b, 17,
editor's translation).[33]

In this way, writing and thinking in the bilanguage definitely does not imply a return to the inner self, but "nothing but critical trans-formations" (1983b, 24). This new shift in priorities, places, proper-ties, and reappropriations (of words, thought, language, and civiliza-tion) cannot occur without putting in place a new economy of sexual identity. Indeed, if everything (in language, in the Maghrebian self) is always composed of at least two languages, two cultural scenes, and two bodies (habitus), then, consequently, no limit can be ascribed to what separates one sex from another. In "whiting out" the relation-ship to language (to languages in general), Khatibi also "whites out" the relationship to sexual difference. To simplify, one cannot venture to change languages without "changing (its) sex."

> One day—and this only recently—he loved a woman, changed sex. Sex in circumcised sex, two-tongued sex, like a snake. From his anus emerged the face of an invisible god. He was then violated by the foreign tongue. Thrown to the ground, he suffered hideously. But—bizarre sensation—he was behind his violator, not taking his turn as penetrator but rather penetrated by the tongue's orgasm—his homosexuality filed in the diction-aries of the whole world. (Khatibi 1990, 47)[34]

Mama ware ein besserer Name, Wenn man nur hinter ihm nicht "Mutter" sich vorstellte. "Mama" would be preferable, if it were pos-sible not to imagine "Mutter" *behind* this word, said Kafka. One day, someone will have to write the "history" of this *hinter ihm,* the "one behind" that haunts our languages and our discourse, of this "invisi-ble God" that violates language's transparency (to itself) and calls into question the self-identity of all things. The atopical figure of the androgyne in Khatibi's writing is an element of those "histories," inseparable from the shifts brought on by the bilanguage: "To trans-late purity into impurity, prostitution into androgyny was an adven-ture which had to be lived without holding back in any way. He wan-dered from country to country, from body to body" (Khatibi 1990, 23).[35]

Such an adventure demands to be lived "without restraint" be-cause, here too, it is less a question of adopting, or "toppling" into, one sex or the other—a move that would not in itself constitute an adventure and would assume that the question of sexual difference was resolved—than of maintaining oneself *between* the sexes, all sexes. Not bisexual or transsexual, but androgynous, not one and the other, but the other of both sexes (of both languages). Since the two sexes do not exist as such in a natural state, the situation of the androgyne—and that of the bilanguage writer—is connected to its "mixed" status, as Plato said of the sophist. The "mix" is a fold in relation to which "there is" man and woman, male and female, being and nonbeing. The result is a wandering, which that figure, or that "writing," calls for. To echo the excellent analysis Alain Grosrichard has done of the status of the eunuch—another "mixed" figure that has haunted the Western literature of the "Orient"[36]—we might say that, in the logic of multiple displacements that the bilanguage mobilizes, the androgyne "is neither the non-being, nor the being-as-whole, but the very figure of otherness itself, the Other that arouses all others, the tutor of their desire, the bar or the break that relates the sexes (languages) and makes this relation both necessary and impossible, since the androgyne (is that not its very function?) is always between one and the other and, so to speak, in the middle of the bed—even and especially when we are sure that it isn't" (Grosrichard 1998, 161–62, translation modified).[37]

What, then, is an androgyne, unless s/he too is a specialist in mimicry and a producer of simulacra, a being that belongs to the fantastic, and produces before your eyes mirages that leave you agape?

Who cannot see, then, that I've taken a route that, without ceasing and without working, I will continue as long as there is ink ("*ancre*," *sic*)[38] and paper. The reader should make no mistake, however; in proposing this attempt at a "reading" of Khatibi's book—of just a few of its pages, in reality—I will have, in the end, not so much interpreted it as lined up my fantasies alongside those of Khatibi, Derrida, Mallarmé, Milner, Montaigne, Yacine, Grosrichard, and the devil.

[9]

the names of oran

HÉLÈNE CIXOUS

THERE ARE SO MANY names, and each one calls to the other, I could never note them all. I shall let them come here in the order without apparent order in which they come when I pronounce their key-name, which is the color of the chrome with which I buttered language with my brush in order to relish painting.

I say Oran, and the words come running down the boulevards and the alleyways, up the hills, along the cliffs the color of raw meat overhanging the coast, here they are clacking high in my new child's ears, dazzled with sonorous sparkles: le Villaginègre, Ya Ouled, Mémé Eckmühl, Ptivichy, Saha, La Calentica, El Khobz, Djib Batata, Ima Ima, Mleh, Fissa fissa, Khlass, El Bab, Mers El Kébir, toflah, sbakh al Kheir, Baba, achraâl, Tlatin douro, l'ahmar, Dolorès, old Mrs. Flörsheim, Promenade de l'Etang, Boulevard Galliéni, Ya Benti, Lycée Lamoricière, Lycée Stéphane Gsell, Oran-Républicain, la Marine, Ain Temouchent, Canastel, Alberplage, Clairefontaine, Cap Falcon with its dunes, la Kemia, Aïd-el-Kebir, lmaâ, and on Sunday the family took the word *les Planteurs* and we went up the slopes of the Moorish cemetery, climbing to the Belvedere, then across the rocky scrub, in the direction of the word *Santacruz*, and when my father took us we made a stop at the word *Marabout*.

And all of this—these explorations, these communions, these ascensions—was Arabic, the Arabic we spoke at *rue Philippe*, on the corner of the *Placedarmes* in Oran.

All the beach-words, the theater-words, the street-words were both strange and strangers, and, "common" or "proper," they fluttered in the form of magic, incantatory verbal spirits, without ever making sentences but making "things," "places," "goods," dwellings, scintillate and appear, themselves, the words, being musical houses where

This chapter was translated by Eric Prenowitz.

sorceries kept watch. These word-names with powerful charms were accompanied in Oran by odors, aromatics, whose red ocher gold powders clogged the thick jute sacks of the spice shops. The names of Oran smelled. They had the perfumes of the Orient that are called *species*. Because language knows that the aromatic is the species itself and that the *spice* is the substance of the word. The name-words were spices of spices. They came to me by air. I sniffed them. Spices of species. Nutmegs cumin chili peppers trails paths led me from one being to another by the tip of my nose and the tip of my tongue. Oran has an odor. The Oran-odor. Privilege and wealth of fragrant countries. India also begins with odor. But the odor India is a mix of perfumes and dejecta: rose and excrement unite. The name of Oran smells of the Bible and incense.

Standing before the lions, real lions of eternal cast iron, or else it was bronze, between the palm trees, with the municipaltheater to my right, and, to my left, the emergencypharmacy flanked by the two grottos where liquors and metamorphoses ferment, I always had that peculiar sensation of having-just-arrived. I was the voyager girl passing in a city-house-theater; no sojournment, no repetition, no duration, ever softened the acuity of my aboarding. I was always standing before between on the doorstep of a foreign country of mine, because of all these name-words, this fauna, which I could not put down on paper and which enveloped me in transparent sonorous forests. Oran was always the book before writing, everything took word, and the word was a name and the names were the precious pieces of a mobile mosaic that I collected and constantly arranged in new combinations, just as at the beach I gathered mother-of-pearl which I worshipped in a multifaceted and precise cult.

The spellbinding charm of this jewelry came from the fact that I knew nothing about transcription. The language one does not know how to write has a magic authority. It is she who spoke to me, and at her words I traveled. I lived in a living illustrated dictionary where the word *cyclorameur* came to light beside the word *araucaria* and the word *créponné* to form groups of intensely erotic elements through incongruous and compatible contiguities. And just as the *Dolorès* group—laundry blue—the royal blue color of the round detergent tablets—the song of the boiling in the laundry boiler—the clean smell of the dish towels—the gallery—the washboard—the *savondeMarseille*—which the words *Bésamé-Bésamémucho* lifted with melancholy, was inseparable from and prophetic of passions I knew nothing about, in the same way the *Mohamed* group—the tin dish of chickpeas in broth—the coat of rag-strips—the darkness of the staircase that sheltered his abode—the solitude of the silent man in the cage—the mystery of his definitive move, as planned by our gods, to the back of the entryway in the four-story house, was part of the most intimate aspect of my existence and I was as attached to those slightly mute living as to very sensitive parts of my body. Thus I lived in the bosom of Oran, bathing in a dissemination of signifiers that lulled and moved my heart, I was in this language intangible in its totality, elusive compact, and which I could never hold in my mouth.

It was not French.

What Is a Language?

I shall never know if it was Arabic that gave me German or German that gave my ear the taste for Arabic and not just any German but precisely the one that was my first food, the German language of Omi my grandmother who arrived from Germany just in time at the end of 1938 to initiate my palate to the mix of words and cabbage with potatoes, or else if it was my father's voice with its rhythmic and persuasive inflections. I did not like to eat. Luckily the grownups bewitched me. I am sitting at the table facing my adversary the plate. The attacks of the plate. Everything displayed there was examined by my hostility. Ah, if only I could have lived without vegetables, but not without words or sound!

By luck and patience, my fostering parents translated the mouthfuls into delicious words for me. First Omi transformed the cabbage purée, that pallid paste, into a field plowed with regular furrows. And it was Austerlitz. Already it was no longer exactly cabbage. Then came the story. I only swallow the cabbage with the sentence. For the carrots, it takes all of my father. I only gave in to carrots smothered in jokes.

What Is a "Tongue"?

Later in Algiers Omi would rather buy a veal tongue. But in Oran it was ox tongue. According to me it began well, with the compact well-shaped muscular end and it finished horrible burgeoning fatty exhibiting the torn strips from being wrenched from the mouth of a flayed animal which left me inconsolable. At the market among the entrails impaled on metal hooks frequented by flies and dripping with blood, they were the blood-stained primitive incarnation of the spirit of the Greek and biblical tragedies. I saw Absalom Oedipus the gouged-out ones the decapitated ones there was no species barrier to my eyes between a raw meat stripped of its organic modesties, exposed, crucified, and another meat. Omi took the thing in her eminent cook's hands hefted it, and began to transfigure it partially. First it is scalded and the thick skin that sheathes it is removed without difficulty, liberating the delicate tenderness of the flesh. According to my father the organ is fixed by the posterior end (the end I abhorred) to the floor of the mouth and owes its admirable mobility to the seventeen striated muscles innervated by the upper hypoglossal. According to Omi there was no relation between *diese schöne Zunge* and *die deutsche Sprache* ["this beautiful tongue and the German language-tongue'"]. That is why she peeled the *Zunge* with a detached expertise. Whereas for me there was only one tongue, which was that of the sacrifice and the butcher, meat itself whose soul dispersed in the hot and odorous air into millions of sounds could never be made into stew.

The one we spoke in Oran my native city was entirely foreign to me and thus desirable. I love my mother tongue—but which one—to begin with it *h*eaves, it *h*aspirates, it rasps, it calls me enticing me, it *ch*atches me, it *h*ails me, it *h*élène's me, it holds me back and drags me with this imperative H, the breath of YaHaweh himself, it cannot be disobeyed, it gives me the impetus and the summons from out of this H that inaugurates me and does not exist in French, but in Arabic-German it aspirates the turmoil [*émois*] along its path.

H, the name of the note *ti* in German.

I bear the German name of my great-grandmother Helene Meyer.

My first name is German, the French language swipes it from me, extinguishes its *ti*, decapitates me. My second name the bizarre one has always medusa-dumbfounded the French. And why? I know not what sound hidden in its phonemes produces the surprise and the minor revulsion that is caused by a spider crab. People don't really know where to grasp it by which leg to stop it. It is a name that won't be tamed. Is it the X that puzzles the star with four points, is it the effect of the CIX that drives them back? No matter how much my name and I spell ourselves, we are not received. We finish the ordeal with a scratch, our C is suppressed, we are disfigured, we are impossible. So: there exists a name that the tongue in which I play with writing recognizes instantaneously to be unpronounceable, indomitable, inaudible, escaping the ear, the voice, and the orthographic corset. Cixous an apotropaic name. My proper hedgehog.

But in Algerian it is at home and as familiar as can be, as unsavage, as crumbly as can be and not spicy at all. As *Kouskous* I am spread semolina in a large dish rolled, rubbed, kneaded by the solid palms of mémé-couscous, moistened, steamed, and accompanied with vegetables meats juices and sauces. No one in Algeria can do without my name I am the daily bread. I am the wheat that does not wound. I am the good repetition, the relief on the tongue, the most common of common names. The most consumed of dishes. All of North Africa lives by it.

What is there in this name, which in the north is poison and in the south is gift? There is a secret.

But I did not know it, neither in Oran, nor in Algiers, nor later in Paris when I said I was Cixous with a C at the beginning, when I tried at lycée Fromentin to slip the word by in French, which repelled it, I didn't know that I was hard wheat flour. The family had a secret, but it was a completely unknown secret. No one has ever heard of it.

One day—it was during a "Salon du Livre," [a book fair]—I was there—but who was I, who are you when you're sitting in the place called Salon du Livre—and these questions are a part of the event that happened then and which I am going to recount—I was there, sitting at a little table, next to myself, I next to myself sitting under my name, under the name of the author Hélène Cixous—a somewhat crazy situation but which luckily only lasts for an objectively limited length of time—because the place called "Salon du Livre" is indeed the only one where I am swapped and appear in good health though crazy as my own fiction. And on this stage not only do I look like the person I know the least, but in addition I respond in her place unavowedly. I am not the only one, in this situation, to be crazy. The people who move around this fair are all crazy in different ways, each one mistaking the other for someone else hundreds of strangers recognize one another they think and all is quid pro quo. It is frightening. Dangerous. But salutary. One is rapidly covered with phantoms and false photos. There is no more reality. But in its place, no Dream. I was sitting surrounded with books I had neither read nor written

but what matter, and above me on the wall the portraits of our favorite actresses kept watch. I was sitting under Liv Ullmann. An en-
thusiastic man assured me he had seen all my films. Did I have a
blonde look? Such is the magic of the fair.

A young woman came to alight in front of me. Smiling, she folded
her wings and struck me with her brilliant beauty. She seemed to me
the opposite of Liv Ullmann. Brunette, tall, keen, with narrow eye-
brows, well-defined lips, very white cheeks.

"You are a Berber," she says to me. She was a Berber, I could see.

"No," I say.

Her brilliant green eyes came and went on my face, along my eye-
brows, around my ears.

"You have my aunt's eyes," says the stranger.

"False!" I cry.

"My mother's lips exactly." She smiles firmly at me. "You are
from our village. I have already seen you."

"Sorry," I say, "I am not a Berber." And I pushed back her smile.

"The spitting image of my sister."

"You are mistaken."

"You deny? So be it."

I defended myself with a violent frown. Upon which she vanished
from before me. And the portals closed.

I felt a sad sensation of victory and immediately afterwards regret
and thereupon grief.

I have defended the truth, I said to myself, but do I know it? Who
did I defend? Who haunts me? Yet I am very sure. But of what. I dis-
owned an unknown person who is dear to me, I thought sadly, I myself have chased off the Secret. I didn't even ask her name. A letter arrived for me and I sent it back. And yet she resembled my father like
a daughter, but I refused her and I don't even know why. I will never
know who had written to me at my address.

Could I be a Berber? Could I have been invented centuries ago in
the Atlas Mountains? It is a non-impossibility.

In my father's family memory begins in 1867. But before 1867
there stretches a vast unexplored uninhabited forgetting, no one in
the family remembers ever having forgotten anything. And before the
immense depopulated forgetting stretched a craggy landscape with
hills climbed by goats and planted with pines. The events that oc-

curred among the sizzling rocks are comparable to the beds of oueds that remember having known white-water rapids. The insistent drought is witness to these disappearances.

A story has been entirely lost I know not where or when. A cloth was cut and ripped, a bridge collapsed, a sin was buried, a love was punished, a promise was not kept. I would so like to know the names of the woman and the man who were buried beneath time and whose tongues still move in my mouth.

My father speaks French, Spanish, English, Arabic, and since Omi entered the home, he also speaks German Charabia, that is, Algharbiya, that is, Berber crossed with Westphalian. It is a language that makes use of everything it encounters, incomprehensible beyond the apartment, a language of signs and *Witz*, a tongue of apes and cats. If the cat asks: "Who took my dictionary?" my father raises his left arm points the index finger of his right hand at his left armpit, and says: "*soulbra.*" Sometimes he only says "soulbra" without the mime. "Soulbra" means "I do not know" in Westphaloberber Charabia. The etymology of *soulbra* is as follows: Soulbra, from: what is there *sous-le-bras* [under-the-arm]? There is *sueur*, French for "sweat." In German: *Schweiß; in Schweiß gebadet*, drenched in sweat; *Schweißtuch:* shroud; *Schweißblatt:* dress shield; *ichSchweißnicht:* I-do-not-know. *IchSchweißnicht* is what Omi the German immigrant says dozens of times a day, because she can hardly speak French. So we go Charabia-wise from one tongue to another juggling from syllable to syllable. Our tongue is preferably terse, accentuated, tonic, laryngeal. Language is a hoax. Omi cooks the ox tongue in *Sauerbraten* and always saves me the tip. Doctor Adida, the dentist, raises *dindons* (turkeys) on the balcony across the street. Whereas we have only a hen. "Can you hear Adida's-chubby-turkey?" cries my father, or rather: *le dindondodudadida*, and he promptly obtains a bonus of pleasure from the dentist across the street. Meanwhile my mother puts K's everywhere (at our house we eat Karrots, at grandma's they are still carrots). But what I prefer are the *Kha*, the *ach!* their severe sweetness, their sweet severity, the rasping of their muffled exclamation which to my great regret does not exist in French, and which I only encounter, with their flower of bitterness mixed with the voice of anguish, in the double consonant, my X, my Ks, my Chi, the single unknown that counts for ten.

Arabic, for me, was always the sweet harshness of the German language, which grates the fur of its young, the mixture of the firm hand and the combing, the rubbing of the silky muscle of the sexual organ between the teeth, the crossing of dryness and breath, at the edge of expiration.

When I listen to myself write I hear the Arabic of *rue Philippe* shaking the roots of its wings in my ears. I like the word *arbre* (tree). It is a survivor. There are not many RBR in French. Nor many SKS. Or KFK. I like the name Franz Kafka its rustling of wings in the branches.

And to think that I do not speak Arabic, yet Arabic speaks (to) me.

When I was ten, happiness sadness, my father gave me the last gift: he gave me two teachers, one of Arabic, the other of Hebrew, and then he died. Without knowing that he was the author of a condemned tale. I don't know if it was a letter; it was a will that I did not read. It was surely a message but brutally posthumous. I struggled for a while. The two men resembled each other the two alphabets imitated replaced approached repelled each other. "What did you say?" I cried at my father who was becoming more distant, "what did you want to tell me?"

But a porch was closed. What have I done? Was this a legacy? An inheritance? Should I speak Hebrew arabically? Should I join prefer separate should I betray love contaminate be a hound hunting for hares fly two wings one white the other black flow a river from one bank to the other. Or exhausting myself in the competition flee the division the vertigoes of the verb *doubler* stop harnessing myself to two carts?

In the end I took up French as a foreign language.

"Is that what you wanted?" I cried. "Perhaps?"

In the distance behind the eternal windowpane my father raised his left arm and gestured to me: "*Soulbra.*"

Upon returning, on my first visit to Algeria, I was struck with the exhilaration of the miracle: I had never imagined this event. Rediscovering the native country. It seemed so unlikely, too far off to arrive in time. Stowed away in the memory of my losses. In my surprise, I wanted to bring everything out, to recall the images, to open the tombs. And I wanted to free the tongue from its long silence. I would hoist its golden sail, I would unfold its tablecloths and its ornaments. I open, I take out the precious linens and fabrics. It was torn, moth-eaten, rusty, like mémé's wedding sheets. I set about collecting my possessions. I went back over the premises, I haunted myself.

To think of the treasure I acquired over the course of a few months in Algiers. I see myself clearly sitting at the desk of my father who died in 1948, it took place in his clinic and not in our wild house. The Arabic teacher, soft peachsmooth calm patient slightly absent, his color a thick transparent brown. How many? Twenty words per lesson? I enriched myself quickly without thinking about it, I was *ohne Verstand* [without understanding] as Omi said, it wasn't worth much I was at the school of the Law and I swallowed so as to be done with it and not so as to begin. I must have possessed five hundred at least. I knew how to read, write, count, make sentences. I had surprises. I discovered that certain syllables which were as familiar to my ears as the banana or medlar trees were to my eyes my hands my tongue and which I had taken to be voiced fruits had a meaning hidden under the noise. Thus el Bab pivoted opened and closed as a door. This pleased me and displeased me. I lost the opacity of old mysteries. The names which were rock and god were humanized. Everything signified. It was exalting and sad. I lost music and grace. It was as if the sentence of my delight had been flayed and quartered, my forever favorite: "Open Sesame!" It was as if Open-Sesame the beautiful the enigmatic had been blanched and peeled. It was as if a teacher had told me *sesame* means: open up in Arabic. Whereas all the power of the sentence is in this or its, masculine or feminine, [*ce ou cette ou son ou sa*] Sesame, the word one must absolutely not forget and which cannot be grasped rationally by logiferating memory, this word Sesame, handsome as a young girl can be handsome promising, promised, he or she, and which opened onto all the riches of the East on the condition that it be pronounced with naïveté belief obedience and the submissiveness of a donkey. Because the untranslatable is what I love. This is why Sesame is so powerful.

But the teachers taught me the equivalents and the synonyms and in an obscure way I feared losing my cavern of treasures kept pure and unusable. Beautiful.

I possessed, I acquired and I was dispossessed, this was translated in my ignorant soul as a timid uprising of my disobediences. I accumulated but there was no future in it. Luckily the Arabic took cover to some extent in the German.

Then I decided to head for ruin. No doubt they were doomed—all this took place in the back of my thinking—Arabic and Hebrew, Arabic as Hebrew and Hebrew as nothing other than Hebrew—a language that was still without streets and without markets—condemned to descend below the earth with their deceased father mother. After the death of the father who had elected and loved them they fell from my lips like dead skins.

The two languages suffered the same fate as Fips our dog, they also suffered the indifference of the family, and the three animals formerly adopted by my father wasted away and were abandoned to dereliction. I did not struggle to save them from oblivion and laden as they were with my sins I let them wander in the desert like three emaciated goats burdened with our misfortunes.

Later on I was always haunted by the three phantom dogs.

Already, in my mouth, on my lips, the two tongues were fading, particularly Hebrew, but I do not know why. Perhaps by chance, but is there chance?—what is it that we call *hasard* in French with the name of a dice-playing Prince in Arabic?—is chance, *hasard*, Arab or Arabic? Is the Arabic *hasard* more seductive and chancy than *aléa*?— perhaps the Arabic teacher was more rounded glistening musical elegant nearly mute and a trifle absent his polished surface offering less hold for the blows of effacement because he was himself handsomely effaced? I do not know.

And immediately afterwards I went off to conquer German and English—the two sisters my cousin mother-aunts, one because it was the language of the country of my mothers whom I cherished, the other to rekindle my mother's quest, my mother who at nineteen left Dresden and Osnabrück to discover England. I bit into the two tongues with relish.

The Words That Remain

When Ali Baba in person came home to me in Paris, I quickly began to collect my possessions. In loss I am rich! I have not finished doing the accounts. I lost the word milk. It's one I miss. And it was so close so familiar so sweet and morning-fresh. My brother and I went to fetch it. In Oran and then in Algiers. Everything is kept fresh. In Oran on the other side of the *Placedarmes* during the war with a ticket and we carried the milk can carefully. In Algiers in the Clos Salembier the same can and we went early to the store run by Madame Bals a pig–turned–grocer to stand in line the two little Jews with the little Algerians, our foreheads lowered before the thundering ladle of

Madame Bals who scolded us and poured the foaming liquid drawn from her casks with cylindrical measures. We bought half a liter or a liter, the poor held out the money for a quarter liter. In the downpour of excremental insults spewed at us we contemplated: *Le Lait*. Each precious drop like a maternal kiss. We loved it so much.

I have lost the word. But it is enough for me to take Boulevard Laurent–Pichat in the Clos Salembier and in a few steps, on the asphalt across from the barbed–wired lot, among the heavy perfumes of pink oleanders, the words inseparable from the Algerian air and street burst out, they cross above my head the little girls in tears crying Ima Ima Mama! Mama. Then stop short. And the little boys lower their torn shorts, open their fly and point their pistols while proclaiming *le Zeb le Zeb!* Le Zeb king of street words. My myopia hid the object from me when it appeared more than two meters from me. But I've seen a collection of Zeb up close, and even in my hand and it is an unforgettable word. I still hear this mix of Zeb and bay leaves, the war cry has remained.

I am waiting for the word milk to return murmuring in Arabic. I'm waiting for it. It shall return. May it return.

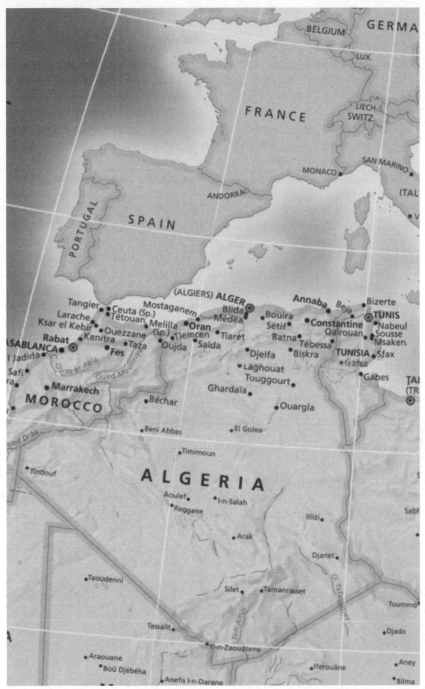

FIGURE 2. Facing each other across the sea: France and Algeria

notes

INTRODUCTION

1. It is interesting to note that the law of 26 December 1990, which extended the resolution of December 1980 concerning the Arabization of education, to all areas of public life, was passed at the end of the year, when the first pluralist elections since independence were held. See Guy Pervillé, "The Frenchification of Algerian Intellectuals," in *Franco-Arab Encounters*, 441 and 443).

2. On this issue, see Hafid Gafaïti's "Monotheism of the Other" in this volume.

3. "L'Algérie musulmane est un peuple ayant sa langue maternelle, sa religion, son passé glorieux, ses penseurs, ses héros et ses traditions islamiques. Nous restons aujourd'hui, malgré la colonisation, très attachés à ce passé." Quoted in Stora 1998, 26–27.

4. In *The Multiple Identities of the Middle East* (1998), an overview of Arabic-speaking countries, from the Machrek to the Maghreb and Turkey, Bernard Lewis reminds the reader that newspapers are a French invention, and indeed, a French import, to the Middle East: "The first newspapers in the region were products and instruments of the French Revolution, published by the French embassy in Istanbul and Bonaparte's administration in Egypt" (95).

5. See, in particular, the 17 January 1976 issue of the Arabophone daily *Ash-Sha'b* (quoted in Grandguillaume 1983, 131, 169). The year 1976 was a high point in Boumediene's politics of Arabization.

6. It would be wrong to describe the Berber cultural movement as "separatist" or "nationalist"; hence my use of "culturalist." On this issue, see Hafid Gafaïti's essay and my own discussion of Berberism in this volume.

7. The internal political and personal feuds of the Kabyle culturalist movement have led to a split within the MCB, which, in the mid-1990s, resulted in the creation of a "Mouvement de la culture Berbère II."

8. Harbi quotes a 1949 document issued by several excluded "Berberists." In this document, entitled "L'Algérie libre vivra" (which can mean either "Free Algeria will come to life," or "Free Algeria will live on"), the authors defend individual freedom against enforced religious and eth-

nonational affiliations; quoting the slogan of Pan-Germanism, "the German nation is everywhere where German is spoken," they refute linguistic national fundamentalism (Harbi 1992, 79). This document was released for publication only in the late 1980s.

9. The GIA is a dissident and radical offspring of the AIS (Armée Islamique du Salut, or Islamic Salvation Army), which is the "regular" armed branch of the FIS. At some point in the negotiations between the government and the FIS, the AIS agreed to a cease-fire, while the GIA never stopped staging attacks against the civilians.

10. See, for instance, Assia Djebar's work in the last ten years or so, in particular, *Le blanc de l'Algérie* (1995) and *Vaste est la prison* (1995b).

11. Among others, Mohamed Benrabah, a political scientist exiled in France, has been a prolific commentator of the linguistic conflict in the French media. See Benrabah 1995, 35–47.

12. Given the censorship (official until 1988, then unofficial) of the Algerian press, the vitality and quality of the debates taking place in the Algerian media are striking.

13. Anderson (1990) explores the complex workings of bi- and tri-lingualism in the Indonesian colonial and postcolonial framework. He reflects on the special power that the new national Indonesian draws from its status as a language without a past; he also stresses the quasi-magical power held by "uncomprehended language(s)," in this instance, Koranic Arabic. According to Anderson, the peculiar power of the latter on the Indonesian cultural scene stems from the very fact that it is learned by rote by the Muslim majority without being understood (127).

14. In her suggestive essay on language and gender in Algeria, Tassadit Yacine (2000) makes similar remarks. She notes that the very notion of "language" is gendered differently across cultures. In Algerian Arabic and Berber, which, like French, have grammatical genders, a specific language or idiom is usually referred to in the feminine. Of somebody who speaks French or English, for instance, one says: he or she speaks French ("she-French") or English ("she-English") (Yacine, 196). In French, however, language in this sense is masculine; one speaks or writes "le français" (he-French) or "l'arabe" (he-Arabic). But, Yacine adds, it seems as if languages change genders when one crosses the Eastern border of Algeria. From Tunisia to the Machrek, languages tend to be designated in the masculine in both standard and dialectal Arabic (see Yacine 2000, 196, note 1.)

15. Note that the judicial administration was one of the first institutions to be "Arabized," and successfully so.

16. On this issue, see of course the works of Assia Djebar, starting with *L'amour la fantasia* (1985). In *L'amour la fantasia*, Djebar calls French itself

a "langue marâtre". As Tassadit Yacine again pointed out during a conference held at the University of Paris 8 (see Yacine, 2001), the notion of the
"marâtre" takes on added connotations in a Maghrebian context. The
"marâtre" is not only the bad stepmother, as the suffix in "âtre" indicates
in French. She is also the second (or other) spouse of the father in a polyga-
mous setting. As such, she is or might be both the rival of the mother and
the love object of the father; in Djebar's case, she came to love the love object of her father, the "langue marâtre," out of love for him. Yacine (2001)
pointed to similar complications with regard to Berber or Tamazight. She
noted that Tamazight, "the mother tongue" of Berberophone Kabyles, was
perceived as the language of the father (because it is the language of tradition, of the ancestors and the fatherland), yet, of a father socially and culturally dominated by women on the one hand, and by Arabic culture and, to
a lesser degree, French culture, on the other hand.

17. On the use of French as the language of writing, see the famous statements of Assia Djebar in *L'amour la fantasia* (1985):

"Ecrire en langue étrangère, hors de l'oralité des deux langues de ma ré-
gion natale—le berbère des montagnes du Dahra et l'arabe de ma ville—
écrire m'a ramenée aux cris des femmes sourdement révoltées de mon enfance, à ma seule origine. . . . Ecrire ne tue pas la voix, mais la réveille. (229)
(Writing in a foreign language, not in either of the [oral] tongues of my native country—the Berber of the Dahra mountains or the Arabic of the town
where I was born—writing has brought me [back] to the cries of the women
silently rebelling in my youth, to my true [and only origin]."
"Writing does not silence the voice, but awakens it" (204, translation
modified).

18. The French word *charabia*, which means "gibberish speech," apparently referred at first to the language of the French immigrants from the
Auvergne (a province of central France). It was first recorded in 1802,
roughly the time of Napoleon's "expedition" in Egypt. Interestingly, it is
supposedly borrowed from the Arabic *algharabiya*, which designates the
"language of the West," namely, Berber.

19. On the issue of metalanguage, see also Derrida (1998b): "Il n'y a pas
de métalangage traductologique qui ne soit assujetti, comme idiome, encore, au drame qu'il prétend formaliser ou traduire à son tour. On ne parle
jamais de la traduction dans un langage universel, hors d'une langue na-
turelle (intraduisible—à traduire)" (223). (There is no such thing as a metalanguage of translation which would not still be subjected, as an idiom, to
the [linguistic] drama it purports to formalize or translate. One never
speaks of translation in a universal language, outside a natural language [as
such untranslatable—in need of translation]) (my translation).

20. Diglossia, once again, has to be distinguished from formal bilingualism, which, for instance, officially characterizes Québec. In Québec, French and English are spoken by neighboring but separate communities. When Francophone Québécois speak English, and, conversely, when Anglophone Québécois speak French, they speak them as foreign (albeit familiar) languages; in contrast, many Algerians, perhaps the majority, live in several languages, often switching from one to the other in the same sentence.

CHAPTER 1. THE MONOTHEISM OF THE OTHER

1. And not "classical" or "Koranic" Arabic as it is often and wrongly called. I consider this decisive distinction below.

2. I am grateful to Patricia M. Pelley for her comments on an earlier version of this text.

3. With Mohammed Harbi, the dissident and rigorous historian, I prefer to use the term "Kabyle culturalists" instead of "Berberists," for two reasons. First, the term "Berberist" has been used since 1948 with a derogatory connotation, and was later appropriated by the FLN and the opponents of any expression of Berberitude in North Africa. Second, the Kabyle ethnic activists tend to appropriate the term "Berber" and use it to designate all Berber groups, who are ethnically, culturally, and politically diverse, in a monolithic and hegemonic manner.

4. The Front de Libération Nationale (National Liberation Front) organized the Algerian resistance to French colonialism. Transformed into a political party, and operating under various forms and designations, it has been ruling Algeria since independence in 1962.

5. In fact, there are as many as seventeen languages spoken in Algeria.

6. However, although it constituted a step toward the principle of political liberalization, the "loi # 90 du 3 avril 1990" or "décret Hamrouche" maintained the state monopoly on the supply of paper and on the material production and distribution of newspapers through ownership and control of the printing presses in the country. This means that the government gave a relatively formal freedom to individuals interested in producing new, so-called independent publications, but continued to control them indirectly. Furthermore, as noted by Arezki Métref (1990) in his "Une presse dans le dégel: Genèse d'une ambiguïté," the decisively important audiovisual media, that is, the national radio stations and the country's only television channel, remained under the direct and total control of the presidency. Obviously, the liberalization of information has remained restricted. In this context, the use of Arabic has continued to be a means of state control and censorship. Moreover, within the context of the increasingly violent political crisis and the explosive situation developing in Algeria, the regime has issued a series of laws that not only drastically jeopardize the previous gains, but also put the press and its members under unbearable constraints.

On 9 February 1992, the government enacted a statute replacing the previous legislation with martial law. This was followed by the 30 September 1992 law on terrorism and subversion, which allows the Ministry of the Interior to order the arrest of journalists or the suspension of newspapers at any time. On 7 June 1994, in the nation's increasingly critical sociopolitical context, the Ministry of the Interior and the Ministry of Communication issued a confidential decree that imposed a veto on coverage or information related to security issues. In brief, this means that journalists were subject to systematic censorship and could not work independently. Two years later, these laws were complemented by the 11 February 1996 governmental decision to appoint to every publishing house "reading committees" consisting of civil servants whose function was to verify the content and treatment of security-related information by newspapers before it could be published. Although these committees were eliminated in early 1998, the exercise of other forms of direct censorship is widely maintained. According to Marc Marginedas (1998), "on the basis of this series of laws, in the last few years the government has ordered the imprisonment of more than twenty-five journalists and the arrest of more than forty members of the media. It also banned or suspended a large number of newspapers and confiscated a great number of publications. In this context, the authoritarian and unilateral implementation of Arabization adds to various deplorable censorship policies and maneuvers that could ultimately kill the Francophone press and handicap part of the Algerian public and its culture in general."

7. For a full account of Kassim's contributions to Arabization and "Islamization," see Hassan 1996, 180–82.

8. Front Islamique du Salut (Islamic Salvation Front), the political party at the center of the Islamist movement in Algeria.

9. For a systematic study of this important dimension of Arabization policy, see the thorough and well-documented work of Martinez 1998, particularly 87–90. Nevertheless, in an otherwise novel view of the sociopolitical situation in Algeria, it is regrettable that Martinez does not take into account the important democratic and feminist movements on the country's new sociopolitical map.

10. The "volunteers" from the Service National Actif were young draftees with a college education who did their time in the military abroad and served as instructors, usually in developing countries (editor's note).

11. It should be noted, first, that there are notable exceptions among members of this elite, those who refused to be co-opted and, second, that, like the majority of Algerians, the Kabyle lower classes did not benefit from French policies, which explains their active participation in the anticolonial war and the tremendous suffering of Kabylia during the 1954–62 war of national liberation.

12. It is important to stress that Algeria also has many genuine friends and supporters among the French people, especially on the left and among the intelligentsia.

13. The mathematician Al Khawarizmi invented trigonometry and developed the concept of algorithms, as his name indicates; Al Hallaj was a poet of genius and philosopher, nicknamed the "Christ of Islam."

14. At the invitation of a Catholic religious order, the Saint-Eugedio meeting took place in Italy and brought together party leaders from the FLN, FIS, Ennahdah (a "moderate" Islamist organization), MDA (Mouvement pour la Démocratie Algérienne) and FFS (Front des Forces Socialistes), along with other politicians who, after decades of direct participation in the oppressive policies of the regime or in totally undemocratic practices in their own organizations—even in the supposedly progressive FFS—called themselves democrats and advocated national "reconciliation." At the same time, they refused to denounce terrorism and the fascist ideology that contributed to creating it!

15. I would like to stress that the French left is diverse and that the Socialist Party (PS), which is fundamentally a social democratic party, does not reflect all the movements or organizations that constitute it. Furthermore, it is important to note that the PS is itself composed of different currents and that some do not always agree with the social democratic policies and opportunistic discourse.

16. In her research on the colonial and postcolonial histories of Vietnam, for example, Patricia M. Pelley (1993) has identified similar dynamics:

"The transition to romanized Vietnamese *(quoc ngu)* created a clear rupture between the Vietnamese present and the Vietnam past in that the traditional canon had been redacted either in classical Chinese or in a phonetic adaptation of Chinese characters (known as *nom)*. In other ways as well the shift to romanized Vietnamese marked a dramatic break with the past: in precolonial times, very few Vietnamese—and only men—had access to formal education (in Chinese); in colonial times, formal education was astonishingly uneven and in new ways, also extremely limited. Colonial rhetoric about language reform only emphasized this sense of rupture: for Paul Bourde, for example quoc ngu' presented the chance for the natives to 'de-chinese' themselves *(se déchinoiser)*. But the ambivalence that revolutionaries such as Tran Huy Lieu and Ho Chi Minh felt toward quoc ngu' stemmed from other sources as well. In the mid-to-late-nineteenth century, just as they began to enact language reforms more aggressively, French administrators publicly debated about the merits of the indigenous language. In 1889, Etienne Aymonier, who was director of L'Ecole Coloniale in Paris, explained to his readers in *Le Temps* that the 'Annamite language'—meaning quoc ngu'—was adequate for everyday purposes, but in literary and scientific discussion, he maintained, it no longer sufficed. . . .

"What is interesting, of course, is the extent to which colonial attitudes towards Indochina converge with late-eighteenth- and nineteenth-century Parisian ideas about the non-Parisian part of France. In 1794, Henri Grégoire referred to the 'primitive idioms' of the provinces that 'extended the infancy of reason.' In 1884, the Cahors Committee of Primary Education declared that the southern dialects were inferior to Parisian French. In the 1860s officials from the Ministry of Education suggested that the other languages of France were remnants of barbarism. In 1889, Ernest Renan insisted that no work of science or philosophy or political economy could be produced in patois. The parallelism between Parisian imperialism in provincial France and French Imperialism in Indochina could not be more striking" (46–48).

French attitudes toward Vietnamese a century ago correspond nearly identically to the Algerian case.

17. It should be noted that the majority of Francophone Algerian journalists are of Kabyle origin and are generally members or supporters of the Kabyle culturalist movement.

18. Let it be clear that I am referring here to the pathological legacies of both Arab and French colonialism.

CHAPTER 3. THE IMPOSSIBLE WEDDING

1. On the links among death, representation, and memory in Anderson's theory of nationalism, see Anthony D. Smith (1998, 132).

2. "One notes the primordialness of languages, even those known to be modern. No one can give a date for the birth of any language. Each looms up imperceptibly out of a horizonless past. . . . Languages thus appear rooted beyond almost anything else in contemporary societies" (Anderson 1992, 144).

3. This seems to be Anderson's answer to the question raised by A. D. Smith in his commentary of *Imagined Communities:* "How do we get from knowing and imagining the nation to feeling it and loving it?" (Smith 1998, 140).

4. To put his assertion in a global perspective, Lewis starts by saying: "The implantation of Latin in much of Western Europe and the permanent Latinization, in the linguistic sense, of France, Spain, and Portugal was a remarkable achievement. It was, however, rendered easier by the fact that there were no previous advanced or written civilizations in these countries. The same may be said, with the exception of Mexico and Peru, of the later implantation of Spanish and Portuguese in Central and South America. But

these achievements pale into insignificance in comparison with the Arabization of South West Asia and North Africa" (53).

5. "Unlike the peoples of Western Europe, who threw off the bonds of bad Latin and raised their vernaculars to the level of literary languages, the peoples of the Middle East are still hampered by the constraints of diglossy and of increasingly archaic and artificial medium of communication. There were some attempts to escape—the late-eighteenth-century Egyptian historian al-Jabarti wrote in a language which, while remaining in form literary Arabic, acquired some of the vigor and vitality of the spoken language. But this promising start was stifled by the neoclassicists of the Arabi revival in the nineteenth century and after. For them, this was not living Arabic; it was just incorrect Arabic. Literary neoclassicism acquired a political dimension with the rise of pan-Arab nationalism in the twentieth century . . .

"The various Arabic vernaculars, as well as the common written language, are all called 'Arabic'—rather as if the same name 'Latin' had been used in Europe to denote the Latin of ancient Rome, . . . of the Renaissance humanists, and, in addition, French, Spanish, Italian . . ." (Lewis 1998, 52–53).

6. Hugues Didier, a long-time teacher in Algeria, gives the following figures, quoted from Nora 1961: on the eve of independence, "one Muslim man out of seven spoke French, but only one out of eighteen or twenty could write it; as for women, one out of one hundred and fifty was able to read and write French" (Didier 1998, 55, my translation).

7. The historian Guy Pervillé (1996) gives the following figures: "The percentage of eligible Muslim children in school reached 5 percent in 1914, 10 percent in 1950, 15 percent in 1955, and 30 percent in 1962" (417).

8. There were and are still some "lycées français" in Algeria, an effect of France's foreign cultural policies.

9. "Nous corrigeons par le biais de cet enfant la langue de sa famille" ("Through this child, we are correcting the language of his family," my translation). Official instructions; see Greffou, 36, quoted in Didier 1998, 74.

10. French actually remained the primary language of education until the late 1970s. According to Pervillé (1996), "in 1977 nearly three-quarters of the university graduates of that year had studied in French" (436).

11. The measure was announced before the election of President Bouteflika. Whether and how it will now be implemented remains to be seen.

12. On this issue, see the work of Mohammed Harbi. For a summary of his recent work, see Harbi 1998, 51–57.

13. See, in particular, Grandguillaume 1983.

14. The institution of the women's "harem" is of course the clearest example of the connection between the "intimate" and the *haram* (that is, the forbidden).

15. The Koran commands women to veil their chests (sura 24) and their faces (sura 33). But the chest veil is called a *khimar* and the face veil a *jalabib*.

16. See suras 17, 19, and 33.

17. Djamila Saadi mentions another "theory" of the origin of dialectal Arabic, which links it to ancient Punic languages. This theory is obviously the result of the perceived symbolic differences between dialectal and standard Arabic.

18. See again Lewis (1998) on the treatment of local languages in Arabophone countries.

19. See Grégoire 1975: "It was said about Quinault that he had made our language go limp by resorting to the most effeminate gallantry and to the most abject forms of adulation. . . . The time has come to do away with that deceitful style and those servile formulas. It is time that language shows everywhere the character of veracity and laconic pride which is the privilege of republicans" (my translation).

20. Some say disparagingly that dialectal Arabic was the only language Boudiaf could master. As for President Bouteflika, he alternates shrewdly among standard Arabic, dialectal Arabic, and French, depending on the context of his public speeches.

21. "On admet mal que ces écrivains puissent dire l'être intime et secret dans la langue de l'autre" (People have a hard time admitting that these [the Francophone] writers can tell the intimate and secret being in the language of the other) (Mimouni 1993, 340).

22. "So much so that 'colonialism' and 'colonization' are only high points [*reliefs*], one traumatism over another, an increasing buildup of violence, the jealous rage of an essential *coloniality* of *culture*, as shown by the two names" (Derrida 1998a, 24). Derrida points here to the linguistic connection between "colonization" and "culture," which were originally the same Latin word (colo, ere).

23. The subtitle of Toumi's piece is "What Do They Really Speak in the Maghreb?" To this question he answers: they speak "Farabé" (French-Arabic-Berber), a playful nickname by which Algerians sometimes designate their own brand of vernacular.

CHAPTER 4. CIVIL WAR, PRIVATE VIOLENCE, AND CULTURAL SOCIALIZATION

1. Concerning the first case, and by comparison with France in the 1940s, we know the importance of informing under Vichy, the extent of the black market knowingly aided and even organized by the Nazis, and the infamy of shady maneuvers aimed at appropriating Jewish property.

2. This premise will inform my text. One would need, of course, to situate the analysis by comparing several Arabic countries, or the Lebanese and

Algerian civil wars. I will confine myself to an internal comparison and an endogenous Algerian logic, to shed as much light as possible on the singularity of the current endemic violence.

3. The "sand wars" and the "green march" were part of the dispute (which continues today) between Morocco and Algeria regarding the status of the Western Sahara (editor's note).

4. For a bracing overview of political violence, see Leca (1993). For a comparative overview of violence in a specific sociohistorical context, see the exemplary study by Daniel Pécaud (1987).

5. See Philippe Braud, *La violence politique dans les démocraties européennes occidentales*, Paris: Harmattan, 1993.

6. In the growing gap between state and society, this tension was (super)imposed on former conflicts between populists and communists, Ulema and the PPA, factions of the MTLD and of the FLN, as well as Arabists and Berberists. The memory of those conflicts are far from fading for the older generations, but they no longer have any meaning for the younger ones. (Editor's note: the MLTD, Mouvement pour le Triomphe des Libertés Démocratiques, was founded by Messali Hadj in the 1940s and was the legal arm of the PPA. In 1954, the centralists opposed the Messalists within the MLTD, a crisis that led to the dissolution of the party and its replacement by the FLN.)

7. The ALN (Armée de libération nationale) is the armed branch of the FLN (editor's note).

8. The complementarity, even complicity, between civilians and soldiers never ruled out tension between them, and especially tension among civilians and within the military. The old conflicts of 1960–65—between the military brass and the GPRA (Gouvernement provisoire de la révolution algérienne, the provisional government of the Algerian revolution), between the Oujda group and the Tizi Ouzou group, resistance fighters and border guards, renegades of the French army and officers from the resistance or trained in the Middle East—left deep traces, without preventing wide-ranging reclassification and reorientation under Boumediene and Chadli. These two men incited new struggles for influence, or more muted splits between generations of officers, army sectors, types of training, and ideological sensibilities, while the path to promotion remained under the control of successive dominant clans. The specific nature of the military, its esprit de corps, does not shelter it from internal divisions, which are similar to those inherent in society as a whole.

9. The "Baathists" refer to the followers of the Baath movement in Algeria. The "Baath" movement (i.e. "rebirth" in Arabic) was created in Syria in the 1940s by Michel Aflak, a Christian, and Salah ad-Din Bitar, a Muslim. In Syria, Egypt, and Iraq, it became the Baath Arab Socialist party, which

held power at various times. With such leaders as Gamal Abdel Nasser in Egypt and Saddam Hussein in Iraq, the Baath became, in the second part of the twentieth century, a strong expression, not only of a kind of revolutionary nationalism, but also, and most importantly, of a secular pan-Arabism. The Islahists are the proponents of a reformist Islam (Islah), as opposed to the Salafists or fundamentalists, who advocate a return to "salaf," the original form of Islam from the time of the califs. Both currents run through the FIS (editor's note).

10. Many from the young bi- or trilingual generation—the most talented and the least implicated in the old internecine battles, the least greedy for material riches, the most concerned with setting the country aright while progressively integrating modern ways—paid with their lives, such as, outside the government, Tahar Djaout, or, within it, Djilali Llabès and Mohammed Boukhobza. Their deaths were probably the result less of the political intelligence of Armée Islamique du Salut (AIS) or Groupes Islamiques Armés (GIA) emirs than of the wars among politico-military clans, where some favored the elimination of common enemies. This is also the case for the assassination of top political figures, however different they may have been in terms of generation or political responsibilities and positions. Kasdi Merbah, Abou Bekr Belkaid, and especially Mohammed Boudiaf are examples.

11. The entire interplay, with its double games, its alliances and ruptures, its repudiations and reconciliations, was obviously activated by the rapid reorganization of the international scene, the fall of the Berlin Wall, the collapse of the Soviet Union, and the Gulf War.

12. In 1974, the symbolism of November was at its peak. Boumediene had succeeded in drawing a parallel between oil income and symbolic income, international recognition at the UN, where he preached a new international economic order, and internal recognition, where his social policies of redistribution (free schooling and health services) promoted the ideal of social justice and the memory of the dead.

13. Ernest Lavisse produced a monumental history of France, whereas Albert Mallet and Jules Isaac are history professors known for their textbook versions of French history (editor's note).

14. The "Vulgate" is the name given to the authorized translation of the Bible into Latin by St. Jerome, on which all Catholic translations of the Holy Book into Romance languages were subsequently based (editor's note).

15. Ahmed Urabî declared war on Britain in 1882 and was arrested. Saad Zaghlûl Pasha (1850–1927) was one of the earliest leaders of anticolonial and nationalist resistance in Egypt. He was also arrested after the revolts of 1882, then exiled. In 1919, he founded the first Egyptian nationalist party, the Wafd (editor's note).

16. An important religious festival, the Aï'd commemorates the sacrifice of Abraham; this sacrifice is understood by Muslims as the ultimate act of faith, and therefore becomes an allegory of their faith; the festival takes place ten days after the return from the pilgrimage to Mecca (editor's note).

17. The *shahid* is a martyr who dies for the cause of God and Islam while reciting the *shahada*, that is, the Muslim profession of faith (editor's note).

18. On Ben Badis, the reformist cleric from Constantine who helped foster a national identity on cultural grounds in the 1930s, see the introduction to this volume (editor's note).

19. There is a continuum from the state—which was formed by revolutionary guerilla forces—or the national army, to the generation that came out of postindependence schools. That generation would produce imitators of Bouyali—a former FLN underground soldier converted to the Islamist underground in about 1980—as it was confronted with the conversion of former mujahideen into bureaucrats and businessmen, and with the reorganization, either separately or in concert, of traditional allegiances and patronage into "regionalist" and Islamist groupings.

20. "Babor Australia" refers to the fantasy of emigrating as far away as possible from Algeria (and if possible to the Western world construed as a hospitable place of opulence and freedom), a fantasy entertained by the desperate youth of the 1980s and 1990s. Countless stories, comics, and songs were produced that talked about taking the boat to Australia or Canada (editor's note).

21. Islam, in Algeria and elsewhere, is rearming. It is setting off once more against the dissolute, materialistic Christian West, dominated by Zionism, increasingly stigmatized in its ingrained errors and moral drift, yet increasingly envied and imitated for its mighty economic and technical power. The rearmament is moral: the rest will follow.

22. Personality types and countertypes are constructed on roles and ranks that organize society over the long term, without major changes.

23. Significant advancements have been made in secretarial work in certain sectors of the economy and the administration. In addition, women are beginning to enter more prestigious professions, which, by the same token, are becoming feminized: primary school teaching and medicine. The nurse, and especially, the grade school teacher, are the positive figures of the new Algerian woman. Many female students manage to clear the hurdles to university teaching and other professions; they become lecturers, doctors, dentists, and pharmacists. In the 1980s, they even became state ministers.

24. More precisely, it is the model of the European couple from the 1950s and 1960s. In decline in Paris after 1968, it flourished in Algiers until the early 1980s, and even today is not about to disappear.

25. The traditional white veil worn by Algerian women before they took to the hidjab (editor's note).

26. The Princes' Mirror (Miroir des Princes) was a generic type of writing practiced since antiquity by clerics and jurors. It aimed at educating the Powerfuls and Kings-to-be by providing guidance in moral and political matters. Machiavelli's famous political treatise belongs to the tradition of the Princes' Mirrors (editor's note).

27. Mustapha Bouyali was a guerilla fighter against France during the war for independence; he then founded one of the first Islamist guerilla groups at the end of the 1980s. François Guizot, a famous French historian and statesman under the "July Monarchy" (1830–48), is better known as a proponent of the free market and modern capitalism in France. He coined the slogan: "Laisser faire, laisser passer," which advocates the abolition of trade barriers. "Bouyali no longer masked Guizot" means that the revolutionary rhetoric could not hide anymore Algeria's adhesion to the practices of unabashed capitalism (editor's note).

28. Abassi Madani and Ali Benhadj are the two principal leaders of the FIS. The former is "old," the latter young. They were imprisoned soon after the 1991 elections were canceled (editor's note).

29. This discourse of exclusive nationality—"Algeria is not France, does not want to be France, could not be France even if she wished it"—coincided with a heavily ambiguous formulation of the Sheikh of Constantine, who attempted to construct a theory of generic (*gensiya*) and political (*siyassiya*) dual nationality.

30. The word *takfir* is the equivalent of "excommunication," whereby anyone, even a fellow Muslim, can be declared unfaithful and therefore a stranger to the community (editor's note).

CHAPTER 5. THE EXPERIENCE OF EVIDENCE

1. In France, part of the trial was televised on the news, and Reuters released a news story entitled "Widowed and Raped, Algeria's Women 'Try' Islamists" (1995), which later circulated on the Web, with the names of the women involved concealed for their protection. See also "Algérie: Journée de la Femme" 1995.

2. Interviews were conducted by the Algerian journalist Mohamed Benmohammed with women who described how they had been raped.

3. See, for example, the comments of the "Collectif des familles de disparus en Algérie" (Collective of families of the "Disappeared" in Algeria) in Amnesty International 1998b.

4. There is some question about what constitutes classical Arabic. Some use the term interchangeably with Koranic Arabic, some with the language of classical Arabic poetry, and some even with Modern Literary

Arabic, drawn from Modern Standard Arabic. Although there is no doubt that Arabic in some form is an international language, even the apparently standard terms (such as "classical") lead to some confusion.

5. *Le Monde* has recently published letters written by victims of and witnesses to these atrocities (Bernard and Herzberg, 1998). It is interesting to read them against testimonies of women from the Algerian War of Independence (Amrane, 1994).

6. I acknowledge that the terms "terrorism" and "torture" have racist connotations in English and French because of their use by the English- and French-language press to report the activities of groups outside the United States and Western Europe, and primarily in North Africa and the Middle East. See the works of Edward Said (1981), Noam Chomsky (1986 and 1988), and Edward Herman (1982), who have discussed this important issue extensively. I would contend, however, that although the terms are used in a derogatory manner to report on particular peoples and regional and religious conflicts, it is important to remember that some acts are terrorism, and some constitute war crimes and torture that should not be permitted by the international community. I use the terms as part of a critique of First World assumptions about the nature of violence in the postnuclear period. In addition, the term "jihad" is frequently used in the non-Muslim press to connote political struggles of all kinds, which are misleadingly conflated as an Islamic holy war (see Said 1981, 107–8). However, in this instance, I am arguing that, *for political reasons*, Islamists in Algeria have posited a continuity in the political battle between the decolonization movement and the current civil war, and have identified the latter as a holy war, thus conflating politics and religion, and state law (both the Shari'a and other laws) and holy law (the means to religious salvation).

7. See, for example, the letter from the parliamentary delegation of the FIS circulated on the Web on 17 March 1995. "The FIS Parliamentary Delegation reiterates its commitment to the Rome Accord (the National Contract) which condemns and calls for an end to attacks against innocent civilians and the destruction of public properties. We insist on the Accord's call for an independent Commission of Inquiry to investigate those acts as well as all other violations of human rights." The FIS has insisted on an independent inquiry, which has also been urged by Amnesty International, to determine whether the source of much of the violence is the state and the military, or indeed, Islamists. See Amnesty International's persistent call for such an inquiry at (http:www.amnesty.org) (1998a). For a persuasive argument that questions the ethics of outlawing the FIS, given its protest against violence, see Entelis 1997, 43–74.

8. Many have discussed the establishment of the family code and Arab-

ization as concessions by the FLN to more conservative wings of the government. See Entelis and Naylor 1992 for strong statements on this issue.

9. For an analysis of the family code that situates it within Algerian politics more generally, see Lazreg 1994, Entelis and Naylor 1992, 151–170, and 171–216.

10. That violent destruction of memory in some postcolonial African nations (though not in Algeria) has received treatment in Werbner 1998.

11. Gisèle Halimi was condemned by the French Federation of the FLN in spite of her work for eight years during the war on behalf of Algerians. See Halimi 1990, 300–301. After the FLN's kidnapping of Djamila Boupacha, who was with Gisèle Halimi, a communiqué was circulated in Tunis and reproduced in *Le Monde*, denouncing "the publicity operation attempted for her own personal ends by the lawyer Gisèle Halimi, in connection with our sister Djamila Boupacha" (*Le Monde*, 3 May 1962).

12. See, for example, Marie-Aimée Hélie-Lucas, "Bound and Gagged by the Family Code," in Davies 1987.

13. Alek Baylee has recently written a play in which Sartre and de Beauvoir return from the dead to participate in the burial of a murdered writer. They are kidnapped by the GIA. Baylee invokes the ghosts of the past to imagine the possibilities of intellectual argument with the GIA, which has been responsible for the slaughter of so many. See Baylee 1996, 5 103.

14. This, of course, would run counter to the argument of Richard Sennett in *The Fall of Public Man* (1974).

15. Even before that time, the Ministries of Justice and Religious Affairs conducted their business largely in Modern Literary Arabic, which gave rise to tensions between the state and some of the elite communities within the state apparatus and outside it. See Entelis 1981, 191–208.

16. Numerous essays on the language problem have been published recently. See, for example, Benrabah 1998, *Parallax* 1998, and Stone 1997.

17. Entelis, "Elite Political Culture and Socialisation in Algeria," 196.

18. There are many studies of British colonial policy in India. Recent books by Gauri Vishwanathan (1989) and Sara Suleri (1992) are instructive.

19. For a commentary on the problems women faced in this system in postcolonial India, see Rajeswari Sunder Rajan's work (1993) on the Shahbano case.

20. For a recent consideration of the notion of the mother tongue in the Algerian Jewish context, see Derrida 1996, 1998a. For a consideration of bilingualism in the Maghrebian context, see Khatibi 1983, 1990.

21. For an alternative reading of the trial, see Murphy 1995, 263–97.

22. For a review of these letters that considers the Algerian question, see Gonfond-Talahite 1998, 143–46.

23. In Camus 1960, see, in particular, "Algeria: Preface to Algerian Reports," 111–30.

24. *Le Monde* was thought to be largely sympathetic to the Algerian cause. For arguments that both support and contest this claim, see *Cahiers de l'IHTP* 1988; Vidal-Naquet 1986, 3–18; Khane 1993, 129–48.

25. Maran 1989 offers an important analysis of the human rights issues involved in torture in the Algerian War.

26. Many books have emerged over the past few years on the subject of trauma studies, most of them concerned specifically with the Holocaust. For good representations of the field, see Felman and Laub 1992; and Caruth 1996.

27. This has been recently discussed at length regarding rape in the former Yugoslavia and how to assess it as a war crime. See Niarchos 1995, 649–90; and Philipose 1996, 46–62.

28. In their rereading of Freud's "Mourning and Melancholia" in light of Sandor Ferenczi's distinction between introjection and incorporation, Nicolas Abraham and Maria Torok (1994) draw on Ferenczi's account of introjection as a normal part of psychic growth through assimilation. In melancholia, in contrast, what takes place is "incorporation," that is, the blocking of introjection, and consequently, unsuccessful assimilation. In this case, narcissism is pathological. The lost object becomes a constant point of reference, but the relationship to it as a separate entity is always marked by identification. The terms are elaborated in "Maladie du deuil" in *L'écorce et le noyau*. See, in particular, the subsection "La notion ferenczienne de l'introjection des pulsions opposée à celle d'incorporation de l'objet" (Abraham and Torok 1978, 233–35; 1994, 125–38).

29. For another commentary on mock trials in postcolonial literature, see Boire 1991, 5–20.

30. As in Gilles Deleuze's *Difference and Repetition* (1968, 1994).

CHAPTER 6. THE SCHEHERAZADE SYNDROME

1. Rachid Mimouni (1945–95) attended elementary school in his village in Algeria, high school in a small town, and college in Algiers. He spent two years in Montreal (Canada), but did not spend time in France. He published, in French, *Le printemps n'en sera que plus beau* (1978), *Le fleuve détourné* (1982), *Tombéza* (1984), *L'Honneur de la tribu* (1989; translated into English as *Honor of the Tribe*, 1992), *La ceinture de l'ogresse* (1990; translated into English as *Ogre's embrace*, 1993), and *La malédiction* (1993).

2. The Algerian war of liberation lasted from November 1954 to 1962. A bloody war, it brought down the Fourth Republic in France before leading to Algerian independence.

3. Berberist writers are those who defend a Berber identity against the

national, religious unity imposed by the Algerian state. Boukhalfa Bitam and Mourad Oussedik belong to that category. Other writers with a Kabyle background (such as Tahar Djaout and Rabah Belamri) did not become the apologists for Berber culture. I am grateful to Alain Mahé for sharing his Kabyle library with me.

This case and the following ones (of Jews and Frenchmen) are only one aspect of the politicization of ethnicity that occurred in Algeria and in other countries of the Arab world in the process of nation building.

4. Native Algerian Jews became French citizens with the Crémieux decree of 1870. By the end of the colonial period, most of the Jews thought of themselves as Frenchmen and were seen as such. Very few shared the nationalist ideals of Muslim Algerians.

5. For a protest against such an exclusion, see Jean Pelegri, "Les signes et les lieux. Essai sur la genèse et les perspectives de la littérature algérienne," in Toso Rodinis 1991, 9–36.

6. In a preface to a book by Yamina Mechakra (1979), Kateb Yacine states: "Dans notre pays, une femme qui écrit vaut son pesant de poudre" (In our country, a woman who writes is worth her weight in gunpowder). He thus emphasizes the subversive value attached to writing, especially for women.

7. Following Kateb Yacine, Assia Djebar underscores the subversive value of writing. She said in an interview, "to write is to expose oneself. If, in spite of everything, women write, theirs is the status of dancers, that is of frivolous women" (*Le Monde*, 1987b).

8. Tahar Djaout wrote *L'exproprié* (1981), *Les chercheurs d'os* (1984), *Les rêts de l'oiseleur* (1984), *L'invention du désert* (1987), and *Les vigiles* (1991). Rachid Boudjedra wrote *La répudiation* (1969, translated into English as *The Repudiation*, 1995), *L'insolation* (1972), *Topographie idéale pour une agression caractérisée* (1975), *L'Escargot entêté* (1977), *1001 années de nostalgie* (1979), *Le vainqueur de coupe* (1981), *Le désordre des choses* (1990), and *Timimoun* (1994). First published in Arabic, then translated into French by the author were *La macération* (1984), *Le démantèlement* (1982), *La pluie* (1987a), and *La prise de Gibraltar* (1987b). Assia Djebar (b. 1936), was educated in Paris as a historian and published her first novel at the age of twenty (*La soif*). She is renowned as a novelist, filmmaker, and feminist writer. Among her novels are *Les impatients* (1958), *Les enfants du Nouveau Monde* (1962), *Les alouettes naïves* (1967), *Femmes d'Alger dans leur appartement* (1980, translated into English as *Women of Algiers in their Apartment*, 1992), *L'amour, la fantasia* (1985, translated into English as *Fantasia, An Algerian Cavalcade*, 1989), *Ombre sultane* (1987a, translated into English as *Sister to Scheherazade*, 1988), *Loin de Médine* (1992), *Vaste est la prison* (1995b), *Le Blanc de l'Algérie* (1995), and *Oran, langue morte*

(1997). Rabah Belamri (1946–95) was born in a village to illiterate parents. He went blind in 1962, studied in France and settled there in 1972, translated and published folktales, and wrote poetry and novels.

9. Boutet de Monvel (1994) also mentions Boudjedra's involvement as an adviser to the Ministry of Information and Culture in 1977 and as a reader for the national publishing house in 1981–82.

10. See Grandguillame 1983 on the general issue of Arabization.

11. See Bourbonne 1985. See also Ben Jelloun 1985: "En cherchant dans ce passé (de l'Algérie coloniale), elle découvre que la langue française qu'elle écrit est entachée de sang. . . . Je suis, dit-elle, l'héritière de ceux qui tuent. J'ai testé par ce livre qu'il y a du sang dans l'héritage de la langue. (By searching the past [of colonial Algeria], she discovers that the French language she writes in is stained with blood. . . . I am, she says, the heiress of killers. I have borne witness in this book that there is blood in the inheritance of the language)." Ben Jelloun suggests, however, that by writing in French Djebar is finally emerging from childhood.

12. See the interview with Djebar in *Jeune Afrique*, June 27, 1984. She adds apologetically that she is still involved in translating works from Arabic in order to confront the Arabic language (*me confronter à la langue arabe*). Her views on French and Arabic are expressed again in *Le Blanc de l'Algérie* (1995).

13. See Cheniki 1986. Cheniki says: "Recognition from elsewhere, a suspect here," and criticizes the publication of the novel in France. Twice, the interviewer presents the success of Mimouni's book in France as "récupération" (co-optation). See Gafaïti 1991 on the reception of Mimouni in France and Algeria.

14. A violently negative review appeared in *El Moudjahid*, 11 April 1991. Although the author was for a time the adviser to the national publishing house, he was also accused by the national press of plagiarizing a novelist who wrote in Arabic.

15. See, for example, in Gafaïti 1987, Boudjedra's ambiguous statements about his love for the French language, coupled with his denunciation of "francophony" as "subtle neo-colonialism" (128).

16. See his strong answer to a perfidious question, grotesque in its formulation, in an interview for *Le Soir d'Algérie* on 10 October 1992. "Question: En dernier lieu, quelle est, d'après toi, la place de la littérature algérienne *de graphie française* dans la culture nationale et au-delà de nos frontières, sachant que peu d'oeuvres d'Algériens publiées en France se retrouvent sur le marché algérien?" (my emphasis) (Question: Finally, what, in your opinion, is the place of Algerian *literature in French characters* in both national culture and beyond our borders, considering that few

Algerian authors published in France will be found in the Algerian market?). "R. B: Voilà plus de quarante ans que la littérature algérienne de langue française a acquis une légitimité en Algérie et hors de l'Algérie. Imposée par l'histoire, elle est, qu'on le veuille ou non, une réalité nationale. Vouloir chasser de notre mémoire littéraire Amrouche ou Sénac, Kateb ou Mammeri, est une aberration, un comportement d'automutilation. L'anathème jeté sur cette part de notre culture est franchement scandaleux. Il constitue une atteinte à la liberté d'expression et de création" (It has been more than forty years since Algerian literature written in French has achieved legitimacy both within and outside of Algeria. Imposed by history, like it or not, this literature has a national reality. To want to drive Amrouche or Sénac, Kateb or Mammeri out of our literary memory is an aberration, an act of self-mutilation. The anathema cast on this aspect of our culture is, frankly, a scandal. It constitutes an attack on freedom of expression and creation).

17. The "maquis" is a typical Mediterranean landscape, made of dense bushes. Traditionally, people who had committed crimes or misdemeanors used it to hide from the authorities. During World War II, it became one of the first places where civilian fighters against Nazi occupation gathered and hid. As a result, the "resistants" in general became known as "maquisards." From then on, the "maquis" has become a synecdochic and familiar way of designating any form of civilian armed resistance. "Prendre le maquis" therefore means to "resist" an oppressive power and engage in guerilla warfare (editor's note).

18. The critique of the Algerian regime can also be found in other novelists, such as Mourad Bourboune, writing in French, or Tahar Ouattar, in Arabic.

19. Djemai, born in 1948, published *Saison de pierres* (1986), *Mémoires de "Nègre"* (1991), *Sable rouge* (1996), and *Un été de cendres* (1997).

20. See Djebar's "Retour non retour" (1996, 41–53) where a mother pushes her daughter to her death.

21. In Mimouni's *La malédiction*, the doctor is murdered by his brother, who has become a Muslim activist. In Belamri's *Femmes sans visage*, a young woman is murdered by her own brother after being raped by a Muslim soldier in the French army. The narrator's father kills his best friend. In Djaout's *Les vigiles*, the character who is forced to commit suicide had earlier been sentenced to death by his comrades-in-arms in the maquis and saved at the last minute.

22. An early exception is Vatin 1975.

23. See *Le blanc de l'Algérie* by Assia Djebar, about the long list of writers who died prematurely or were murdered.

CHAPTER 7. DIGLOSSIA

1. In French, "la perte d'un secret *d'avec* les siens." *D'avec* is an irreducibly ambiguous preposition; the modification of *avec* (with) by *de* usually negates the connection implied by *avec*, but may also rhetorically underscore the connection. Thus the *de* of *d'avec* performs the severing of the link Khatibi describes here (translator's note).

2. "Jamais je n'ai cessé, même aux jours de succès près de l'institutrice (française), de ressentir au fond de moi cette seconde rupture du lien ombilical, cet exil intérieur qui ne rapprochait plus l'écolier de sa mère que pour les arracher, chaque fois un peu plus, au murmure du sang, aux frémissements réprobateurs d'une langue bannie, secrètement d'un même accord, aussitôt brisé que conclu. . . . Ainsi avais-je perdu tout à la fois ma mère et son langage, les seuls trésors inaliénables—et pourtant aliénés, les seuls trésors inaliénables et pourtant aliénés."

3. "J'ai suggéré—et Kateb l'a déclaré très nettement—que l'écrivain arabe de langue française est saisi dans un chiasme, un chiasme entre l'aliénation et l'inaliénation (dans toutes les orientations de ces deux termes): cet auteur n'écrit pas sa langue propre, il transcrit son nom propre transformé, il ne peut rien posséder (si tant soit peu on s'approprie une langue), il ne possède ni son parler maternel qui ne s'écrit pas, ni la langue arabe écrite qui est aliénée et donnée à une substitution, ni cette autre langue apprise et qui lui fait signe de se désapproprier en elle et de s'y effacer. Souffrance insoluble lorsque cet écrivain n'assume pas cette identité entamée, dans une clarté de pensée qui vit de ce chiasme, de cette schize."

CHAPTER 8. MULTILINGUALISM AND NATIONAL "CHARACTER"

1. "Je dois le signaler d'emblée: je n'ai aucun espoir d'apprendre jamais cette langue. Ce n'est pas l'envie qui me manque, encore moins les occasions extérieures, *c'est quelque chose d'autre.* J'essaie depuis quelque temps déjà de m'exprimer *comme les gens du pays.* Je constate que, dans les discussions, *je dis non ce que je veux dire,* mais *ce que je peux dire.* Ce n'est pas du tout pareil, on le conçoit facilement. On présumera qu'il s'agit *d'un état troublant, mais passager,* qu'une étude approfondie pourrait y remédier. Il est *malheureusement inutile de l'espérer. Ce n'est pas seulement une question de vocabulaire ni de syntaxe.* Parlons plutôt d'*un certain habitus,* que je ne vois pas la possibilité d'acquérir. Avec un peu plus de ténacité, à la longue, je pourrais peut-être dire avec des phrases américaines que dans certains tableaux américains le ciel et les arbres me font l'impression d'être fardés, comme des êtres soucieux avant tout de sex-appeal. Mais je ne saurai jamais prendre l'attitude nécessaire pour exprimer ces choses sans choquer. Il faudrait que j'apprenne à devenir un 'nice fellow' " (Brecht 1970, 229–34, my emphasis).

2. On these issues, see Gilles Deleuze and Félix Guattari's indispensable work, *Kafka, Introduction à la littérature mineure* (1975) esp. chapters 3 and 4. For a "historical" and "political" perspective on the problems raised by bilingualism, diglossia, and tetraglossia, see Gobard 1976.

3. See Thevenin 1969, 56 seq.

4. Here I am playing with Fredric Jameson's expression in *The Prison-House of Language: A Critical Account of Structuralism and Russian Formalism* (1972).

5. Khatibi is the author of a poem entitled: "Le lutteur de classe à la manière taoiste" (1976).

6. It has not escaped me that Khatibi is not the "first" Maghrebian author to raise the question of bilingualism. It does seem to me, however, that he is the first to put it at the center of his thinking, and to inscribe that theoretical problematic in the very body of his "poetic" texts. To pastiche Barthes, I might say that bilingualism, born *in practical and aesthetic terms* with writers such as Kateb Yacine, for example, was still waiting for its *theoretical entry* in the Maghreb. With Khatibi, this entry became plain: inaugurated by *La mémoire tatouée* et *La blessure du nom propre*, this problematic finds its strongest expression in *Amour bilingue* and, in a frankly theoretical form, in *Maghreb pluriel*.

7. "La bi-langue? Ma chance, mon gouffre individuel et ma belle angoisse d'amnésie. Énergie que je *ne sens* pas, c'est bien curieux, comme déficience; mais elle serait ma troisième oreille. Atteint par quelque désintegration je me serais développé . . . *en un sens inverse, dans la dissociation de tout langage unique*. C'est pourquoi j'admire, chez l'aveugle cette *gravité du geste*; et chez le sourd, *cet amour désespéré, impossible de la langue*" (Khatibi 1983a, 5).

8. "Dès lors se construit la scénographie des doubles. Un mot: déjà deux: déjà un récit" (1983a, 11).

9. The author is referring to the polysemic potential of the French word *geste*, which in the masculine means "gesture," but in the feminine "chanson de geste," a medieval genre of epic poetry (translator's note).

10. "Je t'avais baptisée: *bi-langue*. Et maintenant plurilangue. *En somme, une question de traduction*, à défalquer de mes nuits blanches. J'épelais *le sans nom et le sans fondement* comme éléments de mon épreuve, partout où l'incommunicable me tenait auprès de lui. J'avais traversé ensuite l'innocence des choses, la confusion des langues et tout langage antérieur de révélation" (Khatibi 1983a, 113).

11. To think of the "confrontation" of the two languages (French/Arabic) in terms of "repression" is insufficient. On Khatibi's complex position regarding repression, see "Pensée-autre" in Khatibi 1983b, esp. 11. In the

same book, see also "Bilinguisme et Littérature," on Abdelwahab Meddeb's beautiful *Talismano* (1979).

In writing these notes, I have come to realize that, in a way, Khatibi already prefaced what I am trying to put in place here, after the fact. At the very beginning of the article on *Talismano*, which re-marks my "reading" of Khatibi's book, we read:

"So long as the theory of translation, of bilanguage, and of plural-language does not progress, certain Maghrebian texts will remain intractable to a formal or functional approach. The 'mother' tongue operates within the foreign language. A permanent translation and an infinite dialogue extremely difficult to uncover, take place between one and the other. . . . Where does the violence of the text trace itself out, if not in this chiasmus of the two languages, at their impossible intersection? It is necessary to acknowledge this violence within the text itself: Yes, one has to take on the French language, but in order to name this fault and this pleasure in the foreign, one has to work continuously at the margin, that is to say, for its own sake, in isolation" (editor's translation).

"Tant que *la théorie de la traduction, de la bi-langue et de la pluri-langue* n'aura pas avancé, *certains textes maghrébins resteront imprenables selon une approche formelle et fonctionnelle.* La langue "maternelle" *est à l'oeuvre dans la langue étrangère.* De l'une à l'autre se déroulent une *traduction permanente* et un *entretien en abyme* extrêmement difficile à mettre au jour . . . Où se dessine la violence du texte, *sinon dans ce chiasme, cette intersection, à vrai dire, irréconciliable*? Encore faut-il en prendre acte DANS LE TEXTE MEME: *assumer la langue française,* oui, pour y nommer cette faille et cette jouissance de l'étranger qui doit *continuellement travailler à la marge,* c'est à dire pour son seul compte, solitairement" (Khatibi 1983b, 179).

12. "Une certaine unité de la langue se réalisa dans son corps. Ses états d'âme, qui changeaient au jour le jour, étaient limpides, prévenants, prodigieusement inattendus. La grande souffrance? terminée. Le reniement? de l'affirmation, rien que de l'affirmation" (Khatibi 1983a, 119).

13. "Cette fois, il ferma les yeux avant de prêter toute son attention: une présence qu'il sentait là, mais *invisiblement,* inaudible. Aucun sifflement, pas de bruit, mais bientôt une musique *silencieuse,* un chant intérieur à la mer"(Khatibi 1983a, 39)."

14. "Une fois, j'ai lu un auteur bizarre: pour se débarrasser de son maître, il avait changé de langue. Coup de génie, cette mutation si rare" (Khatibi 1983a, 14).

15. The passage that follows plays on the multiple meanings of the noun *louche* (literally, cross-eyed; figuratively, shifty, dubious, suspicious) and

the verb "loucher" (literally, to look cross-eyed, figuratively, to peer at, to eye), as well as on a rarer sense of louche given in the text (translator's note).

16. See Derrida 1967, chapter entitled "L'écriture avant la lettre"; see also Derrida 1972a, chapter entitled "La différance"; finally, see how Derrida develops this concept in *Positions* (1972b), esp. 108.

17. "Ce *début* du texte *semblait dévorer le récitant*, qui le lisait sans relâche. Il s'approchait chaque fois *de ce début qui l'excluait*: un récit *sans personnage*; ou s'il y en avait, ce serait le *récit lui-même*, s'entendant dire ce seul mot: Recommence" (Khatibi 1983a, 12).

18. "Qui s'était formulée toute seule" (p. 9 in French-language text; p. 3 in English).

19. "Il partit, repartit. Il décida de partir définitivement. Le récit devrait s'arrêter ici, le livre se fermer sur lui-même" (9).

20. Il n'oubliait pas que, dans son lexique, la séduction (*fitna*) est cette *homographie de guerre et de séduction proprement dite*, cette passion chevaleresque qui ne chante que les absents du désert, les aimés inconnus.

"En cela, la séduction les portait sur *une double scène dans la volupté de la langue*. Comment savoir? Comment savoir dans la moindre parole, le moindre fait, l'ordre des lois mortelles—leur désordre?

"*Mort:* pour se donner la vie dans le mot, *il fallait parcourir toute la force destructice de la bi-langue*. Dans son parler maternel, la mort est cet au-delà céleste, ce paradis d'enfant. *Il se devait de disséminer en lui*, non point ce rappel—il en était enchanté—mais l'*illusion d'anges invisibles*, pour enfin glorifier, célébrer toute rencontre aimante" (Khatibi 1983a, 17–18).

21. "Tout était blanc. Clarté palpitante du jour. Il sentit une grande fatigue. Tout à l'heure, il méditait encore ou rêvassait, assis, silencieux, *devant un livre ouvert*. *Glissement de la lumière:* plus le jour avançait, plus il avait l'impression de feuilleter un *livre blanc*.

" . . . De nouveau, il lisait. Son regard passait sur les lettres, *pour autant qu'il s'évanouissait dans leur graphie, selon les plis de ce magnifique volume*" (Khatibi 1983a, 46).

22. "C'est alors que les mots défilèrent devant lui en voltigeant, *puis ils s'écroulèrent les uns sur les autres avec fracas: la langue était folle*.

"Se lever? Il ne le pouvait pas: *à la place d'un mot en débris, plus de lieu pour aucune chose visible:* la mer elle-même avait sombré dans la nuit. Et *en français*—sa langue étrangère—le 'mot' est près de la mort, *il ne lui manque qu'une seule lettre:* concision de sa frappe, une syllabe, extase d'un sanglot retenu. Pourquoi croyait-il que la langue est plus belle, plus *terrible* pour un *étranger*?"

"Il se calma d'un coup, lorsque apparut le 'mot' arabe 'kalma' avec son équivalent savant 'kalima' et toute la chaîne des diminutifs, calembours de son enfance: 'klima' . . . la diglossie 'kal(i)ma' me revint sans que disparût ni s'effaçât le mot 'mot.' Tous deux s'observaient en lui, précédant l'émergence maintenant rapide de souvenirs, fragments de mots, onomatopées, phrases en guirlandes, enlacées à mort: indéchiffrables. Scène encore muette" (Khatibi 1983, 10, my emphasis).

23. "Lorsqu'il s'agit *d'écarter une ligne d'une autre ou de séparer,* comme pour les notes, *un texte plus fort d'avec un moindre,* c'est au moyen d'interlignes, ou de lignes de blancs composées de cadrats, qu'on augmente les intervalles. Cela s'appelle BLANCHIR OU JETER DU BLANC."

24. *Blanchir* retains the dual meaning of the French *blanc,* both "blank" and "white"; in keeping with the spirit of the author's use of typographical vocabulary, the technical term "white out" for the creation of blank space in a printed text is used here (translator's note).

25. "La casse contient donc, *outre les caractères,* diverses sortes *non apparentes au tirage,* qui font partie des blancs; ce sont les cadrats, les cadratins, les demi-cadratins, les espaces dont nous venons de parler. Les espaces séparent les mots; *il en est de plusieurs forces ou épaisseurs.* Les cadratins se placent en tête de chaque alinéa, et les cadrats à la fin de la ligne qui le termine, quand cette ligne n'est pas completée par le texte même" (Claye 1874, 18–19).

26. "De nouveau, il lisait. Son regard passait *sur les lettres,* pour autant qu'il s'évanouissait dans leur graphie, selon les plis de ce magnifique volume. Par instants simultanés, il lui semblait que sa lecture, *bien qu'intelligible et déchiffrable, tournait autour d'un mot insaisissable qui n'appartenait pas au texte.* Insaisissabilité harcelante qui dévaste, d'un coup, les pages, les mots, les lignes et la ponctuation, *à travers une tache noire flottant entre ses yeux et le livre.*

"Bientôt, *le livre allait s'illuminer autour de ce mot méconnaissable encore,* qui laissait le livre s'écrouler *hors de ses feuilles,* et marquer au passage, de page en page, ce point de strabisme qui sortait de son regard pour que *brillât,* devant lui, le signe de la nuit. La nuit entrait, sortait du livre, effaçant, en quelque sorte, le blanc par le noir, sans qu'il pût se dégager de sa fascination" (Khatibi 1983a, 46).

27. Here I am using for my own purposes certain aspects of the fine analyses Jean-Claude Milner has proposed on the status of Ferdinand de Saussure's anagrams in *L'amour de la langue* (1978). See in particular "Un linguiste désirant," 85–98.

28. "Nostalgie qu'il aimait *prononcer* (sic), penser aussi dans le mot arabe: 'Hanine,' *anagramme* d'une double jouissance. Il *décomposa* ce mot 'h' spirante du pharynx, puis 'a' murmuré, avant 'n-î-ne,' *modulation*

soutenue par le 'i' long. A dire ce mot, à le répétcr, comme un baiser de souffle qui vibre encore dans le pharynx, souffle régulier, sans déchirure, mais extase locale, un appel euphonique, à lui seul un chant" (Khatibi 1983a, 14).

29. "Avec un Dieu invisible sur le dos, un seul geste: lui couper la parole" (1983, 30).

30. "Plus tard, j'avais appris le braille et les langages des handicapés. Peut-être ne puis-je écrire que *pour les handicapés bilingues:* en tout cas, *ce sera trop tard pour me rejoindre!* T'avais-je perdue avant de te rencontrer? Il faut absolument que je me fasse traduire en braille, *avant que l'ordinateur n'emballe tout dans le communicable*" (Khatibi 1983, 31).

31. "Une (pensée) essentiellement minoritaire, fragmentaire, et inachevée."

32. "Une (pensée) trouée de marges, d'écarts et de questions silencieuses" (17).

33. "La pensée du 'nous' vers laquelle nous nous tournons ne se place, ne se déplace plus dans le cercle de la métaphysique (occidentale), ni selon la théologie de l'islam, mais à leur marge. Une marge en éveil" (17).

34. "Un jour—et c'est récent—il aima une femme, *changea de sexe.* Un sexe dans le sexe circoncis, *sexe à double langue, comme un serpent.* De son anus, émergeait la figure d'un Dieu invisible. *Il fut violé alors par la langue étrangère.* Jeté à terre, il souffrait atrocement. Mais—sensation bizarre—*il était derrière son violeur,* non pas à son tour le pénétrant, *mais il etait pénétré par la jouissance de la langue*—son homosexualité fichée dans les dictionnaires du monde entier" (Khatibi 1983a, 55).

35. "Traduire l'impur dans le pur, la prostitution dans l'androgynie était une aventure, qui exigeait d'etre vécue sans aucune réserve. Il errait de pays en pays, de corps en corps, de langue en langue" (Khatibi 1983a, 30).

36. See Grosrichard (1979), esp. chapter 3, "L'ombre du sérail."

37. "[L'androgyne] n'est ni le non-être, ni l'être comme tout, mais il *est la figure de l'alterité même,* l'Autre qui suscite tous les autres, l'instituteur de leur désir, la barre ou la coupure qui met les sexes (les langues) en rapport et qui rend ce rapport à la fois nécessaire et impossible, puisque toujours (n'est-ce pas sa fonction?) l'androgyne est entre l'un et l'autre et, pour ainsi dire, dans le mitan du lit—même et surtout, lorsqu'on est sûr qu'il n'y est pas" (1979, 201–202).

38. The author concludes with a parody of Montaigne: "Qui ne voit dès lors, aussi que j'ay pris une route par laquelle, sans cesse et sans travail, j'iray autant qu'il y a d'ancre et de papier au monde?" (translator's note).

works cited

Abraham, Nicolas, and Maria Torok. 1978. *L'écorce et le noyau*. Paris: Flammarion.

——. 1994. *The Shell and the Kernel*. Translated by Nicholas Rand. Chicago: University Of Chicago Press.

Achour, Christiane. 1985. *Abécédaires en devenir: Idéologie coloniale et langue française en Algérie*. Preface by Mostéfa Lacheraf. Algiers: Enterprise Nationale de Presse.

Ageron, Charles-Robert. 1991. *Modern Algeria: A History from 1830 to the Present*. Translated by Michael Bret. London: Hurst.

Aïssa, Salim. 1987. *Mimouna*. Algiers: Laphomic.

Alahite, Fatiha. 1983. *Travail domestique et salariat féminin. Essai sur les femmes dans les rapports marchands. Le cas de l'Algérie*. Oran. Magistère de sciences économiques, University of Oran.

"Algérie: Femmes victimes terrorisme." 1997. France 2, *Le journal de 20H00*, broadcast of 25 February.

"Algérie: Journée de la Femme." 1995. TFI (Télévision Française I), broadcast of 8 March.

Amnesty International. 1998a. "Algerian Mothers of 'Disappeared' Come to London." Amnesty International On-line news release.

——. 1998b. "Collectif des familles de disparus en Algérie." Amnesty International On-line news release. 9 July.

Amrane, Djamila. 1991. *Les femmes algériennes dans la guerre*. Paris: Plon.

——. 1994. *Des femmes dans la guerre d'Algérie: Entretiens*. Paris: Karthala.

Anderson, Benedict. 1990. *Language and Power: Exploring Political Cultures in Indonesia*. Ithaca: Cornell University Press.

——. 1992. *Imagined Communities: Reflections on the Origin and Spread of Nationalism*. Revised edition. London: Verso.

Aouli, Smaïl, and Ramdane Redjala. 1995. "La Kabylie face à la dérive intégriste." *Les Temps modernes* 580 (January/February): 196–208. Special issue: *Algérie, La guerre des frères*.

Arezki, Métref. 1990. "Une presse dans le dégel: Genèse d'une ambiguité." *Monde arabe: Maghreb-Machrek* 154: 61–67. Special issue: *Algérie, la fin de l'unanimisme: débats et combats des années 80 et 90*.

Arkoun, Mohamed. 1984. *Essai sur la pensée islamique.* Paris: Maison-neuve-Larose.

Arrivé, Michel, Françoise Gadet, and Michel Galmiche. 1986. *La Grammaire d'aujourd'hui: guide alphabétique de linguistique française.* Paris: Flammarion.

Badie, Bertrand. 1987. *Les deux Etats: Pouvoir et Société en Occident . . . d'Islam.* Paris: Fayard.

Bagtache, Merzac. 1997. "Calamus." *Algérie Littérature/Action* 10–11 (April—May): 7–132.

Barère, Bertrand. 1961. "Rapport du Comité de Salut Public sur les idiomes." *Archives Parlementaires,* 1st series, vol. 83. Paris: CNRS.

Barrouhi, Abdelazis. 1995. "Widowed and Raped, Algeria's Women 'Try' Islamists." *Reuters,* Tunis, 8 March.

Baylee, Alek. 1996. "Madah Sartre." *Algérie Littérature/Action* 6 (December): 5–103.

Beauvoir, Simone de. 1963. *La force des choses.* Paris: Gallimard.

——. 1965. *Force of Circumstance.* Harmondsworth: Penguin.

——. 1998. *A Transatlantic Love Affair: Letters to Nelson Algren.* London: Norton.

Beauvoir, Simone de, and Gisèle Halimi. 1962a. *Djamila Boupacha.* Paris: Gallimard.

——. 1962b. *Djamila Boupacha: The Story of the Torture of a Young Algerian Girl Which Shocked Liberal Opinion,* translated by Peter Green. London: André Deutsch and Weidenfeld Nicolson.

Belamri, Rabah. 1992. *Femmes sans visage.* Paris: Gallimard.

Bengharbit-Remaoun, Nouria. 1993. "Les jeunes en situation scolaire, représentations et pratiques." *Naqd* 5 (April–August): 34–41. Special issue: "Culture et système éducatif."

Benhedouga, Abdelhamid. 1997. *"Je rêve d'un monde. . . ." Algérie Littérature/Action* 15/16 (November/December): 5–168.

Ben Jelloun, Tahar. 1985. Review of *L'amour la fantasia* by Assia Djebar. *Le Monde,* 10 May.

Benkheira, Mohamed. 1997. *L'amour de la loi. Essai sur la normativité en Islam.* Paris: PUF.

Benrabah, Mohamed. 1995. "La langue perdue." *Esprit* 208 (January): 35–47. Special issue: "Avec l'Algérie."

——, ed. 1998. *Les violences en Algérie.* Paris: Odile Jacob.

Berger, Anne-Emmanuelle. 1998. "The Newly Veiled Woman: Irigaray, Specularity and the Islamic Veil." *Diacritics* 28, no. 1: 93–120.

Bernard, Philippe, and Nathaniel Herzberg, eds. 1998. *Le Monde: Lettres d'Algérie.* Paris: Gallimard.

Betts, Raymond. 1961. *Assimilation and Association in French Colonial Theory, 1899–1914.* New York: Columbia University Press.

Bitam, Boukhalfa. 1986. *Les Justes.* Algiers: ENL.

Boire, Gary. 1991. "Tribunalations: George Ryga's Postcolonial Trial 'Play.'" *Ariel* 22, no. 2 (April): 5–20.

Bois, Marcel. 1986. "Tendances nouvelles du roman algérien de langue arabe." In *Nouveaux enjeux culturels au Maghreb,* edited by Jean-Robert Henry. Paris: CNRS.

Bonn, Charles. 1985. *Le roman algérien de langue française.* Paris: L'Harmattan.

Botiveau, Bernard, Mohamed Al-Ahnaf and Franck Fregosi, eds. 1991. *L'Algérie par ses islamistes.* Paris: Karthala.

Boudalia-Greffou, Malika. 1989. *L'école algérienne d'Ibn Badis à Pavlov.* Algiers: Laphomic.

Boudjedra, Rachid. 1969. *La répudiation.* Paris: Denoël.

——. 1972. *L'insolation.* Paris: Denoël.

——. 1975. *Topographie idéale pour une agression caracterisée.* Paris: Denoël.

——. 1977. *L'escargot entêté.* Paris: Denoël.

——. 1979. *1001 années de nostalgie.* Paris: Denoël.

——. 1981. *Le vainqueur de coupe.* Paris: Denoël.

——. 1984. *La macération.* Paris: Denoël.

——. 1987a. *La pluie.* Paris: Denoël.

——. 1987b. *La prise de Gibraltar.* Paris: Denoël.

——. 1990a. *Le démantèlement.* Algiers: Bouchène.

——. 1990b. *Le désordre des choses.* Paris: Denoël.

——. 1994. *Timimoun.* Paris: Denoël.

——. 1995. *The Repudiation.* Translated by Goda Lambrova. Colorado Springs: Three Continents Press.

Boukous, Ahmed. 1989. "Les études de dialectologie berbère en Algérie." In *Langue et Société au Maghreb: bilan et perspectives.* Rabat: Publications de la Faculté des Lettres et des Sciences Humaines de Rabat.

Bourbonne, Mourad. 1985. Review of *L'amour la fantasia* by Assia Djebar. *Jeune Afrique,* 15 April.

Bourdieu, Pierre. 1979. *Algeria 1960: Essays.* Cambridge: Cambridge University Press.

Boutet de Monvel, Marc. 1994. *Boudjedra, l'insolé. L'Insolation, racines et greffes.* Paris: L'Harmattan.

Braud, Philippe. 1993. *La violence politique dans les démocrats européennes occidentales.* Paris: L'Harmattan.

Brecht, Bertolt. *Ecrits sur la politique et la société.* Paris: L'Arche, 1970.

Burgat, François. 1996. *L'islamisme en face.* Paris: La Découverte.

Cabral, Amilcar. 1970. *National Liberation and Culture.* Translated by Maureen Webster. Syracuse: Syracuse University Press.

Cahiers de l'IHTP [Institut d'Histoire du Temps Présent] 10 (1988).

Carlier, Omar. 1992. "De l'islahisme à l'islamisme, la thérapie politico-religieuse du FIS." *Cahiers d'Etudes Africaines* 32 (2): 185–220. Reprinted in *Entre Nation et Jihad.* Paris: Presses de la fondation nationale des Sciences politiques, 1995.

Camus, Albert. 1953. *Actuelles III.* Paris: Gallimard.

——. 1960. *Resistance, Rebellion and Death: Essays.* Translated by Justin O'Brien. New York: Vintage.

Carré, Olivier. 1993. *Le nationalisme arabe.* Paris: Petite Bibliothèque Payot.

Caruth, Cathy. 1996. *Unclaimed Experience: Trauma, Narrative and History.* Baltimore: Johns Hopkins University Press.

Chaker, Salem. 1986. "Langue et identité berbères (Algérie/Emigration): Un enjeu de société." In *Nouveaux enjeux culturels au Maghreb,* edited by Jean-Robert Henry. Paris: CNRS.

Cheniki, Ahmed. 1986. Interview of Rachid Mimouni. *Révolution africaine,* 26 December.

Cheriet, Boutheina. 1992. "Islam and Feminism: Algeria's 'Rites of Passage' to Democracy." In *State and Society in Algeria,* edited by John Entelis and Philip Naylor, 171–216. Boulder: Westview.

Chomsky, Noam. 1986. *Pirates and Emperors: International Terrorism in the Real World.* New York: Claremont University Press.

——. 1988. *The Culture of Terrorism.* Boston: South End.

Christelow, Allan. 1985. *Muslim Law Courts and the French Colonial State in Algeria.* Princeton: Princeton University Press.

Claye, Jules. 1874. *Typologie: Manuel du compositeur apprenti.* Paris: J. Claye.

Colas, Dominique. 1992. *Le glaive et le fléau, généalogie du fanatisme et de la société civile.* Paris: Grasset.

Colona, Ugo. 1992. "L'Algérie en chiffres." *Revue Autrement* 60. Special issue: Algérie 30 ans.

Colonna, Fanny. 1975. *Instituteurs algériens 1883–1939.* Paris: Presses de la Fondation nationale des Sciences politiques.

Crouzet, Denis. 1997. "La Saint-Barthélémy: Religion et barbarie." *L'Histoire* 214: 32–35.

Dakhia, Jocelyne. 1998. *Le divan des rois. Le politique et le religieux dans l'islam.* Paris: Aubier.

Déjeux, Jean. 1986. "Les éditeurs de romans, recueils de nouvelles et recueils de poèmes maghrébins de langue française de 1945 à 1984." In

Nouveaux enjeux culturels au Maghreb, edited by Jean-Robert Henry. Paris: CNRS.

———. 1994. *La littérature féminine de langue française au Maghreb*. Paris: Karthala.

Deleuze, Gilles. 1968. *Différence et répétition*. Paris: PUF.

———. 1994. *Difference and Repetition*. Translated by Paul Patton. New York: Columbia University Press.

Deleuze, Gilles, and Felix Guattari. 1975. *Kafka, Introduction à la littérature mineure*. Paris: Minuit.

Derrida, Jacques. 1967. *De la grammatologie*. Paris: Minuit.

———. 1972a. *Marges de la philosophie*. Paris: Minuit.

———. 1972b. *Positions*. Paris: Minuit.

———. 1981. *Dissemination*. Translated by Barbara Johnson. Chicago: The University of Chicago Press, 1981.

———. 1995. "Passages—from Traumatism to Promise." In *Points . . . Interviews 1974–1994*, edited by Elisabeth Weber, translated by Peggy Kamuf et al. Stanford: Stanford University Press.

———. 1996. *Monolinguisme de l'autre: ou la prothèse de l'origine*. Paris: Galilée.

———. 1998a. *Monolingualism of the Other, or, the Prosthesis of Origin*. Translated by Patrick Mensah. Stanford: Stanford University Press.

———. 1998b. Roundtable intervention. In *Idiomes, Nationalités, Déconstruction*, edited by Fehti Benslama, 218–35. Casablanca and Paris: Toubkal and Intersignes.

Didier, Hugues. 1998. "L'Algérie dans ses langues." In *2000 ans d'Algérie*. Vol. 2 of *Carnets Séguier*. Biarritz: Atlantica, 47–76.

Djaout, Tahar. 1981. *L'exproprié*. Algiers: Entreprise Nationale du Livre.

———. 1984a. *Les chercheurs d'os*. Paris: Seuil.

———. 1984b. *Les rets de l'oiseleur*. Algiers: Entreprise Nationale du Livre.

———. 1987. *L'invention du désert*. Paris: Seuil.

———. 1995. *Les Vigiles*. Paris: Seuil.

Djebar, Assia. 1958. *Les impatients*. Paris: Julliard.

———. 1962. *Les enfants du nouveau monde*. Paris: Julliard.

———. 1967. *Les Alouettes naïves*. Paris: Julliard.

———. 1980. *Femmes d'Alger dans leur appartement*. Paris: Des Femmes.

———. 1984. Interview. *Jeune Afrique*, 27 June.

———. 1985. *L'amour la fantasia*. Paris: Jean-Claude Lattès.

———. 1987a. *Ombre sultane*. Paris: Jean-Claude Lattès.

———. 1987b. Interview. *Le Monde*, 19 May.

———. 1990. *Les romans d'Assia Djebar*. Algiers: Office des Publications Universitaires.

——. 1991. *Loin de Médine: filles d'Ismaël*. Paris: Albin Michel.

——. 1993. *Fantasia: An Algerian Cavalcade*. Translated by D.S. Blair. Portsmouth, N.H.: Heineman.

——. 1995a. *Le Blanc de l'Algérie*. Paris: Albin-Michel.

——. 1995b. *Vaste est la prison*. Paris: Albin-Michel.

——. 1996. "Retour non retour." *Nouvelle Revue Française* 521 (June): 41–53.

——. 1997. *Oran, langue morte*. Arles: Actes Sud.

Djeghloul, Abdelkader. 1986. "La formation des intellectuels modernes (1880–1890)." In *Aspects de la culture algérienne*, 51–82. Paris: Centre Culturel Algérien.

Djemaï, Abdelkader. 1986. *Saison de pierres*. Alger: Entreprise Nationale du Livre.

——. 1993. *Le lapsus de Djedda Aicha: et autres histoires à lire à haute voix*. Paris: L'Harmattan.

——. 1995a. *Camus à Oran*. Paris: Éditions Michalon.

——. 1995b. *Un été de cendres*. Paris: Gallimard.

——. 1996. *Sable Rouge*. Paris: Éditions Michalon.

——. 1998. *31, rue de l'Aigle*. Paris: Gallimard.

——. 1999. *Mémoires de nègre*. Paris: Éditions Michalon.

——. 2000. *Dites-leur de me laisser passer et autres nouvelles*. Paris: Michalon.

Elimam, Abdou. 1997. *Le maghribi, langue trois fois millénaire, exploration en linguistique Maghrébine*. Algiers: ANEP.

Entelis, John. 1981. "Elite Political Culture and Socialisation in Algeria: Tensions and Discontinuities." *Middle East Journal* 35, 2 (spring).

——. 1997. "Political Islam in the Maghreb: The Non-Violent Dimension." In *Islam, Democracy and the State in North Africa*, edited by John Entelis. Bloomington: Indiana University Press.

Entelis, John, and Philip Naylor, eds. 1992. *State and Society in Algeria*. Boulder: Westview.

Eveno, Patrick. 1994. *L'Algérie*. Paris: Le Monde.

Fanon, Frantz. 1959. *L'an cinq de la Révolution algérienne*. Paris: François Maspéro.

——. 1965. *Studies in a Dying Colonialism*. Translated by Haakon Chevalier. London: Earthscan.

Felman, Shoshana, and Dori Laub. 1992. *Testimony*. New York: Routledge.

Fregosi, Franck. 1994. "Fondamentalisme islamique et relations internationales : Le cas du FIS." *Trimestre du Monde* 25: 29–40.

Gafaïti, Hafid. 1985. "Entretien avec Rachid Mimouni." *Voix Multiples* 10 (Oran): 94–100. Special issue: "Réflexions sur la littérature algérienne." Reprinted in *Tombéza*, Algiers: Laphomic (1987).

——. 1987. *Boudjedra ou la passion de la modernité.* Paris: Denoël.

——. 1991. "Rachid Mimouni entre la critique algérienne et la critique française." In *Poétiques croisées au Maghreb* 14, second semester 1991, 26–36.

——. 1997. "Between God and the President: Literature and Censorship in North Africa." *Diacritics* 27, no. 2 (1997): 59–84.

Gallissot, René. 1995. "Arabo-musulman versus arabo-berbère: Communauté religieuse et identité nationale à partir de l'exemple algérien." In *Identité-Communauté: Les cahiers du CEFRESS*, edited by Nadif Marouf. Paris: L'Harmattan.

Gaudemar, Antoine de. 1991. "Entretien avec Rachid Boudjedra." *Libération*, 31 May.

Gobard, Henri. 1976. *L'aliénation linguistique, analyse tetraglossique*, preface by Gilles Deleuze. Paris: Flammarion.

Gonfond-Talahite, Claude. 1998. "Simone de Beauvoir et l'Algérie." *Algérie Littérature/Action* 17 (January): 143–46.

Grandguillaume, Gilbert. 1983. *Arabisation et politique linguistique au Maghreb.* Paris: Maisonneuve et Larose.

—— 1986. "Langue arabe et Etat moderne au Maghreb." In *Nouveaux en jeux culturels au Maghreb*, edited by Jean-Robert Henry. Paris: CNRS.

——. 1998. "Langues et représentations identitaires en Algérie." In *2000 ans d'Algérie*. Vol. 1 of *Carnets Séguier*. Biarritz: Atlantica.

Grégoire, Abbé. 1975. "Rapport sur la nécessité et les moyens d'anéantir les patois et d'universaliser la langue française" (1794). Reprinted in *Une politique de la langue: La Révolution française et les patois*, edited by M. de Certeau, D. Julia, and J. Revel. Paris: Gallimard.

Grosrichard, Alain. 1979. *Structure du sérail: La fiction du despotisme asiatique dans l'Occident classique.* Paris: Seuil.

Haddab, Mustapha. 1979. *Éducation et changements socio-culturels: Les Moniteurs de l'enseignement élémentaire en Algérie.* Algiers: Office des Publications Universitaires.

——. 1998. *The Sultan's Court: European Fantasies of the East.* Translated by Liz Heron. New York: Verso.

Halimi, Gisèle. 1978. "La libération pour tous . . . sauf pour elles?" *Nouvel Observateur* (10 July).

——. 1990. *Milk for the Orange Tree.* Translated by Dorothy Blair. London: Quartet.

Harbi, Mohammed. 1980. *Le FLN, mirage et réalité.* Paris: Jeune Afrique.

——. 1992. *L'Algérie et son destin. Croyants ou citoyens.* Paris: Arcantère.

——. 1995. "Violence, nationalisme, Islamisme." *Les Temps Modernes* 580 (January–February): 24–33. Special issue: "Algerie: La guerre des frères."

——. 1997. "Le complot Lamouri." In *La guerre d'Algérie et les Algériens, 1954–1962*, edited by Charles-Robert Ageron. Paris: Armand Colin, 151–79.

——. 1998. "Naissance d'une nationalité." In *2000 ans d'Algérie*. Vol. 1 of *Cahiers Séguier*. Biarritz: Atlantica, 51–57.

Hassan. 1996. *Algérie, Histoire d'un naufrage*. Paris: Seuil.

Hélie-Lucas, Marie-Aimée. 1987. "Bound and Gagged by the Family Code." In *Third World Second Sex*. Vol. 2. Edited by Miranda Davies. London: Zed.

Herman, Edward. 1982. *The Real Terror Network: Terrorism in Fact and Propaganda*. Boston: South End.

"Horizons Maghreb." 1984. In *Le Français dans le Monde*, 189 (November–December).

Jameson, Fredric. 1972. *The Prison-House of Language: A Critical Account of Structuralism and Russian Formalism*. Princeton: Princeton University Press.

Kafka, Franz. *The Diaries of Franz Kafka*, edited by Max Brod. Vol 1. New York: Schocken Books, 1948.

Khane, Mohammed. 1993. "*Le Monde* and the Algerian War During the Fourth Republic." In *French and Algerian Identities from Colonial Times to the Present*, edited by Alec Hargreaves and Michael Heffernan, 129–48. Lewiston: Edwin Mellen.

Khatibi, Abdelkebir. 1976. *Le lutteur de classe à la manière taoiste*. Paris: Sindbad.

——. 1982. *La mémoire tatouée*. Paris: Denoël.

——. 1983a. *Amour bilingue*. Montpellier: Fata Morgana.

——. 1983b. *Maghreb pluriel*. Paris: Denoël.

——. 1986. *La blessure du nom propre*. Paris: Denoël.

——. 1990. *Love in Two Languages*. Translated by Richard Howard. Minneapolis: University of Minnesota Press.

Khatibi, Abdelkebir, and Mohamed Sijelmassi. 1994. *L'Art calligraphique de l'Islam*. Paris: Gallimard.

Klossowski, Pierre. 1969. *Nietzsche et le cercle vicieux*. Paris: Mercure de France.

Knauss, Peter. 1992. "Algerian Women since Independence." In *State and Society in Algeria*, edited by John Entelis and Philip Naylor, 151–70. Boulder: Westview.

Lacheraf, Mostefa. 1964. *L'Algérie, nation et société*. Paris: Maspéro.

Larej, Waciny. 1996. "La gardienne des ombres." *Algérie Littérature/Action* 3/4 (September–October): 9–161.

Lazreg, Marnia. 1994. *The Eloquence of Silence*. London: Routledge.

Leca, Jean. 1993. *La "rationalité" de la violence politique.* Paris: IEP.

Leca, Jean, and Jean Claude Vatin. 1975. *L'Algérie politique.* Paris: Presses de la FNSP.

Lewis, Bernard. 1998. *The Multiple Identities of the Middle-East.* New York: Schocken Books.

Limqueco, Peter, Peter Weiss and Ken Coates, eds. 1971. *Prevent the Crime of Silence: Reports from the Sessions of the International War Crimes Tribunal Founded by Bertrand Russell.* London: Allen Lane.

Lippert, Anne. 1987. "Algerian Women's Access to Power: 1962–1985." In *Studies in Power and Class in Africa,* edited by Irving Leonard Markovitz, 209–32. Oxford: Oxford University Press.

Lorcin, Patricia M. E. 1995. *Imperial Identities: Stereotyping, Prejudice and Race in Colonial Algeria.* London: I. B. Tauris.

Mahe, Alain. 1996. "Entre le religieux, le juridique et le politique : l'éthique. Réflexions sur la nature du rigorisme moral promu et sanctionné par les assemblées villageoises en Grande Kabylie." *Anthropologie et sociétés* 20, no. 2 (spring): 85–109. Special issue: "Algérie aux marges du religieux."

Maran, Rita. 1989. *Torture: The Role of Ideology in the French-Algerian War.* New York: Praeger.

Marginedas, Marc. 1998. "L'information asservie en Algérie." *Le Monde Diplomatique,* (September): 19.

Martinez, Luis. 1998. *La guerre civile en Algérie.* Paris: Karthala.

Mazouni, Abdallah. 1969. *Culture et enseignement en Algérie et au Maghreb.* Paris: Maspéro.

Meddeb, Abdelwahab. 1979. *Talismano.* Paris: C. Bourgois.

Méchakra, Yamina. 1979. *La grotte éclatée,* preface by Kateb Yacine. Algiers: S.N.E.D.

Médiene, Benamar. 1996. "Aujourd'hui l'Algérie: Crise sociale ou crise du sens." Paper delivered at "Algeria in and out of French: A Conference on Politics and Culture in Postcolonial Algeria," Cornell University, October.

Milner, Jean-Claude. 1978. *L'amour de la langue.* Paris: Seuil.

Mimouni, Rachid. 1982. *Le fleuve détourné.* Paris: R. Laffont.

——. 1984. *Tombéza.* Paris: R. Laffont.

——. 1988. *Le printemps n'en sera que plus beau.* Algiers: Entreprise Nationale du Livre.

——. 1989. *L'honneur de la tribu.* Paris: R. Laffont.

——. 1990. *La ceinture de l'ogresse.* Paris: Seghers.

——. 1992. *The Honor of the Tribe: A Novel.* Translated by Joachim Neugroschel. New York: Morrow.

——. 1993a. *La malédiction*. Paris: Stock.

——. 1993b. *The Ogre's Embrace*. Translated by Shirley Eber. London: Quartet Books.

——. 1993c. "L'Algérie sans la France." In *L'Algérie des Français*, edited by Charles-Robert Ageron, 335–41. Paris: Seuil.

Munier, Henri. 1991. "Les systèmes d'enseignement. Résultats quantitatifs, mais dégradation qualitative." In *L'Etat du Maghreb*, edited by Yves Lacoste and Camille Lacoste. Casablanca: Le Fennec.

Murphy, Julien. 1995. "Beauvoir and the Algerian War: Toward a Postcolonial Ethics." In *Feminist Interpretations of Simone de Beauvoir*, edited by Margaret A. Simons. University Park: Pennsylvania State University Press.

Niarchos, Catherine N. 1995. "Women, War, and Rape: Challenges Facing the International Tribunal for the Former Yugoslavia." *Human Rights Quarterly* 17, no. 4 (November): 649–90.

Nora, Pierre. 1961. *Les Français d'Algérie*. Paris: Julliard.

Pécaud, Daniel. 1987. *L'ordre et la violence. Evolution socio-politique de la Colombie entre 1930 et 1953*. Paris: Editions de l'EHESS.

Pelégri, Jean. 1991. "Les signes et les lieux. Essai sur la genèse et les perspectives de la littérature algérienne." In *Le banquet maghrebin*, edited by Guiliana Toso Rodinis, 9–36. Rome: Bulzone.

Pelley, Patricia N. 1993. "The New History in Political Vietnam." Ph.D. diss, Cornell University.

Pervillé, Guy. 1996. "The Frenchification of Algerian Intellectuals: History of a Failure?" In *Franco-Arab Encounters*, edited by L. Carol Brown and M. S. Gordon, 415–45. American University of Beirut.

Philipose, Liz. 1996. "The Laws of War and Women's Human Rights." *Hypatia* 11, no. 4 (fall): 46–62.

Prochaska, David. 1990. *Making Algeria French:Colonialism in Bône, 1870–1920*. Cambridge: Cambridge University Press.

Rajan, Rajeswari Sunder. 1993. *Real and Imagined Women: Gender, Culture and Postcolonialism*. London: Routledge.

Rapport de prise en charge du dossier amazigh (1995/1998). 1998. Algiers: Ministère de l'Education nationale.

Renan, Ernest. 1990. "What Is a Nation?" Translated by Martin Thom. In *Nation and Narration*, edited by Homi K. Bhabha, 8–22. London: Routledge.

Rey, Alain. 1985. "Pour une critique de la crise." In *La crise des langues*, edited by Jacques Maurais. Québec: Conseil de la langue française.

Rousseau, Jean-Jacques. 1966. "Essay on the Origins of Languages," translated by J. H. Moran. In *On the Origin of Language: Rousseau and Herder*. New York: F. Ungar.

Ruedy, John. 1996. "Chérif Benhabylès and the Young Algerians." In *Franco-Arab Encounters*, edited by L. Carol Brown and M. S. Gordon, 345–69. American University of Beirut.

Saadi-Mokrane, Djamila. 1985. *La charte nationale algérienne, analyse de discours*. Algiers: Office des Publications Universitaires.

Said, Edward. 1981. *Covering Islam*. New York: Pantheon.

Sanneh, Lamine. 1989. *Translating the Message*. Maryknoll: Orbis Books.

Santucci, Jean-Claude. 1986. "Le français au Maghreb, situation générale et perspectives d'avenir." In *Nouveaux enjeux culturels au Maghreb*, edited by Jean-Robert Henry. Paris: CNRS.

Sartre, Jean Paul. 1948a. "Orphée Noir." Preface to *Anthologie de la nouvelle poésie nègre et malgache de langue française*, by Léopold Sédar Senghor. Paris: PUF.

——. 1948b. *Qu'est-ce que la littérature?* Paris: Gallimard.

——. 1958. Introduction to *The Question*, by Henri Alleg. New York: George Braziller.

——. 1967. *What is Literature?* Translated by Bernard Fretchman. Bristol: Methuen.

——. 1968. *On Genocide*. Boston: Beacon.

——. 1976. *Black Orpheus*. Translated by S. W. Allen. Paris: Présence Africaine.

Scarry, Elaine. 1985. *The Body in Pain: The Making and Unmaking of the World*. Oxford: Oxford University Press.

Sennett, Richard. 1974. *The Fall of Public Man*. New York: Knopf.

Smith, Anthony D. 1998. *Nationalism and Modernism*. London: Routledge.

Souriau, Christiane. 1975. "L'arabisation en Algérie." In *Introduction à l'Afrique du Nord contemporaine*, 375–98. Paris: Centre National de la Recherche Scientifique.

Sraïeb, Noureddine. 1975. "Enseignement, décolonisation et développement au Maghreb." In *Introduction à l'Afrique du Nord contemporaine*, 131–54. Paris: Centre National de la Recherche Scientifique.

Stone, Martin. 1997. *The Agony of Algeria*. New York: Columbia University Press.

Stora, Benjamin. 1995. "Deuxième guerre Algérienne?" *Les Temps Modernes* 580 (January–February): 242–61.

——. 1998. *Algérie: Formation d'une nation*. Biarritz: Atlantica.

Suleri, Sara. 1992. *The Rhetoric of British India*. Chicago: University of Chicago Press.

Taleb-Ibrahimi, Khaoula. 1993. "A propos de *L'école algérienne d'Ibn*

Badis à Pavlov de M. Boudalia-Greffou: quelques réflexions sur les pratiques didactiques dans l'enseignement de la langue arabe dans le système éducatif algérien." *Naqd* 5 (April–August): 65–73. Special issue: "Culture et système éducatif."

———. 1997. *Les Algériens et leur(s) langue(s).* Algiers: El Hikma.

Théolleyre, Jean-Marc. 1997. *Juger en Algérie 1944–1962.* Paris: Seuil.

Thévenin, Paule. 1969. "Entendre/Voir/Lire." *Tel Quel* 30 (fall).

Toso Rodinis, Giuliana, ed. 1991. *Le banquet maghrébin.* Rome: Bulzone.

Toumi, Alawa. 2000. "Creolized North-Africa." In *French Cultural Studies: Criticism at the Crossroads,* edited by M. P. Le Hir and D. Strand, 69–80. Albany: SUNY Press, 2000.

"Translating 'Algeria.' " 1998. *Parallax* 7 (May).

Turin, Yvonne. 1971. *Affrontements dans l'Algérie coloniale. Ecoles, médecines, religion, 1830–1880.* Paris: Maspéro.

Vatin, Jean Claude. 1975. "Littérature et société au Maghreb." In *Culture et société au Maghreb,* edited by Jean Claude Vatin, 211–31. Paris: CNRS.

Vidal-Naquet, Pierre. 1986. "Une fidélité têtue: La résistance française à la guerre d'Algérie." *Vingtième Siècle* (April–June): 3–18.

Vishwanathan, Gauri. 1989. *Masks of Conquest.* New York: Columbia University Press.

Werbner, Richard, ed. 1998. *Memory and the Postcolony: African Anthropology and the Critique of Power.* London : Zed.

Willis, Michael. 1997. *Islamist Challenge in Algeria: A Political History.* New York: New York University Press, 1997.

Yacine, Rachida. 1993. "The Impact of the French Colonial Heritage on Policies in Independent North Africa." In *North Africa: Nation, State, and Region,* edited by George Joffé, 221–32. London: Routledge.

Yacine, Tassadit. 2000. "Langue et représentations sexuelles ou sociales." *Journal des anthropologues* 82–83: 195–213.

———. 2001. Oral intervention at the conference "Algérie à plus d'une langue," organized by Mireille Calle-Gruber. Centre de Recherches en Etudes Féminines, University of Paris 8, 16 June.

Youssi, Abderrahim. 1991. "Un trilinguisme complexe." In *L'Etat du Maghreb,* edited by Yves Lacoste and Camille Lacoste. Casablanca: Le Fennec.

Zola, Émile. 1898a. "J'accuse." *L'Aurore,* 13 January 1898.

———. 1898b. *The Trial of Emile Zola.* New York: Benjamin R. Tucker.

——— 1974. "J'accuse." In *The Fall of Public Man,* by Richard Sennett. New York: Knopf.

contributors

RÉDA BENSMAIA is professor of French and Francophone literature in the French Studies department and in the Department of Comparative Literature at Brown University. He has published numerous articles on twentieth-century French and Francophone literature, on film theory, and on contemporary philosophy. He is the author of *The Barthes Effect: The Essay as Reflective Text* (Minneapolis: University of Minnesota Press, 1987); *The Year of Passages* (Minneapolis: University of Minnesota Press, 1995); and *Alger ou la maladie de la mémoire* (Paris: L'Harmattan, 1997). He is also the editor of two special issues on Gilles Deleuze: "Gilles Deleuze!" *Lendemains* 53, no. 1 (1989); and "Gilles Deleuze: A Reason to Believe in this World," *Discourse* 20, no. 3 (fall 1998). He is currently working on a book entitled *Experimental Nations* dealing with contemporary North African Francophone writers.

ANNE-EMMANUELLE BERGER is professor of French literature at Cornell University. She is the author of *Le banquet de Rimbaud* (Seyssel: Champ-Vallon, 1992) and coeditor of *Lectures de la différence sexuelle* (Paris: Des Femmes, 1994). She has written numerous articles on poetry and poetics, the Enlightenment, women writers, contemporary thought, and the cultural politics of the veil. She is currently completing a book on the relation of modern poetry to modern forms of poverty.

OMAR CARLIER taught Algerian history at the University of Oran until 1993 and is currently associate professor (*maître de conférences*) at the University of Paris I, Sorbonne. He is a researcher at the Center for African Research (Paris I) and at the Center for Social History of Mediterranean Islam (Ecole des Hautes Etudes en Sciences Sociales). He is the author of *Entre Nation et Jihad: histoire sociale des radicalismes algériens* (Paris: Presses de la Fondation Nationale des Sciences Politiques, 1995). Recent publications include "L'élection présidentielle comme analyseur de la société politique algérienne contemporaine," in *L'Algérie contemporaine: Bilan et solutions pour sortir de la crise*, edited by G. Meynier (April 1991); *Espace maghrébin, la force du local?* (Paris: L'Harmattan, 1996); and "Les enjeux sociaux du corps. Le hamman maghrébin (XIXe—XXe)," *Annales* 6 (November/December 2000): 1303–34.

HÉLÈNE CIXOUS was born in Algeria in 1937 into an atypical Jewish family. She grew up in Oran and Algiers before moving to France in 1955. The author of more than thirty-five books of poetic fiction, a dozen plays and scenarios, and several collections of critical work, as well as countless shorter pieces, she has recently published *Les rêveries de la femme sauvage* (Paris: Galilée, 2000), which deals with her Algerian childhood. She was instrumental in founding the experimental Université de Paris 8 (1969). In 1974, she created the *Centre de recherches en Etudes Féminines*, the first, and still the only, French doctoral program in women's studies. She has been actively involved in many political struggles, including the cause of Algerian refugees and artists. Of her many books published in English translation, the question of Algeria is perhaps most explicitly present in *Hélène Cixous, Rootprints* (London: Routledge, 1997) and *Stigmata: Escaping Texts* (London: Routledge, 1998).

HAFID GAFAÏTI is the Jeanne Charnier-Qualia Professor of French and Francophone Studies at Texas Tech University. He has written extensively on contemporary Francophone literature, feminism, and on cultural issues in a postcolonial setting. He is the author or co-author of six books and numerous articles. His most recent publications include *Rachid Boudjedra: Une poétique de la subversion*, Vol. 1, *Autobiographie et histoire* (Paris: L'Harmattan, 1999); Vol 2, *Lectures* critiques (Paris: L'Harmattan, 2000); *French Feminism across the Disciplines* (Texas Tech: Intertexts, 1998), and *Les femmes dans le roman algérien* (Paris: L'Harmattan, 1996). Currently, he is working on a book-length study entitled *The Pact of Censorship* and is serving as editor for *Language and National Identity in Postcolonial Contexts* and *Problématiques identitaires au Québec*. Hafid Gafaïti is editor-in-chief of *Etudes Transnationales, Francophones et Comparées/Transnational, Francophone and Comparative Studies*, published by L'Harmattan.

RANJANA KHANNA is assistant professor of English at Duke University, where she teaches feminist and postcolonial literature and theory. She has two books in progress: *Dark Continents: Psychoanalysis and Colonialism* and *Algeria Cuts: Women and Representation 1830 to the Present*.

ABDELKEBIR KHATIBI is a Moroccan novelist, poet, essayist, and critic. A prominent proponent and analyst of Maghrebian polylingualism, he lives in Rabat. He has published a dozen books and numerous essays. His works include: fictional texts such as *Amour bilingue* (Montpellier: Fata Morgana, 1983) and *Un été à Stockholm* (Paris: Flammarion, 1990); essays on cultural issues such as *Maghreb pluriel* (Paris: Denoël, 1983) and *La blessure du nom propre* (Paris: Denoël, 1986); essays on art and literature (*Figures de l'étranger dans la littérature française*, [Paris: Denoël, 1987] and *The Splendor of Islamic Calligraphy*, with Mohammed Sijelmassi, [New York: Thames and Hudson, 1996]), and political works (*L'alternance et les partis politiques* [Casablanca, 1998]).

DJAMILA SAADI-MOKRANE has taught French linguistics and Maghrebian literature at the University of Algiers. She is currently associate professor (*maître de conférences*) at the University of Lille 3 in France. Her work is largely in the field of sociolinguistics: linguistic practices in Algeria and the current use of French in France, for example. She is also interested in semiotic questions regarding popular culture in the Maghreb and among Maghrebian immigrants in France working in various genres, such as painting, music, and stories.

LUCETTE VALENSI was born in Tunisia. She is *directrice d'études* at the Ecole des Hautes Etudes en Sciences Sociales (Paris) and director of the Institut d'Etudes de l'Islam et des Sociétés du Monde Musulman. Among her books available in English are *On The Eve of Colonialism: North Africa before the French Conquest* (New York: Africana, 1977); *Tunisian Peasants in the Eighteenth and Nineteenth Centuries* (Cambridge: Cambridge University Press, 1985); *The Last Arab Jews: The Communities of Jerba, Tunisia* (with A. L. Udovitch, [New York: Harwood, 1984]); *Jewish Memories* (with N. Wachtel, [Berkeley: University of California Press, 1987]), and *Venice and the Sublime Porte: The Birth of the Despot* (Ithaca: Cornell University Press, 1993).

index